The Coming King

The Coming King

The Coming King

By
James Edson White
and Alonzo L. Baker

TEACH Services, Inc.
P U B L I S H I N G
www.TEACHServices.com • (800) 367-1844

World rights reserved. This book or any portion thereof may not be copied or reproduced in any form or manner whatever, except as provided by law, without the written permission of the publisher, except by a reviewer who may quote brief passages in a review.

The author assumes full responsibility for the accuracy of all facts and quotations as cited in this book. The opinions expressed in this book are the author's personal views and interpretations, and do not necessarily reflect those of the publisher.

This book is provided with the understanding that the publisher is not engaged in giving spiritual, legal, medical, or other professional advice. If authoritative advice is needed, the reader should seek the counsel of a competent professional.

Facsimile Reproduction

As this book played a formative role in the development of Christian thought and the publisher feels that this book, with its candor and depth, still holds significance for the church today. Therefore the publisher has chosen to reproduce this historical classic from an original copy. Frequent variations in the quality of the print are unavoidable due to the condition of the original. Thus the print may look darker or lighter or appear to be missing detail, more in some places than in others.

Copyright © 2018 TEACH Services, Inc.
ISBN-13: 978-1-57258-366-5 (Paperback)
Library of Congress Control Number: 2006907368

www.TEACHServices.com • (800) 367-1844

Table *of* Contents

	PAGE
THE CREATOR	9
THE CREATED	13
THE REDEEMER	17
THE GOSPEL IN THE OLD TESTAMENT	23
THE LEADER OF ISRAEL	27
THE GREAT TEACHER	31
THE MAN OF SORROWS	39
CHRIST OUR SACRIFICE	45
THE RESURRECTION	53
THE LORD'S ASCENSION	59
CHRIST OUR MEDIATOR AND ADVOCATE	63
HE WILL COME AGAIN	66
WHEN SHALL THESE THINGS BE?	75
DESTRUCTION OF JERUSALEM	79
GREAT TRIBULATION	105
DARKENING OF THE SUN	112
THE FALLING STARS	123
THE DAYS OF NOAH	130
FALSE CHRISTS AND FALSE PROPHETS	134
PARABLE OF THE FIG-TREE	137
INIQUITY SHALL ABOUND	140
THE CHURCH APOSTATIZING	157

Table *of* Contents---*Continued*

	PAGE
FAMINES	163
PESTILENCE AND EARTHQUAKE	171
STORMS AND TIDAL WAVES	178
CAPITAL AND LABOR	183
WARS AND RUMORS OF WARS	194
TALKING PEACE BUT PREPARING FOR WAR	205
GOSPEL TO ALL NATIONS	216
ONE TAKEN, ANOTHER LEFT	219
THE REVELATION	222
THE FIRST ANGEL'S MESSAGE	226
THE SANCTUARY	246
THE SECOND ANGEL'S MESSAGE	258
THE THIRD ANGEL'S MESSAGE	265
SABBATH REST	275
A SEALING MESSAGE	298
THE COMING KING	307
THE KING'S REWARD	312
THE NEW JERUSALEM	315

List *of* Illustrations

	PAGE
The Coming King	FRONTISPIECE
The Word of God was Christ, who was "made flesh"	11
The Week of Creation	14
Christ heals a blind man	19
Christ cured lepers	22
The baptism of the Holy Spirit at Pentecost	24
Christ led Israel from Egypt to the promised land	28
Christ taught the Samaritan woman at the well	30
The descent of the Holy Spirit on Christ at His baptism	33
The Law of God in the Old Testament and the New	35
Christ mocked and scourged before His crucifixion	40
The temptation of Christ	43
Christ, our Sacrifice, before the rabble	47
"He is risen"	52
Christ appears to His disciples after His resurrection	54
The Saviour shows His nail prints to Thomas	56
He ascended from among His disciples	58
Christ, our Advocate, reconciles us to one another	62
The transfiguration of Christ	69
"So shall also the coming of the Son of man be"	73
Christ curses the fig-tree	80
Christ driving the money changers from the temple	84
The Roman army taking Jerusalem	88
The wailing wall at Jerusalem	94
The stoning of Stephen	106
Paul in chains preaches to a Roman officer	110
The dark day of 1780	115
The falling of the stars in 1833	126
"My words shall not pass away"	129
Modern, atheistic Russians scoff at the Christian religion	132

List *of* Illustrations---*Continued*

	PAGE
The arrest of women communists	141
Many of the "movies" are a menace to morals	147
A swift journey from the marriage altar to the divorce court	151
Demoralizing drugs destroyed by the New York police	154
The theory that man ascended from the ape	158
Famine victims in Russia	164
The destructive fruit fly	167
Fruit injured by fruit fly	169
Scene after the great earthquake in Japan	173
Refugees after the Japan earthquake	174
The awful hurricane in Miami, Florida	179
A tornado in the distance	181
A parade of labor to denounce capitalism	186
A racing auto capable of 300 miles an hour	193
The glare and shadow of war stalks everywhere	195
Swarms of bombing planes	211
A medical missionary on the border of Tibet	217
"Two women shall be grinding at the mill"	221
Child preachers in Scandinavia	234
Chart of the 2300 days	239
The scapegoat	249
The day of atonement	252
The second angel denounces the fallen churches	259
The prophet saw a beast with seven heads	266
Sabbath and worship	276
Paul preached till daybreak	285
Paul preached to the Gentiles on Sabbath	294
The joys and glories of the new earth	318

The Creator

HOW great must be that mighty One, who could make an earth like ours; who could make the grass and trees, fruits and flowers, to grow and flourish; who could cause the intelligent creatures of the world in which we live, to move, and think, and love!

"In the beginning God created the heaven and the earth." Genesis 1: 1. The way in which God created all things is in harmony with His greatness. The psalmist says, "He spake, and it was done; He commanded, and it stood fast." Psalm 33: 9. Hence the Creator *spake*, and His word, as spoken through Christ, made the world.

"The worlds were framed by the word of God, so that things which are seen were not made of things which do appear." Hebrews 11: 3. The world was not made of anything that we can see, but was the product of the Creator's word.

The apostle tells us that life dwells in the Word, and that this life is "the light of men." (John 1: 4.) Men live, and think, and act because of the power of God's word. This word, which created the worlds in the beginning, has the same power today which it had then.

Christ is the Word of God. The apostle writes, "The Word was made flesh, and dwelt among us." John 1: 14. The helpless Babe, born in a manger at Bethlehem, was in reality the Being who created the world in the beginning. He was the Son of God, the Only-begotten of the Father, and had been with God before the creation of the world.

The prayer of Jesus makes plain the above statement regarding the pre-existence of Christ. "And now, O Father, glorify Thou Me with Thine own self with the glory which I had with Thee before the world was." John 17: 5.

And Micah 5:2 states that His "goings forth have been from of old, from everlasting." (Heb. "from the days of eternity.")

Christ was from eternal ages a sharer in His Father's heavenly glory, but by a miracle altogether beyond our comprehension, came to the earth to be a man among men, to carry our griefs, and to share our experiences, that finally we might share His glory. (Hebrews, 2:9, 14.) Jesus prayed, "Father, I will that they also, whom Thou hast given Me, be with Me where I am; that they may behold My glory, which Thou hast given Me: for Thou lovedst Me before the foundation of the world." John 17:24.

John also said, "In the beginning was the Word, and the Word was with God, and the Word was God. The same was in the beginning with God." John 1:1, 2. Christ was with the Father when the world was planned and made.

Of the part that Christ took in the creation of the world, the apostle John says, "All things were made by Him; and without Him was not any thing made that was made." "He was in the world, and the world was made by Him." John 1:3, 10.

In John 1:1 the Word (Christ) is called God. The Father himself declares, "Thy throne, O God, is for ever and ever: a scepter of righteousness is the scepter of Thy kingdom." Hebrews 1:8; Psalm 45:6. In these texts the Son is called God by the Father.

Isaiah, giving the names that apply to Christ, says, "For unto us a Child is born, unto us a Son is given: and the government shall be upon His shoulder: and His name shall be called Wonderful, Counselor, The Mighty God, The Everlasting Father, The Prince of Peace." Isaiah 9:6.

These titles, as applied to Christ, are very appropriate when we consider His exalted position as stated by Paul: "Who, being in the form of God, thought it not robbery to

Autotype Fine Art Co., Ltd.
The Word of God was Christ, His Son, who was "made flesh" in the son of Mary.

be equal with God." Philippians 2: 6. Standing equal with the Father in the realm of heaven, and in all the created universe, it can be plainly seen that He should bear the titles of the Creator.

Of the glory of Christ, Paul writes: "Who is the image of the invisible God, the first-born of every creature: for by Him were all things created, that are in heaven, and that are in earth, visible and invisible, whether they be thrones, or dominions, or principalities, or powers: all things were created by Him and for Him: and He is before all things, and by Him all things consist." Colossians 1: 15-17.

The same apostle also says, "God . . . hath in these last days spoken unto us by His Son, whom He hath appointed heir of all things, by whom also He made the worlds; who, being the brightness of His glory, and the express image of His person, and upholding all things by the word of His power, when He had by Himself purged our sins, sat down on the right hand of the Majesty on high." Hebrews 1: 1-3.

Jesus, the Son of God, our Redeemer, created the heavens and the earth, as well as the other planets of the universe, and all they contain. He not only created all things, but He sustains, or holds together, all that He has created. One day follows another, the seasons come and go, because, by the word of His power, all things consist and remain. It is the word of His power that keeps the earth, the sun, the moon, and the stars in their places.

Such a Saviour may well be trusted with our all. We may rest in Him as in a faithful Creator, knowing that "there hath not failed one word of all His good promise" (1 Kings 8: 56) to the children of men; and that, accepting His word, we too shall be upheld even as all things are upheld "by the word of His power."

The Created

THE first chapter in the Bible tells of the most wonderful week the world has ever known. In it this earth was made. "Thus the heavens and the earth were finished, and all the host of them." Genesis 2: 1. At first it was all dark, surrounded by mists, and covered with water. "And the earth was without form, and void; and darkness was upon the face of the deep." Genesis 1: 2.

"In six days the Lord made heaven and earth, the sea, and all that in them is." Exodus 20: 11. On the first day of this week, the voice of God caused the light to shine where all was darkness before. On the second day the mists were collected into clouds, and the firmament was made. On the third day the dry land appeared, and out of it God made to grow the trees, the grass, the beautiful flowers, and all vegetation.

On the fourth day He appointed the sun to shine by day, and the moon and stars to rule the night. On the fifth day He made great whales, the fish, and all the animals that live in the sea, and the birds and fowls that fly in the air.

The work done on the sixth day was most wonderful of all. On this day God made the beasts of the field, the cattle, and all creeping things. But last, and best of all, God made man, His "noblest work" because made "in His own image." "And God blessed them, and God said unto them, Be fruitful, and multiply, and replenish the earth, and subdue it: and have dominion over the fish of the sea, and over the fowl of the air, and over every living thing that moveth upon the earth." Genesis 1: 27, 28.

Not only was man made absolute ruler of everything in it, but the earth itself was given to him. "The heaven, even

The Week of Creation

the heavens, are the Lord's: but the earth hath He given to the children of men." Psalm 115: 16.

"And the Lord God planted a garden eastward in Eden; and there He put the man whom He had formed. And out of the ground made the Lord God to grow every tree that is pleasant to the sight, and good for food." Genesis 2: 8, 9.

What a beautiful garden home this must have been! No curse rested upon it; no weeds nor briars grew in its soil. Everything that heart could desire was provided for our first parents.

And God caused to grow "the tree of life also in the midst of the garden." This was a wonderful tree, for its fruit would keep one alive as long as he had the privilege of eating it. As long as he would obey God, he could eat of the fruit, but as soon as he should disobey, he would no longer have any right to it, and so would become subject to death.

In the garden was another tree, called "the tree of the knowledge of good and evil." The fruit which it bore appeared luscious, and as inviting as that which grew elsewhere. But God said, "Thou shalt not eat of it: for in the day that thou eatest thereof thou shalt surely die." Genesis 2: 17. God could have prevented man from eating of that fruit; but had He done so, it could not have been shown whether man intended to obey Him or not. God is pleased only with willing obedience, because it is only by cheerful obedience that we show our love for Him. "God is love," and loving service only is acceptable to Him. So God gives to every one the power of choice, either to obey Him and live, or to disobey Him and die.

Those who truly obey God do so because they love Him, and love His ways. Those who dislike God's ways will not walk in them. He who walks in God's ways grows to be like Him, and so becomes fitted to dwell with God, and to associate with sinless angels.

But we are just as free to disobey as we are to obey. God tells us, as He told Adam and Eve in Eden, what He wants us to do, and what disobedience will bring us; then He leaves us to choose what we will do. If God should force men to obey Him against their will, their hearts would not be changed. If compelled to act in a way contrary to their choice, they would hate God still more; thus their service would neither benefit themselves nor be acceptable to God. For this reason, man is left free to do as he chooses.

Adam and Eve, tempted by Satan, failed to obey God. They chose to eat of the forbidden fruit, and lost their Eden home. God mercifully expelled them from the garden, and carefully guarded every avenue of approach to the tree of life, in order to prevent their partaking of its fruit, thereby perpetuating an existence in sin. (See Genesis 3: 22-24.)

Thus deprived of this wonderful fruit, they had no hope of life. The sentence of death was even then being carried out. How changed their condition! All this because they had chosen Satan as their leader and king.

But the effects of their mistake did not cease with themselves. All the human race came under the same sentence of death. "As by one man sin entered into the world, and death by sin; . . . so death passed upon all men." Romans 5: 12.

All the race would have been lost, had God provided no way of escape from eternal death, but His love found a refuge for all who would believe. "We see Jesus, who was made a little lower than the angels for the suffering of death, crowned with glory and honor; that He by the grace of God should taste death for every man." Hebrews 2: 9. If we, too, see Jesus, as the one who has tasted death for us, and flee to the refuge He has provided, we may confidently hope in His salvation.

The Redeemer

THE eternal purpose of God from the beginning has been that every intelligent being should yield Him obedience and loving service, because by this very loving service man would reach the highest degree of happiness. "God so loved the world, that He gave His only-begotten Son, that whosoever believeth in Him should not perish, but have everlasting life." John 3: 16.

Man was created perfect — in the image of God. Through sin his innocence was lost, condemning him to death. Justice demanded this; but while abhorring sin, God loved the sinner still, because God never changes. (Malachi 3: 6; James 1: 17.)

The heavenly angels loved man also, so all heaven was filled with sorrow when he fell. Man had trampled upon the law of God; and death, which till then was unknown, would now follow everywhere in the track of sin. To the guilty pair there seemed no way of escape.

There was One, however, and only One in the universe, who could pay the debt. He only could redeem who had power to create. The Son of God, the Only-begotten of the Father, could meet man's needs, and He offered Himself as a ransom for sinners.

But does God love the poor sinner enough to make such a sacrifice for him? What a struggle it must have been for the great God to decide to give up His much beloved Son to die for a wretched, guilty race!

Yet He did this very thing, for His love is an "everlasting love." (Jeremiah 31: 3.) So when man fell, "God so loved the world that He gave His only-begotten Son." Not only did Christ die for us, but He has been given to us forever. He is ours, now, and through the endless ages of eternity.

What boundless love is this! It is beyond all human understanding; but it is the love of God toward man.

How different is this from the thought that God is a pitiless Judge, whose desire is to destroy the sinner, and that the constant pleading of Christ alone prevents Him from doing so.

But we can now see that God and Christ are one in counsel, one in purpose, one in love, and one in their desire and effort to "save that which was lost."

It is not God who must be reconciled to man. God's character has never changed; but man, through sinful thoughts, stands unreconciled to God. To teach man to love God, and so to bring him into harmony with God, was the mission of Christ to this earth. This, too, was the work of God, for "God was in Christ, reconciling the world unto Himself." (2 Corinthians 5: 19.)

Therefore, whenever Christ appeared among men, God was working through Him to redeem man. All that Christ said or did was the life of God, showing through Christ, to tell of God's love to fallen humanity.

Man had exchanged his beautiful garments of righteousness and glory for filthy rags. He was wearing the clothing of a convict, and was under sentence of death. The image of God in his character had been marred.

But notwithstanding all this, Christ left His royal robes in heaven, and came to earth to live with, and wear the garb of, criminals. He took their nature. (Hebrews 2: 17; Romans 8: 3.) He was tempted in all points as they were. (Hebrews 4: 15.) He was made "to be sin" for them, though He "knew no sin." (2 Corinthians 5: 21.)

He came to earth in human form, and placed Himself by the sinner's side, in order to show him a perfect life; that is, God's life in human flesh, saying by this to the sinner, "This is what God desires you to be."

Autotype Fine Art Co., Ltd.
Christ heals a blind man; and He was as well the healer of spiritual blindness.

If we will permit Him, He will take from us our sin-stained garments of filthy rags, and clothe us with the beautiful garments of His righteousness.

In Zechariah 3: 3, 4 we read as follows: "Now Joshua was clothed with filthy garments, and stood before the angel. And he [the angel] answered and spake unto those that stood before him, saying, Take away the filthy garments from him. And unto him [Joshua] he said, Behold, I have caused thine iniquity to pass from thee, and I will clothe thee with change of raiment." In this text Joshua represents the sinner both before and after he becomes reconciled to God.

Fallen man cannot earn righteousness by any works he can do. It is the free gift of God to all who will accept it. When a sinner turns to Christ, realizing that in so doing lies his only hope, he is pardoned, justified, by the righteousness of Christ. Christ's righteousness is then imputed to him.

Our Saviour illustrates this in the prayers of the Pharisee and publican: "Two men went up into the temple to pray; the one a Pharisee, and the other a publican. The Pharisee stood and prayed thus with himself, God, I thank Thee, that I am not as other men are, extortioners, unjust, adulterers, or even as this publican. I fast twice in the week, I give tithes of all that I possess.

"And the publican, standing afar off, would not lift up so much as his eyes unto heaven, but smote upon his breast, saying, God be merciful to me a sinner. I tell you, this man went down to his house justified rather than the other: for every one that exalteth himself shall be abased; and he that humbleth himself shall be exalted." Luke 18: 10-14. He was forgiven, justified, made righteous.

Only one way could be devised to save the fallen. Man had broken God's holy law, and cut himself off from God. God's law could not be changed to save the sinner, and even if it could have been, this would not have reconciled man to

God. To change God's law, therefore, would not elevate man; on the contrary, it would lower the standard and destroy the immutability of the word of the Creator of the universe. This could not be, and so the suffering of the Son of God must follow, or the salvation of man be abandoned.

When the eternal purpose of God is finally worked out in the wonderful plan of redemption, "not only men, but angels, will ascribe honor and glory to the Redeemer; for even they are secure only through the sufferings of the Son of God.

"Not only those who are washed by the blood of Christ, but the holy angels also, are drawn to Him by His crowning act of giving His life for the sins of the world. 'And I, if I be lifted up from the earth, will draw all unto Me'— not only earth, but heaven; for of Him 'the whole family in heaven and earth is named.'" John 12:32; Ephesians 3:15. "That in the dispensation of the fullness of times He might gather together in one all things in Christ, both which are in heaven, and which are on earth; even in Him." Ephesians 1:10.

The plan of redemption met immediately the sin and fall of man. God accepted the offer of Christ to die for the sinner. Christ the Creator became the promised sacrifice and Redeemer; hence He is the "Lamb slain from the foundation of the world." Revelation 13:8. Throughout the ages the sacrifice of Christ has been the hope and comfort of the faithful. To the redeemed it will be the theme of praise and adoration throughout the ceaseless years of eternity.

To the repentant sinner the blood of Christ, through faith, brought pardon during the ages before His death, just as surely as it does to us who are living this side of the crucifixion. Their faith looked forward to a Saviour to come; ours looks backward to the crucified Redeemer of Calvary. There has been but one gospel, one way of salvation.

The blood of the innocent lamb, which was offered as a sacrifice by the patriarchs, was a type of the blood of Christ.

Autotype Fine Art Co., Ltd.
Christ cured lepers that He might teach His power to cure the leprosy of sin.

It showed their faith in the coming Redeemer, and brought pardon for their sins. These sacrifices were necessary until Christ should come and die; for "without shedding of blood is no remission." (Hebrews 9:22.) Our acceptance of Christ, by faith, brings pardon for our transgression. Thus the gospel of salvation through Christ is the same both before and after the crucifixion. And through all His ministry for man, "God was in Christ reconciling the world unto Himself."

The Gospel *in the* Old Testament

THE great plan of redemption has been in operation ever since man fell. "Unto us was the gospel preached, as well as unto them." Hebrews 4:2. Jesus Christ is the central figure of this plan. "Neither is there salvation in any other: for there is none other name under heaven given among men, whereby we must be saved." Acts 4:12.

This applies to all ages, for Christ is "the Lamb slain from the foundation of the world." Revelation 13:8. It is a mistake to suppose that there have been two plans of salvation —one for patriarchs and Hebrews living before the cross, and another for Christians of the present dispensation.

It is a mistake to suppose that Old Testament sinners were forgiven and saved through obedience to the law without faith in the atonement and pardoning love of Christ.

It is equally a mistake to suppose that we of the New Testament dispensation are saved by the gospel of Christ while disregarding the law of God. Faith in Christ brings pardon for past sins. His abiding presence, and the transforming power of the Holy Spirit, enable us to obey the requirements of the law of God, and so prepare and fit us to dwell with the holy angels throughout eternity.

The word "gospel" means good news — good news of redemption through Jesus Christ. How long has this gospel been proclaimed? Was it first given in the time of Christ? Or was it first made known to Moses or Abraham?—When God proclaimed to the first guilty pair that the seed of the woman (Christ) should bruise the serpent's (Satan's) head (Genesis 3:15), He gave them the gospel, or good news, that

Autotype Fine Art Co., Ltd.
The baptism of the Holy Spirit, and the preaching of the gospel at Pentecost

Christ would overcome Satan, and open a way of escape for fallen man. In this promise to Adam and his posterity, we find the gospel of the Redeemer as truly as did the shepherds on the plains of Bethlehem, as they listened to the wonderful anthem from the angel choir, "Glory to God in the highest, and on earth peace, good will toward men." Luke 2: 14.

Abel's faith in the gospel of Jesus Christ made his offering acceptable to God. The fire that came from heaven and consumed his sacrifice was the testimony from God that his faith in Christ, and his compliance with the requirements of God, had brought him pardon and justification by faith.

Cain, while professedly obedient, had a heart full of rebellion and unbelief. The love of Christ had no place in his sacrifice; therefore it was rejected of heaven. With it there was no recognition of the wonderful provisions of the gospel; hence his offering brought no forgiveness, no justification, for there was no exhibition of faith.

Envy and hatred of his brother sprang up in the heart of Cain. And then followed the awful tragedy of the murder of Abel, which was the first human death the world had known. "And wherefore slew he him? Because his own works were evil, and his brother's righteous." 1 John 3: 12.

Cain's offering of the fruits of the ground was not in accordance with God's plan. Such an offering could not in any way represent the atoning blood of Christ; for Paul says, "without shedding of blood is no remission." (Hebrews 9: 22.)

The gospel was preached to Abraham. "And the scripture, foreseeing that God would justify the heathen through faith, preached before the gospel unto Abraham, saying, In thee shall all nations be blessed." Galatians 3: 8. Paul here quotes from Genesis 22: 18: "And in thy seed shall all the nations of the earth be blessed." In Galatians 3: 16 Paul says this "seed" is Christ. This was the gospel of justification by faith, the same as we have it.

Moses and the children of Israel had the gospel; for Paul says, "Unto us was the gospel preached, as well as unto them." Hebrews 4:2. Here the apostle treats it as a well-known fact that their fathers had the gospel. And we have the gospel as well as they.

All the sacrifices and offerings of the old dispensation simply showed forth man's faith in the coming of a Messiah. Without this faith, the Levitical sacrifices could be of no more avail than was the offering of Cain.

But this faith was not cherished by those who came out of the bondage of Egypt. Hence they were compelled to wander forty years in the wilderness until their carcasses fell by the way, and a generation that knew God had taken their place. Two faithful ones alone of all the vast company that left Egypt — Caleb and Joshua — finally entered the promised land.

The brazen serpent (Numbers 21:8) was an object-lesson teaching the children of Israel of the Christ to come. "Look and live," is the true test of faith in Christ. As one look at the brazen serpent, set up in view of all the camp of Israel, brought life and health to the sufferer, so one look at the crucified One of Calvary brings life and salvation to the repentant sinner.

Christ gives the connection between the raising up of the serpent in the wilderness and His own crucifixion, thus: "As Moses lifted up the serpent in the wilderness, even so must the Son of man be lifted up." John 3:14. Later He explains the object of this: "And I, if I be lifted up from the earth, will draw all men unto Me." John 12:32.

Through the influence of the Holy Spirit, our Lord is working upon the hearts of men. To the sinner He says, I have been tempted just as you are. There is hope, courage, and salvation in exchange for a look. Only look and live.

The Leader *of* Israel

WHEN the hosts of Israel left Egypt to go to the land of Canaan, they did not go alone. God said to them: "Behold, I send an Angel before thee, to keep thee in the way, and to bring thee into the place which I have prepared. Beware of Him, and obey His voice, provoke Him not; for He will not pardon your transgressions: for My name is in Him." Exodus 23: 20, 31.

Only one Being in the universe besides the Father bears the name of God, and that is His Son, Jesus Christ. Hence this Angel that accompanied Israel in their wanderings was no other than Christ.

But the rebellion of the people was so great that at one time Moses feared that the Lord might leave them, and so he pleaded, "If Thy presence go not with me, carry us not up hence." And the Lord answered, "My presence shall go with thee." Exodus 33: 14, 15.

So, throughout their journeyings, the presence of the Lord went with them as a pillar of cloud by day, which protected them from the intense heat of the desert. In the night this was changed to a pillar of fire, to give them light and comfort. When the Lord would have them journey, the pillar would be lifted, and move in the direction they should take. When it stood still, the camp was pitched beneath its protection.

Soon after leaving Egypt, they came into the desert, where there was no water. When Moses cried to the Lord, He directed him to the rock of Horeb. When Moses smote the rock, as commanded, the waters flowed from it, and supplied all their needs. Ever after, in their wanderings, until they neared the promised land, wherever they camped, there was the cooling stream of water, flowing from the rock.

Paul declares that this was a type of Christ, and that they "did all eat the same spiritual meat; and did all drink the same spiritual drink: for they drank of that spiritual Rock that followed them; and that Rock was Christ." (1 Corinthians 10: 1-4.)

We can now understand the statement of Stephen: "This

It was Christ who led Israel from Egypt to the promised land.

[Moses] is he that was in the church in the wilderness with the Angel [Christ] which spake to him [Moses] in the Mount Sina, and with our fathers: who received the lively oracles [the law of God] to give unto us." Acts 7: 38.

We have found the Angel in the wilderness to have been Christ. The Father and the Son were doubtless both in the mount. But it was the Son as Mediator between God and man, who spoke the ten commandments from Mount Sinai, in the presence of Moses and the children of Israel. Hence we see that Christ is not only the Creator, but He is also the giver of His Father's law to this world. How appropriate, therefore, that He should, when on earth, proclaim Himself

"Lord of the Sabbath," and the expounder of all the precepts of His Father's divine law.

As the Hebrews reached the promised land, under the leadership of Joshua, as they were preparing to attack Jericho, the Lord appeared to Joshua in person. "And it came to pass, when Joshua was by Jericho, that he lifted up his eyes and looked, and, behold, there stood a Man over against him with His sword drawn in His hand; and Joshua went unto Him, and said unto Him, Art Thou for us, or for our adversaries? And He said, Nay; but as Captain of the host of the Lord am I now come." Joshua 5: 13-15.

Christ is the Captain, or Archangel, of the host of heavenly angels. (See Jude 9: 1 Thessalonians 4: 16.) At the command of Christ, "the host of the Lord" threw down the walls of Jericho.

The Spirit of Christ inspired the prophets of the former dispensation. It testified through them of Christ's sufferings at His first advent, and of the glory that should follow at His second coming. Hence the prophets "inquired and searched diligently, who prophesied of the grace that should come unto you; searching what, or what manner of time the Spirit of Christ which was in them did signify, when it testified beforehand the sufferings of Christ, and the glory that should follow." (1 Peter 1: 10, 11.)

We can see, therefore, that it was Christ who has given to us the Old as well as the New Testament. He spoke through the prophets of the Old Testament, the same as He has spoken through Peter, James, John, and Paul in the New. So we have a whole Bible, filled, from Genesis to Revelation, with the wonderful gospel of salvation through our Lord and Saviour Jesus Christ, for which we will praise Him now and evermore.

Autotype Fine Art Co., Ltd.
Christ taught His wonderful truths to the Samaritan woman at the well.

The Great Teacher

BEFORE sin entered the world there was nothing to hinder direct intercourse between God and man, and the Creator could make known to men His purposes and wishes. Sin separated man from God, as a sinner cannot remain in the presence of the holy God.

God still loved man after he had sinned, and at once began the work for his salvation. He purposed, at a later time, to send His Son into the world, but the people needed immediate instruction, and so, from among themselves, God raised up men to whom, in dreams and visions, or in a more direct manner, He revealed His will, that they might make it known to the people.

Noah was one of these; Moses was another; and these teachers were inspired by Christ, who from the beginning took charge of the world which He had created, and which He purposed to redeem.

These teachers prophesied that Christ would come. The prophet Isaiah especially foretold very minutely the sufferings and death of the Saviour. (See Isaiah 53.) Of all of these prophets the apostle Peter declares that "the Spirit of Christ which was in them . . . testified beforehand the sufferings of Christ, and the glory that should follow." (1 Peter 1: 11.)

In the parable of the vineyard Christ describes the treatment these teachers received. He said:

"There was a certain householder, which planted a vineyard, and hedged it round about, and digged a winepress in it, and built a tower, and let it out to husbandmen, and went into a far country: and when the time of the fruit drew near, he sent his servants to the husbandmen, that they might receive the fruits of it. And the husbandmen took his servants, and beat one, and killed another, and stoned another. Again, he sent other servants more than the first: and they did unto them likewise. But last of all he sent unto them his son, saying, They will reverence my son." Matthew 21: 33-37.

Therefore after many other teachers had been sent into the world, Christ came Himself as the greatest teacher that the world ever knew; even His enemies said, "Never man spake like this man." (John 7: 46.)

The public ministry of Jesus began when He was thirty years old. Before beginning to preach, He came to the River Jordan, where John was baptizing, and was baptized by him. Jesus was not a sinner, so John at first hesitated to baptize Him. But when he learned that Jesus desired to set an example for those who should follow Him, he consented.

When Jesus was baptized, as He came up out of the water, "the heavens were opened unto Him, and He saw the Spirit of God descending like a dove, and lighting upon Him: and, lo, a voice from heaven, saying, This is My beloved Son, in whom I am well pleased." (Matthew 3: 16, 17.) Thus strengthened for His soon-coming conflict with Satan, the Saviour went forth to teach the ways of God to the people.

Christ bore a message of love from the heavenly Father to mankind. In the Sermon on the Mount, Jesus taught that those who are poor in spirit, those who mourn because of their sins, those who are meek, those who long for righteousness, the merciful, the pure in heart, the peacemakers, are blessed of God, and that those who are persecuted for righteousness' sake may rejoice even while suffering. (See Matthew 5: 1-11.)

These promises have eased many heartaches, and lighted up with divine glory many an otherwise weary road.

Christ's teaching in regard to the law of the Father deserves careful attention: "Think not that I am come to

Autotype Fine Art Co., Ltd.
The descent of the Holy Spirit on Jesus after He was baptized.

destroy the law, or the prophets: I am not come to destroy, but to fulfill. For verily I say unto you, Till heaven and earth pass, one jot or one tittle shall in no wise pass from the law, till all be fulfilled. Whosoever therefore shall break one of these least commandments, and shall teach men so, he shall be called the least in the kingdom of heaven: but whosoever shall do and teach them, the same shall be called great in the kingdom of heaven." Matthew 5: 17-19.

That the Lord here refers especially to the ten commandments is evident because, following these words, He quotes the sixth and seventh commandments, and shows that hatred is murder and that lust is adultery.

As explained by Jesus, the law takes hold upon the very thoughts of the heart. No one can say, therefore, that he has never broken that law, and that he does not need the blood of Christ to cleanse from sin.

It is very natural for us to love those who love us, and hate those who have injured us; but the Saviour taught a better way, even His way. He said, "Love your enemies, bless them that curse you, do good to them that hate you, and pray for them which despitefully use you, and persecute you." Matthew 5: 44.

How noble is such teaching! Does the law ask too much of us?— No, indeed; obedience would produce universal happiness, for none can be happy while hating others, or seeking to injure them.

As long as God sends His blessings — His sunshine, His rain — on any one, He must love him; and if God loves him, why should not we? Jesus taught us to pray God to forgive our trespasses even as we forgive those who trespass against us. (See Matthew 5: 12-15.) How, then, can we breathe that holy prayer, which Jesus taught us, or hope for God's mercy, while in our hearts we are cherishing hatred against any?

"And thou shalt teach them diligently unto thy children, and shalt talk of them when thou sittest in thine house, and when thou walkest by the way, and when thou liest down, and when thou risest up." Deut. 6:7.

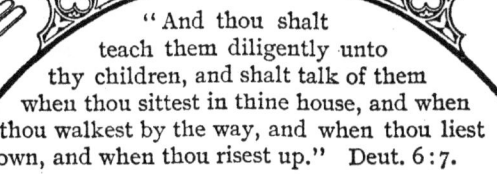

THE LAW OF GOD

I
Thou shalt have no other gods before Me.

II
Thou shalt not make unto thee any graven image, or any likeness of any thing that is in heaven above, or that is in the earth beneath, or that is in the water under the earth: thou shalt not bow down thyself to them, nor serve them: for I the Lord thy God am a jealous God, visiting the iniquity of the fathers upon the children unto the third and fourth generation of them that hate Me; and shewing mercy unto thousands of them that love Me, and keep My commandments.

III
Thou shalt not take the name of the Lord thy God in vain; for the Lord will not hold him guiltless that taketh His name in vain.

IV
Remember the Sabbath day, to keep it holy. Six days shalt thou labour, and do all thy work: but the seventh day is the Sabbath of the Lord thy God. in it thou shalt not do any work, thou, nor thy son, nor thy daughter, thy manservant, nor thy maidservant, nor thy cattle, nor thy stranger that is within thy gates: for in six days the Lord made heaven and earth, the sea, and all that in them is, and rested the seventh day: wherefore the Lord blessed the Sabbath day, and hallowed it.

V
Honour thy father and thy mother: that thy days may be long upon the land which the Lord thy God giveth thee.

VI
Thou shalt not kill.

VII
Thou shalt not commit adultery.

VIII
Thou shalt not steal.

IX
Thou shalt not bear false witness against thy neighbour.

X
Thou shalt not covet thy neighbour's house, thou shalt not covet thy neighbour's wife, nor his manservant, nor his maidservant, nor his ox, nor his ass, nor any thing that is thy neighbour's.

"Think not that I am come to destroy the law, or the prophets: I am not come to destroy, but to fulfill. For verily I say unto you, Till heaven and earth pass, one jot or one tittle shall in no wise pass from the law, till all be fulfilled." Matthew 5:17, 18.

The Law of God in the Old Testament and the New

But the greatest of all Christ's teachings — the one thing that He desires us to know — is that we, poor sinners, can through Him return to God, and find mercy, pardon, and salvation. To teach this, and to teach it so that all would know it, He came to earth.

Jesus mingled with the poor and needy. Free from sin Himself, He associated with sinners. (See Luke 15: 1.) Blessed record; hope of the otherwise hopeless — Jesus received sinners! He receives them still.

How Christ receives sinners He taught in the parable of the prodigal son. "A certain man had two sons: and the younger of them said to his father, Father, give me the portion of goods that falleth to me. And he divided unto them his living. And not many days after the younger son gathered all together, and took his journey into a far country, and there wasted his substance with riotous living.

"And when he had spent all, there arose a mighty famine in that land; and he began to be in want. And he went and joined himself to a citizen of that country; and he sent him into his fields to feed swine. And he would fain have filled his belly with the husks that the swine did eat; and no man gave unto him.

"And when he came to himself, he said, How many hired servants of my father's have bread enough and to spare, and I perish with hunger! I will arise and go to my father, and will say unto him, Father, I have sinned against heaven, and before thee, and am no more worthy to be called thy son: make me as one of thy hired servants." And this interesting record continues:

"And he arose, and came to his father. But when he was yet a great way off, his father saw him, and had compassion, and ran, and fell on his neck, and kissed him. And the son said unto him, Father, I have sinned against heaven, and in thy sight, and am no more worthy to be called thy son.

But the father said to his servants, Bring forth the best robe, and put it on him; and put a ring on his hand, and shoes on his feet: and bring hither the fatted calf, and kill it; and let us eat, and be merry: for this my son was dead, and is alive again; he was lost, and is found." Luke 15: 11-24.

The prodigal son represents a sinner. He has wandered away from his Father's house; but God sends His Spirit to convict him of sin, and if he will yield to that Spirit, he will arise and return to his Father. And how will this sinful son be received?—Oh, when he is yet a great way off, if but his face is turned homeward, the Father will run to meet him. He will not receive him as a servant, but as a son. The best robe is none too good for him; the choicest food is placed before him; there is joy and rejoicing, for a sinner has returned to the Father's house.

This is the lesson that Jesus teaches in this parable. How can one wander from such a loving, heavenly Father? Or, having wandered, how can he longer stay away?

It is easy to believe that the Father loves the Son, but we should believe also that He loves us if we are trying to serve and obey Him. If it were not so, why did He give His Son to die that we might live?

Of those who received His words when here on earth, He said: "I have given unto them the words which Thou gavest Me; and they have received them, and have known surely that I came out from Thee, and they have believed that Thou didst send Me. I pray for them: I pray not for the world, but for them which Thou hast given Me; for they are Thine." John 17: 8, 9.

And not only for those who listened to the words that fell from His lips did Jesus pray, but for all believers even to the end of time; for, continuing, He prayed: "Neither pray I for these alone, but for them also which shall believe on Me through their word; that they all may be one: as Thou,

Father, art in Me, and I in Thee, that they also may be one in us: that the world may believe that Thou hast sent Me." John 17: 20, 21. With such a loving Teacher, whose sole purpose is to do us good, who has given even His life for us, and whose object is to make us holy and happy forever, why should we not make haste to learn the lessons He has set before us?

When this great Teacher came unto His own (the Jewish people), they received Him not; they treated Him as they had treated those He had sent before Him. (See Matthew 21: 38, 39.) Shall He be treated by us in this way? Oh, let us receive His words, that we, like those who then received Him, may become the sons of God.

He said, "Learn of Me; for I am meek and lowly in heart: and ye shall find rest unto your souls." Matthew 11: 29.

Only in Jesus is there rest. Let us sit at His feet, receiving His words, and being baptized with His Spirit. Then, throughout eternity, we shall learn more of the "depth of the riches both of the wisdom and knowledge of God."

The Man *of* Sorrows

IT WAS necessary, in order to carry out the plan of salvation, for the Son of God to come to this earth and die, that lost man might be redeemed. In God's own good time, therefore, Christ left His home in heaven, and the power and glory which He had with His Father "before the world was" (John 17: 5), to accomplish this purpose. To the world He appeared simply as a babe born in a manger in Bethlehem. He grew to manhood, known only as a humble carpenter, working with His earthly father, Joseph.

Even when Jesus began His public ministry, though His teaching was accompanied by mighty miracles, few believed in Him. In their blindness the people could not see in Him and His work the "arm of the Lord." Their unbelief had been foretold by the prophet: "Who hath believed our report? And to whom is the arm of the Lord revealed?" Isaiah 53: 1.

The words, "He was despised and rejected of men; a Man of sorrows, and acquainted with grief," were spoken many years before the advent of the Saviour, and they were literally fulfilled in His life among men. "He was in the world, and the world was made by Him, and the world knew Him not." John 1: 10. His mission to this earth was twofold.

First, He came to redeem man. To redeem is to purchase back that which has been lost. By the sacrifice of Himself, He "purchased back" sinners, in order to free them from the terrible consequences of sin. By His death He secured life for all who would receive Him.

Second, He came to be an example. He lived just such a life as man must live, so that He might be a perfect guide to all who would follow Him. In order to meet man in his fallen condition, He must go to the lowest depths of poverty, tempta-

Autotype Fine Art Co., Ltd.
Christ was mocked and scourged before His crucifixion. He was a "man of sorrows."

The Man of Sorrows 41

tion, sorrow, and suffering. While He was here upon earth, our Saviour passed through every experience of man. Of His poverty it is written: "The foxes have holes, and the birds of the air have nests; but the Son of man hath not where to lay His head." Matthew 8: 20. Even the very poorest have some place which they call home, but our Lord was a homeless wanderer.

Of the temptations that Jesus passed through in His human nature, and of His care for the tempted, we read: "For we have not an High Priest which cannot be touched with the feeling of our infirmities; but was in all points tempted like as we are, yet without sin. Let us therefore come boldly unto the throne of grace, that we may obtain mercy, and find grace to help in time of need." Hebrews 4: 15, 16.

In the wilderness Christ was especially tempted upon the point of appetite and ambition. Our first parents failed on the point of appetite, and Christ won the victory where they had failed.

On the pinnacle of the temple, He was tempted to presume on His Father's care and mercy. The taunts of the enemy, insinuating disbelief of Christ's sonship to God, were hard for His human nature to bear, but He took no step outside the boundaries of His heavenly mission to earth. Had He yielded, the plan of salvation would have been a failure.

On the mount, the tempter sought to lead the Saviour to believe that He could redeem man in an easier way than by the life of suffering He was just entering upon. If He would only bow down and acknowledge Satan as the rightful owner and ruler of the world, the evil one promised to abdicate, and Christ could take possession at once. At such a suggestion the Saviour turned to him in indignation, with words of Scripture upon His lips, and gave the command that compelled the enemy to depart.

Of the inner life of Christ, the prophet said, He was "a Man of sorrows." To us, life brings more of happiness than of sorrow; more of joy than of grief. But the sorrows of a sinful world pressed the heaviest upon the heart of Christ.

Of His sufferings we read, "He was wounded for our transgressions, He was bruised for our iniquities: the chastisement of our peace was upon Him; and with His stripes we are healed." Isaiah 53: 5. His life was one of privation, and often of suffering. His experience in the wilderness, His anguish in Gethsemane, as well as the awful horrors of His trial and crucifixion,— all testify to the truthfulness of this statement. No martyr's suffering in the torture chamber can compare with the keen anguish Christ suffered in mind and in body. He bore the limit of human suffering. Jesus met every form of temptation that can come to man, for a twofold purpose.

First, "For in that He Himself hath suffered, being tempted, He is able to succor them that are tempted." Hebrews 2: 18. To "succor," is to give comfort and help when one is in trouble. This is just what the Lord Jesus does for those who are distressed by the presence of sin. He speaks peace to the troubled spirit, and says to the weary, anxious one, "Come unto Me," I will give you rest.

Second, that whenever we are in deep trial and temptation, we may remembeer that our Saviour passed through the same, and has promised to "make a way to escape" for us in every instance. If we will only let Him, He will bring us in triumph through every temptation. More than this, though He has passed through all these trying experiences, yet, for our salvation, He will, with us, pass through them again, and as the Apostle Paul expresses it, make us "in all these things . . . more than conquerors, through Him that loved us." In view of such great deliverance, is it any wonder that the same apostle should triumphantly exclaim, "Thanks be unto God for His unspeakable gift"?

The Man of Sorrows

Christ was also a "Man of sorrows" on the earth, because He was daily among those who were suffering from the plague of sin. "In all their affliction He was afflicted." These consoling words of the prophet point especially to the work of Christ. When any mourned the loss of dear friends, He sympathized with them. (See John 11: 33-36.) When they

The temptation of Christ

rebelled against Him, He was sorely grieved. (See Mark 3: 5.) When they refused to hear His words of warning, He wept over them. (See Luke 19: 41.)

When, in the garden of Gethsemane, He was preparing to meet death on the cross, He endured such agony that "His sweat was as it were great drops of blood falling down to the ground." (Luke 22: 44.) When brought before Pilate, a legal trial was denied Him, and men were hired to testify falsely against Him. (See Matthew 26: 59-61.) When hanging on the cross, the weight of the sins of the world was so great that He felt forsaken of His Father, and cried out in the deepest agony, "My God! My God! why hast Thou forsaken Me?" (Matthew 27:46.)

All this was borne by the Lord, not only to show how much He loved the fallen race, but that He might bestow on all who would receive Him the fellowship with Him in suffering, and give them His own consolation and glory. To receive the Lord and follow Him, is to pass through similar experiences of trial. "The servant is not greater than his lord. If they have persecuted Me, they will also persecute you; if they have kept My saying, they will keep yours also." John 15:20.

If, however, the world does all these things to the followers of Christ, the fact that He has borne it all before them, can be their consolation. In all these troubles, the assurance is given that by suffering with Him they are preparing to reign with Him. (2 Timothy 2:12.) They should rejoice, because they are partaking of His sufferings. (1 Peter 4:13.)

Christ endured these things; and as we are joint heirs with Him, we, too, must share with Him in His sufferings, if we expect to share His glory. (See Romans 8:17.) But we need not wait to the end for the consolation which comes from sharing with Christ in His sufferings. He has sent us word that "as the sufferings of Christ abound in us, so our consolation also aboundeth by Christ." (2 Corinthians 1:5.)

Just think of this promise: as suffering abounds, so consolation abounds. That is to say, we have enough consolation to balance all the suffering we are called upon to endure. To illustrate this, we may suppose ourselves to be like a pair of balances. On one side suffering is put in against us. This would weigh that side entirely down if nothing were put in the other side; so the Lord balances that with His consolation. We will therefore call the suffering "as" and the consolation "so." *As* the suffering weighs down one side, *so* the consolation weighs down the other, and thus the scales are kept evenly balanced all the time.

Christ Our Sacrifice

WHEN the Lord made man and placed him in the beautiful garden of Eden, He put upon him a test, that he might choose whether he would obey God or not. It was a very simple test. The man was to eat freely of all of the trees of the garden except one, and that was the tree of the knowledge of good and evil. God did not give the fruit of this tree to man. He did not wish man to know evil, as that could come only by disobeying God.

The Lord had stated plainly what the result of disobedience would be. "But of the tree of the knowledge of good and evil, thou shalt not eat of it: for in the day that thou eatest thereof thou shalt surely die." Genesis 2: 17.

Against the express command of God, our first parents, when tempted of Satan, allowed appetite to control them. They did the very thing that God had forbidden them to do, and therefore were driven from the garden. Thus cut off from the tree of life, they became subject to death; and so all their descendants became, in them, a dying race. "Wherefore, as by one man [Adam] sin entered into the world, and death by sin; and so death passed upon all men, for that all have sinned." Romans 5: 12.

Sin is rebellion against God; and as God cannot allow rebellion to continue forever, either the sinner must be destroyed, or some plan must be devised by which his sins could be removed from him. The plan of salvation met this need by providing that Jesus, the Son of God, should die in place of the sinner.

"All we like sheep have gone astray; we have turned every one to his own way; and the Lord hath laid on Him the iniquity of us all." Isaiah 53: 6. "Who His own self bare our sins in His own body on the tree, that we, being dead to sins, should live unto righteousness: by whose stripes ye were healed." 1 Peter 2: 24.

He who never sinned took the sinner's place, received the punishment that man deserved, and henceforth stands ready to give the believing sinner His own righteousness. This does not save the sinner from dying the natural death which comes to all as a consequence of Adam's sin, but it will save him who accepts of it from the "second death," which the unrepentant must suffer for his own sins.

The plan of salvation provided that the sins of all the world should be laid upon Christ, that He should be treated as a sinner, in order that repentant sinners might be made righteous through Him and receive the reward of righteousness. For when we believe on Christ, realizing the great love that led Him to die for us, our hearts are changed; sin becomes hateful to us; we put it away, and the power of God working for us, and through us, makes us "new creatures in Christ Jesus."

As soon as this plan was devised, it provided a Saviour for man, and mercy was at once offered to him. Having given Himself thus for man in the very beginning, Christ is truly described in the Scriptures as the "Lamb slain from the foundation of the world." Revelation 13: 8.

But it was not the design of God that Christ should at once give Him life for man. There were few people in the world in the early ages. God desired to have many witnesses of the death of His Son. At that time, the terrible nature of sin had not been fully developed, nor could it be seen until men should become so wicked that they would not hesitate to take even the life of the Son of God. Thus their hatred and His willingness to die that they might live, would be brought into sharp contrast; the fruit of sin and the fruit of love would be placed so close together that all could see the

Autotype Fine Art Co., Ltd.
Christ, our Sacrifice, before the rabble

difference. The great central event in the history of this world was to be the cross of Calvary.

For the purpose of keeping before men the blessed hope that Christ would come and die for the sinner, the Lord directed that offerings should be presented to Him. These offerings were to be such as would represent Christ,— living creatures that could be slain as He was to be slain. By such offerings, the children of men could show their faith in the promised Saviour.

"In process of time" Cain and Abel brought offerings to God. "Cain brought of the fruit of the ground"; but Abel "brought of the firstlings of his flock." God had respect to Abel's offering, but not to that of Cain. (See Genesis 4: 3-7.) The reason why God accepted Abel's offering is thus told in the Scriptures: "By faith Abel offered unto God a more excellent sacrifice than Cain." Hebrews 11: 4.

What was it that made Abel's offering acceptable?—It was faith. That faith led him to offer a lamb, which represented the Lamb of God. The blood of the lamb represented the blood of Christ to be shed on Calvary,— the innocent dying for the guilty; and that is the principle upon which the plan of salvation rests.

During the long ages between Adam's sin and the advent of Jesus Christ to the world, those who believed in God offered sacrifices in faith, the same as Abel. Abraham, Isaac, and Jacob, wherever they went, offered sacrifices. These offerings were a most important part of the worship of God.

When God, through Moses, took His people out of Egypt where they had been in bondage, He again gave them laws in regard to offerings. The lamb to be offered must be without blemish, so that they would properly represent the perfect Son of God.

Under the Jewish ritual, if one had sinned, and felt that he needed forgiveness, he brought his offering to God. Placing his hand upon the head of the victim, he confessed his sins, which were thus in a figure transferred to the offering. The life of the victim was then taken instead of his own life, which he had forfeited through sin.

When the fullness of time came, God sent His Son into the world to be the divine sacrifice for sin. The blood of animals could not really take away sin; it could only prefigure the spilt blood of Christ, which was to be shed for sin. When John the Baptist saw Jesus coming to him, he exclaimed, "Behold the Lamb of God, which taketh away the sin of the world!" John 1: 29.

Year after year, through long ages, men had looked over their flocks, and selected the choicest lambs for sacrifice; but now God's Lamb had come. God had looked over His great flock, and only One could be found that could redeem the world; and though He was His only-begotten Son, God freely gave Him to bear the sins of the world. Herein is love eternal and all sufficient.

Was Christ not a perfect sacrifice?—No one has yet been able to find any fault in Him. Even Pilate, who, to please the enemies of Jesus, gave orders for His crucifixion, was forced to say: "Ye have brought this Man unto me, as one that perverteth the people: and, behold, I, having examined Him before you, have found no fault in this Man touching those things whereof ye accuse Him: no, nor yet Herod." Luke 23: 14, 15.

Then they led Jesus away to be crucified. Well had the prophet declared: "He is brought as a lamb to the slaughter, and as a sheep before her shearers is dumb, so He openeth not His mouth." Isaiah 53: 7.

Sinner, behold your Sacrifice! See Him fainting underneath the weight of the cross, on the way to Calvary! That little hill near Jerusalem was to become the greatest altar of sacrifice the world ever saw, the place where love conquered hate; the place to which every sinner can look, and say, "Behold, what manner of love the Father hath bestowed upon us," that He should give His Son to die that "we should be called the sons of God!" 1 John 3: 1.

Nailed to the cross, suffering the most terrible anguish, for six hours He hung suspended between the heavens and the earth; and yet He prayed for His executioners. (See Luke 23: 34.)

Though men were unfeeling, nature was not; and a mysterious darkness falling upon the world, with earthquake and rending rock, drew from even the heathen Roman officer who stood by the confession: "Truly this Man was the Son of God." Mark 15: 39. The physical pain which Jesus endured, though great, was but a small part of His sufferings. To be rejected by His own people, and to be delivered by them to the Romans to be put to death, caused Him intense grief. But more than everything else it was the sense of the sins which He bore for all the world, thus separating Himself from His Father, which crushed Him, and caused Him the bitterest anguish.

It was the awful sense of sin which before, in the garden of Gethsemane, had caused Him to sweat as it were great drops of blood falling down to the ground (Luke 22: 39-46); and now,— though nailed to the rugged wood, suffering great physical pain, deserted by His disciples, and entirely given up to His enemies, surrounded by a mob led on by the chief priests and rulers, who, even while the film of death was gathering over His eyes, taunted and derided Him,— it was the sense of His Father's displeasure that caused Him such overmastering grief, and forced from His lips the despairing cry, "My God! My God! why hast Thou forsaken Me?" Matthew 27: 46. To be forsaken of God,— an experience which He must obtain in order to become a perfect Saviour for guilty sinners,— this broke His great, loving heart, and cut short His life.

But the great sacrifice for sin was now made; the plan of salvation is sure because now complète. Christ, the Son of God, had died for man, the just for the unjust, the divine for the human. That which the sacrificial offerings had long pointed forward to was now a reality.

The offering of a lamb is now no longer required; "but we see Jesus, who was made a little lower than the angels for the suffering of death, crowned with glory and honor; that He by the grace of God should taste death for every man." (Hebrews 2: 9.) A worthy sacrifice has been provided by God Himself, and He will surely accept the offering which He has furnished.

This sacrifice is always ready. Wherever we are, whenever we will, we can, by faith, bring this sacrifice before God in prayer, and plead the merits of the Son of God in our own behalf. The promise is: "Whatsoever ye shall ask in My name, that will I do, that the Father may be glorified in the Son." John 14: 13.

He is the Prince of Life and "His name through faith in His name," can bring perfect soundness to every sinful soul.

"He is risen."

The Resurrection

SEVEN hundred years before the crucifixion, Isaiah testified of the Saviour "and He made His grave with the wicked, and with the rich in His death." (Isaiah 53:9.) To make "His grave with the wicked," would have been to cast Him out without burial, with criminals. Bishop Lowthe translates this text as follows: "And His grave was *appointed* with the wicked; but with the rich man was His tomb." The design of His enemies was frustrated. The Jews were foiled in this design, by one of their own wealthy rulers, Joseph of Arimathea, who, in this darkest hour for the followers of Christ, stepped out boldly and took his stand for the crucified Saviour.

Joseph had great influence with Pilate, and begged from him permission to take the body from the cross to give it honorable burial. Pilate, who was conscience stricken because of the weak and wicked part he had acted, readily gave Joseph the desired permission.

Tender, loving hands took the Saviour from the cruel cross, and bore His body to the new tomb, which had never before been used, and there He had laid, thus literally fulfilling the statement of the prophet. Although poor while in life, in death His body was laid in the new, rock-hewn tomb of the wealthy ruler of Israel. No greater honor could have been shown to the dead than was accorded to Jesus by Joseph and Nicodemus. Of His rest in the tomb we read in the beautiful language of David in the Psalms: "Therefore My heart is glad, and My glory rejoiceth: My flesh also shall rest in hope. For Thou wilt not leave My soul in hell [the grave]; neither wilt Thou suffer Thine Holy One to see corruption." Psalm 16: 9, 10.

Autotype Fine Art Co., Ltd. Christ, after His resurrection, appears before His disciples.

[54]

In the hour of death, the faith of Christ clung to the promises of God. He laid down His life in the full assurance that He would soon hear the summons, "Jesus, Thou Son of God, Thy Father calls Thee." Solomon had said, "The heaven and heaven of heavens cannot contain Him." 2 Chronicles 2: 6. Peter, speaking of His death, said: "It was not possible that He should be holden of it." Acts 2: 24.

Early on the first day of the week, a bright and powerful angel appeared at the tomb; the Roman guard fell as dead men before his glorious brightness; the stone was rolled away, and at the command of the heavenly messenger the bands of death were broken, and the Saviour came forth a mighty conqueror. Henceforth the resurrection of the dead was a reality.

It was to this resurrection scene that the apostles looked as the evidence of fulfillment of the promise of the future reward of all the faithful. Said Christ: "I am the resurrection, and the life: he that believeth in Me, though he were dead, yet shall he live." John 11: 25.

Christ died "that through death He might destroy him that had the power of death, that is, the devil." (Hebrews 2: 14.) Satan claimed all who had fallen in death as his subjects. The resurrection of Christ broke the power of death. From that hour, Satan knew that his hold on the human family would sometime be broken, and that his days were numbered.

Paul, looking forward to the general resurrection, which is to take place at the second coming of Christ, describes it in the following words: "The Lord himself shall descend from heaven with a shout, with the voice of the archangel, and with the trump of God: and the dead in Christ shall rise first: then we which are alive and remain shall be caught up together with them in the clouds, to meet the Lord in the air: and so shall we ever be with the Lord. Wherefore comfort one another with these words." 1 Thessalonians 4: 16-18.

The future reward of the righteous is placed at the time of the resurrection, for the Saviour says: "Thou shalt be recompensed at the resurrection of the just." Luke 14: 14.

Paul bases his entire hope of a future life on the resurrec-

Autotype Fine Art Co., Ltd.
The Saviour shows His nail prints to doubting Thomas.

tion of the dead. He says that if there is no resurrection, "then they also which are fallen asleep in Christ are perished." But this is not possible; "for since by man came death, by man came also the resurrection of the dead. For as in Adam all die, even so in Christ shall all be made alive." "For the trumpet shall sound, and the dead shall be raised incorruptible, and we shall be changed." (Read 1 Corinthians 15: 12-22, 52.)

The Resurrection

Isaiah looked beyond the grave when he testified: "Thy dead men shall live, together with My dead body shall they arise. Awake and sing, ye that dwell in dust: for thy dew is as the dew of herbs, and the earth shall cast out the dead." Isaiah 26: 19.

Job was willing to rest his future hope on the resurrection. "If a man die, shall he live again? All the days of my appointed time will I wait, till my change come. Thou shalt call, and I will answer Thee: Thou wilt have a desire to the work of Thine hands." Job 14: 14, 15. Where was Job to wait? Here is his own answer: "If I wait, the grave is mine house: I have made my bed in the darkness." Job 17: 13.

He who conquered the grave, will come to this earth again, and at that time, "the dead shall hear the voice of the Son of God: and they that hear shall live." (John 5: 25.) Then "the wilderness and the solitary place shall be glad for them; and the desert shall rejoice, and blossom as the rose. It shall blossom abundantly, and rejoice even with joy and singing: the glory of Lebanon shall be given unto it, the excellency of Carmel and Sharon; they shall see the glory of the Lord, and the excellency of our God." (Isaiah 35: 1, 2.)

He ascended from among the disciples.

The Lord's Ascension

AS THE time drew near in which the Saviour knew that He must return to the Father, whence He had come, He began to reveal to His disciples something of what the future had in store for them. The prospect of meeting trials without the Saviour to share them brought sadness to their hearts; and lest they should become discouraged, He opened to them the thought that His going away would be an advantage to them; said He, "for if I go not away, the Comforter will not come unto you." (John 16:7.)

These words were full of mystery to the wondering disciples. How would it be possible for another to do as much for them as He had done? Who, indeed, besides Jesus, could feed the hungry multitude, heal the sick, cure loathsome diseases, quiet the angry waves of the sea, and raise the dead at will?

Had they not, too, been constantly instructed by His gracious words, and were they not able, in His name, to cast out devils? Why should they desire a change? Should He leave them, as He declared He must, how would they then be able to do the wondrous things which His presence had enabled them to accomplish? Their hearts were filled with foreboding and perplexity.

Notwithstanding all this, Jesus again assured them that even for their sake, it would be better for Him to go away. Should He remain with them personally, His presence would be confined to one locality at a time, and this would make it necessary for some who wished to meet Him to travel long distances. But the Holy Spirit, which was to come to the earth in His place, could be found by all at one time, wherever they might be.

When on earth in person, Christ was seen by saint and sinner alike; but the Spirit, which He sent to represent Himself while He is away in heaven, is never seen, but may be known through faith in Christ. The unbelieving world does not know this heavenly Visitant, because He is felt rather than seen. (Read John 14:17.)

To those, however, who accept Christ by faith, the Spirit becomes an indwelling power, by which the possessor is enabled to overcome the world and sinful flesh.

As the disciples had been connected with heaven through attachment to, and dwelling with, the personal Christ, so now, since He has gone to heaven, He has provided an indwelling Presence, by which all His believers may have access to Him where He is. So, then, whatever Christ was to His disciples by His personal presence, even such He is now to every one who comes to Him by faith, through the Holy Spirit, which God bestows as freely as He has given His only-begotten Son.

Christ was about to leave this world, where He had spent thirty-three years of earth life, for the throne of glory, which He had once before enjoyed with the Father. But still, He did not for a moment forget those who were to remain behind, and in His place become the light of the world, finishing His work. (See Matthew 5:14-16; Hebrews 2:3; Acts 1:8.)

He had before prayed that God might not take them out of the world, but rather that they might be kept from its evil. (Read John 17:15.) So on the eve of His leaving them, He gave the blessed promise, "Lo, I am with you alway, even unto the end of the world." Matthew 28:20.

Coming near to Bethany, the disciples gathered about the Saviour. As He looked in their faces, a peculiar light seemed to cover His countenance; and as He stretched out His hands in the act of blessing them, He was taken up slowly from them. "And when He had spoken these things, while they beheld, He was taken up; and a cloud received Him out of their sight." Acts 1:9. Gazing at Him in His ascent, the wondering disciples saw Him enter a cloud of bright glory, and He was lost to their sight.

In deep amazement, their gaze was fixed on the point where they had last seen their beloved Lord, when suddenly a voice was heard near them. Turning, they saw two shining beings, who brought them the comforting message, "This same Jesus, which is taken up from you into heaven, shall so come in like manner as ye have seen Him go into heaven." Acts 1:11.

Christ had triumphed. He had come from heaven to earth to take man's nature, and been born in Bethlehem's lowly manger; He had been subject to His earthly parents; had worked by the side of Joseph at the carpenter's trade; had known weariness in His journeyings; had prayed all night on the mountainside; in pity had fed the famishing multitudes; had healed the sick and raised the dead; had been rejected of men, scourged, and crucified; and had ascended in the form of man to sit on the right hand of God. (See Hebrews 8:1, 2.)

Autotype Fine Art Co., Ltd.
Christ, our Advocate, reconciles us to His Father and to one another.

Christ Our Mediator *and* Advocate

IF TWO persons are involved in a difficulty, and cannot agree, it is a common custom for some friend to act as a mediator or arbitrator between the two. In this capacity Jesus Christ acts between God and man. "For there is one God, and one Mediator between God and men, the Man Christ Jesus." 1 Timothy 2: 5. Man is estranged from God. In his sinful condition he is not reconciled to the government of God; for we read that the "carnal [natural] mind is enmity against God; for it is not subject to the law of God, neither indeed can be." (Romans 8: 7.) It must be changed before it can be subject to God's government, and that can be done only by the power of God. Since the fall of man by sin, all men are carnal. Even the apostle Paul said, "I am carnal, sold under sin." (Romans 7: 14.)

In order to save man, it was necessary that a divine sacrifice should be made for the sins of the world. This was provided for by the death of Jesus Christ. But the death of Christ alone could not save man. Christ must rise from the dead, and then, in His divine and human nature blended, act as the Mediator between every repenting sinner and the Father, pleading in the sinner's behalf the merits of His sacrifice.

Before Christ came in the flesh, this office of mediatorship was represented by the priesthood, especially by the high priest of the Jewish nation. As the high priest was to bear upon his shoulders, graven in stone, the names of all the tribes of Israel, representing the people of God (Exodus 28: 9-12), so Christ takes upon Himself the task of bearing all His people, and bringing them into harmony with the government of God.

We should not forget that God has no feeling of hatred toward the sinner; for He so loved mankind that He gave His own Son to die in the sinner's place. He is not a hard master, whose anger must be appeased. He loves the sinner, and because of that love, He gave His Son to die for him, that the sinner might be separated from his sin, which, if not removed, must forever separate him from God and happiness. Through Jesus Christ as mediator, God, though the Author of all things, and the One who has been wronged by sin, takes the first step toward a reconciliation. It is while we were yet enemies that Jesus died for us.

So we read: "All things are of God, who hath reconciled us to Himself by Jesus Christ, and hath given to us the ministry of reconciliation; to wit, that God was in Christ, reconciling the world unto Himself, not imputing their trespasses unto them; and hath committed unto us the word of reconciliation." Christ, having shown by His sacrifice that God still loves the sinner, now sends out His ministers, praying us, praying all mankind, to be reconciled to God. (See 2 Corinthians 5: 17-20.)

Christ comes to us as a friend and helper, as one who has influence and power with God. He brings to us the terms by which, if we accept them, we may be restored to favor with God. These conditions are honorable to God and merciful to us. Since Jesus has died for us, the law of God will not be lowered by our salvation. He can "be just, and the justifier of him which believeth in Jesus." (Romans 3: 26.) Christ, in answer to our faith, gives us His righteousness, which is just what the law of God demands, to cover all our sins. So we have His death for our death, and His life for our life. Accepting this gracious offer, sinners and aliens become children and saints of God.

Christ Our Mediator and Advocate

Christ is also our Advocate. Hence we read: "If any man sin, we have an Advocate with the Father, Jesus Christ the righteous." 1 John 2: 1. An advocate is one who pleads the cause of another. Every being has a case at the bar of God. "We must all appear before the judgment seat of Christ; that every one may receive the things done in his body, according to that he hath done, whether it be good or bad." 2 Corinthians 5: 10. If we have Christ for our Advocate, why should we fear? He is the only begotten of the Father; but it is as man that He represents us and pleads for us. The Mediator, the Advocate, is the "Man Christ Jesus." (Read Hebrews 2: 17, 18.)

Behold the wonderful provisions of divine grace! The Son of God dies as a sacrifice for our sins. He is also the Mediator, pleading with us to accept the gospel of salvation, which, at so great a price He has made it possible for us to secure. With the sweat of Gethsemane upon His brow, with the blood of the sacrifice dripping from pierced hands, feet, and side, in suffering unspeakable, and with love unutterable, He appeals to us, saying, "Come unto Me, all ye that labor and are heavy laden, and I will give you rest." Matthew 11: 28. Then when we come to Him, He bears our case upon His heart; and when we repent, He pleads our case before the Father and obtains for us a pardon.

He Will Come Again

AT THE close of the Passover Supper, just before entering upon His night of agony in Gethsemane, the Saviour told His disciples that He was soon going away from them. This made them very sorrowful; but the Master then gave the words of comfort and assurance which have been the hope of the faithful and true through all succeeding ages:

"Let not your heart be troubled: ye believe in God, believe also in Me. In My Father's house are many mansions: if it were not so, I would have told you. I go to prepare a place for you. And if I go and prepare a place for you, I will come again, and receive you unto Myself; that where I am, there ye may be also." John 14: 1-3.

In these words our Saviour tells of the glorious city, the New Jerusalem, which is being prepared in His "Father's house,"— the home of God. Already there were many mansions in this beautiful city. When Jesus should go back to heaven, He would prepare other manisons for them, and for all the righteous who should live after them.

Abraham looked forward to the time when he should have a home in this city. "For he looked for a city which hath foundations, whose builder and maker is God." Hebrews 11: 10.

The apostle-prophet John minutely describes this city in the twenty-first chapter of Revelation. He tells of its foundations, describes its walls and gates, and gives a very realistic account of this home of the saved.

But to the followers of Jesus, the central thought in these verses is the statement, "I will come again." This is the consummation of the great plan of redemption. Then the "ransomed of the Lord," the victorious of the race that were banished from their inheritance by sin, "shall return, and come to Zion with songs and everlasting joy upon their heads: they shall obtain joy and gladness, and sorrow and sighing shall flee away." (Isaiah 35: 10.)

The doctrine of the second advent is the very keynote of the sacred Scriptures. From the day when the first pair turned their sorrowing steps from Eden, the children of faith have waited the coming of the Promised One to break the destroyer's power and bring them again to the lost paradise.

The Old Testament abounds in prophecies concerning the return of our Lord. Even before the Flood, this grand truth, as well as that of the judgment, was understood. "Enoch also, the seventh from Adam, prophesied of these, saying, Behold, the Lord cometh, with ten thousands of His saints, to execute judgment upon all." Jude 14, 15.

The prophet Zechariah testifies of the same event: "The Lord my God shall come, and all the saints with Thee." Zechariah 14: 5. And the Saviour tells us that "the Son of man shall come in His glory, and all the holy angels with Him." (Matthew 25: 31.)

The "saints" spoken of in the foregoing text are the hosts of angels which accompany our Lord at His second coming to earth. This is made clear by the words of our Saviour in the preceding text. It is "all the holy angels" who come with Him. Heaven will be emptied; for all its bright dwellers will accompany their Lord on His wonderful journey from heaven to earth.

The angels have a most important part to act when the Son of man "appears in the clouds of heaven." For "He shall send His angels with a great sound of a trumpet, and they shall gather together His elect from the four winds, from one end of heaven to the other." (Matthew 24: 31.)

Then when the elect are so gathered, both the "dead in Christ" who have been raised from their graves, and those who "are alive and remain shall be caught up together . . . in the clouds, to meet the Lord in the air: and so shall we ever be with the Lord." Then Paul exhorts us to "comfort one another with these words." (1 Thessalonians 4: 17, 18.)

From the depths of sorrow and affliction, the patriarch Job looked forward to the second coming of Christ for his sure and final reward. "I know that my Redeemer liveth, and that He shall stand at the latter day upon the earth: and though after my skin worms destroy this body, yet in my flesh shall I see God: whom I shall see for myself, and mine eyes shall behold, and not another." Job 19: 25-27.

Job was not alone in this consolation. David, the sweet singer of Israel, contemplating the victorious return of Christ, said, "Let the heavens rejoice, and let the earth be glad; let the sea roar, and the fulness thereof. Let the field be joyful, and all that is therein: then shall all the trees of the wood rejoice before the Lord: for He cometh, for He cometh to judge the earth: He shall judge the world with righteousness, and the people with His truth." "Our God shall come, and shall not keep silence: a fire shall devour before Him, and it shall be very tempestuous round about Him. He shall call to the heavens from above, and to the earth, that He may judge His people." Psalms 96: 11-13; 50: 3, 4.

With burning eloquence, from lips touched with hallowed fire from heaven's altar, the gospel prophet exclaims: "He will swallow up death in victory; and the Lord God will wipe away tears from off all faces; and the rebuke of His people shall He take away from off all the earth; for the Lord hath spoken it. And it shall be said in that day, Lo, this is our God; we have waited for Him, and He will save us: this is the Lord; we have waited for Him, we will be glad and rejoice in His salvation." And of the righteous dead who receive immortal life at this time, he says, "Thy dead men shall live, together with My dead body shall they arise. Awake and sing, ye that dwell in dust: for thy dew is as the dew of herbs, and the earth shall cast out the dead." Isaiah 25: 8, 9; 26: 19.

The apostle Paul testifies: "And unto them that look for Him shall He appear the second time without sin unto salvation." Hebrews 9: 28.

At His first advent, our Saviour bore the sins of the world

Autotype Fine Art Co., ltd.
The transfiguration of Christ was a prophetic picture of His second appearing.

in Gethsemane and on Calvary. At His second advent, He will come bearing no sin, but as the mighty and glorious King, to take all His faithful children to Himself forever. (Read Matthew 25: 31.)

Our Saviour himself says of this coming: "For the Son of man shall come in the glory of His Father with His angels;

and then He shall reward every man according to his works." Matthew 16:27.

All through the ages, the saints of God, suffering for their faith in gloomy prisons, in the torture-chamber, racked upon the wheel, bound to the stake, suffering the tortures of fire and flame,— these have borne blessed testimony to their faith in the personal, literal, and soon coming of their beloved Lord, for the advancement of whose precious cause they counted not their lives as dear.

It was this hope that cheered their weary spirits and buoyed them up amid their sufferings. The wise and gentle Melanchthon, companion of Luther, declared that "this aged world is not far from its end." And, as if echoing the same thought, Luther himself asserted: "I persuade myself verily, that the day of judgment will not be absent full three hundred years. God will not, cannot, suffer this wicked world much longer." "The great day is drawing near in which the kingdom of abominations shall be overthrown."

One of the early Christians declares that "being assured of Christ's personal resurrection, and consequently of their own, at His coming, for this cause they despised death and were found to be above it." If they must sleep in the grave, they were willing, that they "might rise free." By this hope they triumphed over death and the grave.

These godly suffering ones looked for the "Lord to come from heaven in the clouds with the glory of the Father," "bringing to the just the times of the kingdom."

Calvin, the great reformer, urges Christians "not to hesitate, desiring the day of Christ's coming as of all events most auspicious"; "the whole family of the faithful," he declares, "will keep in view that day." He further asserts that "we must hunger after Christ, we must seek, contemplate, till the dawning of the great day, when our Lord will fully manifest the glory of His kingdom."

Baxter declares that "the thoughts of the coming of the Lord are most sweet and joyful to me." "If death be the last enemy to be destroyed at the resurrection, we may learn how earnestly believers should long and pray for the second coming of Christ, when this full and final conquest shall be made." "This is the day that all believers should long, and hope, and wait for, as being the accomplishment of all the work for their redemption, and all the desires and endeavors of their souls." "Hasten, O Lord, this blessed day."

John Knox, Scotland's devoted reformer, exclaimed fervently, "Has not our Lord Jesus carried up our flesh into heaven? And shall He not return?—We know that He shall return, and that with expedition."

Latimer and Ridley, both martyrs for Jesus Christ, and for their faith in Him, rejoiced in the same blessed hope of His second coming. Among the writings of Ridley, we find the following beautiful and inspiring sentiment: "The world without doubt — this I do believe, and therefore I say it— draws to an end. Let us with John, the servant of God, cry in our hearts unto our Saviour, 'Come, Lord Jesus, come.'"

This blessed doctrine, then, was the hope and inspiration of the early church. The "church in the wilderness" rejoiced in it; and the godly reformers, who counted naught dear that they might win Christ, anticipated with joy unspeakable the glorious day when their absent Lord would come again. It is no new doctrine, hatched in the foolish brain of some latter-day enthusiast, and taught by his fanatical followers. Nay, verily; but it has been the one glorious hope of the faithful, from the days of righteous Enoch, until now, when the whole creation, longing to be delivered, indeed "groaneth and travaileth in pain."

The second coming of Christ will be literal and personal, and in view of all the world. As the sorrowing disciples were earnestly looking into heaven to catch the last glimpse of their departing Lord, two shining angels appeared to comfort them with the joyful promise:

"Ye men of Galilee, why stand ye gazing up into heaven? This same Jesus, which is taken up from you into heaven, shall so come in like manner as ye have seen Him go into heaven." Acts 1: 11.

O joyful assurance! "This same Jesus" who had dwelt among them, who had eaten with them, who had taught them, who had walked up and down with them through the cities of Israel, who had preached to the poor, fed the hungry, ministered to the sorrowing, healed the sick, raised the dead, and whom John says "our hands have handled," is coming back to earth again.

"This same Jesus"! With these words ringing in their ears, the disciples returned to Jerusalem with hearts full of joy and with tongues and lips eloquent with the voice of praise. To them the future hope had become a reality. Their Saviour was not lost to them. He would come again.

How will He come?—Listen to the words of the angels: "In like manner as ye have seen Him go into heaven."

How did He go?—Personally, bodily. As He stood among them, commissioning them regarding their future labors, "He was taken up." And as He rose with pierced hands outstretched in blessing, "a cloud received Him out of their sight."

"Shall so come in like manner." They saw Him ascend. On His return, "every eye shall see Him." (Revelation 1:7.)

"A cloud received Him out of their sight." This must have been a cloud of angels who had come to escort Him on His return to His Father's house.

Of His coming back to earth, John says, "Behold, He cometh with clouds." Revelation 1:7. Accompanying Him are all the angels of glory, whose number is given as "ten thousand times ten thousand [a hundred million] and thousands of thousands." (Revelation 5: 11.)

That there will be many deceptions abroad regarding the second coming of Christ is evidenced by His own words of

Herbert Photos, Inc.
"As the lightning ... so shall also the coming of the son of man be."

warning. In answer to the questions of the disciples regarding this event, He said, "Take heed that no man deceive you." He then pointed out some of the deceptions that were to arise.

Some would come, saying, "I am Christ," and many such pretenders have arisen. There were to be "false prophets" who would show "great signs and wonders." Some would say, "Behold, He is in the desert." Others, "He is in the secret chamber."

There will be all kinds of theories and beliefs, to lull to sleep the souls of men. But our Lord brushes all these away with the solemn statement:

"As the lightning cometh out of the east, and shineth even unto the west; so shall also the coming of the Son of man be." Matthew 24:27.

But the deceptions of the enemy are so plausible that "if it were possible, they shall deceive the very elect." (Matthew 24:24.)

To the elect of these days our Lord has left word, "Take heed that no man deceive you." After explicit statements of what might be expected, He says, "Behold, I have told you before." Matthew 24:25. All who fail to heed these warnings will certainly be without excuse when they stand before their Lord at His appearing.

If we study the teachings of Christ and of the apostles who have testified of His second coming, we need not be deceived. Of one thing we may be sure, the conversion of a sinner or the death of a saint cannot fill these requirements.

Close your eyes as firmly as you may, and you cannot hide the sight of the lightning's flash. The light which shines from the bolt that crashes from the cloud in the far east, is seen with equal distinctness at the verge of the western horizon. The appearance of the Son of man in the clouds of heaven will be as visible to the whole world as a flash of lightning.

To those who reject these warnings, the mission of Christ to earth will not be one of peace. Of these the psalmist writes, "Thou shalt break them with a rod of iron; Thou shalt dash them in pieces like a potter's vessel." Psalm 2:9.

When Shall These Things Be?

IN THE Saviour's teachings, He had instructed His disciples in regard to His second advent to the world. But they had but a vague idea when it would take place. They expected Him to set up a temporal kingdom on earth, and probably connected this event with His second coming.

As Jesus was departing from the temple, after His triumphant entry into Jerusalem, His disciples directed His attention to its glory. It was the pride of the Jewish nation, and they supposed it would stand forever. It was a wonderful building; its construction had required the labor of thousands of men for more than forty years. Josephus, in his description of it, said that the stones were fifty feet long, twenty-four feet broad, and sixteen feet thick. (See Mark 13:1. *Antiq. b. 15, c. xi.*)

What must have been the astonishment of the disciples as Jesus turned to them sorrowfully, and said, "See ye not all these things? Verily I say unto you, There shall not be left here one stone upon another, that shall not be thrown down." Matthew 24:2.

All the traditions the disciples had held, and their own beliefs, seemed slipping away from them. They remembered the instructions of their Lord in regard to His second coming, the end of the world, and the setting up of His kingdom; and now He had added to this the plain statement that Jerusalem and the temple would be utterly destroyed. What could it mean? Had they misunderstood Him?

Silently they walked by His side to the Mount of Olives, and when He had seated Himself, they came to Him with questions the answer to which would forever settle the matter. "When shall these things be? and what shall be the sign of Thy coming, and of the end of the world?"

Were their questions out of place? Did the Saviour rebuke them for unseemly curiosity?—No! He knew that their motives in asking were sincere, and He proceeded carefully to instruct them in regard to the events referred to in their questions.

The Saviour was always ready to give full and careful explanation and instruction to all who really desire to understand the truths taught by Him. To be sure, He often spoke in parables, many of which were not readily understood by the hearers, but to all who were interested sufficiently to ask for an explanation, He made His meaning simple and plain. Hence, to the inquiring disciples, the Saviour gave, as recorded in Matthew 24, the prophecy in regard to the events that were to take place on this earth.

In these words of instruction are embodied the full and complete answer to their questions. Neither was it given for the benefit of these disciples alone. It was given to the disciples, that it might be handed down by them to all who would believe on the Saviour in all ages until He should finally come and take the faithful to Himself. It applies to our time, and with much greater force as we are nearing the closing scenes in the events recorded in this wonderful panorama of the remaining history of the world.

It is asserted by some, however, that the second advent is a subject with which we have nothing to do; that all knowledge of this great event is kept as a secret with the Almighty; that He may come in one year, or His coming may be a thousand years in the future. If this is the case, then why did the Saviour take pains to make such definite statements in regard to it? Why did he give such positive waymarks to show when the day of His coming should be near, "even at the door"?

If we can know nothing in regard to this important event which so intimately concerns us, we are forced to accept one of two conclusions: Either the Saviour undertook to make an explanation to the disciples which He should not have entered into, or, trying to explain the matter, He failed to make it clear enough to be understood. Of course we cannot admit either one of these propositions, and hence are forced to believe that the Saviour considered that this subject was important, and intended that we should understand it.

The Lord has given us the most minute description of the events to transpire on this earth, and has also given accurate signs to show when His coming is near, "even at the door." And although we may not know the day and the hour, yet our information is so definite that we may "see the day approaching," and be prepared to meet our King, at His appearing, with joy, and not with grief.

Our Lord knew that the truths in regard to His second coming would be misunderstood. It is the one subject above all others upon which the enemy of all souls desires to keep us in ignorance. The knell of his doom is perceived ringing through every promise of the coming of our Lord.

More than this, there is no subject that so turns the hearts of men to God and converts souls to Christ, as the earnest proclamation of Bible truth in regard to the soon-coming Saviour. Of course Satan will do all in his power to blind the eyes of men to this truth, and to divert their attention from the events clustering around it.

Christ knew that errors would abound in regard to this subject, and prefaces His instruction with the warning, "Take heed that no man decieve you." Matthew 24: 4. Now, in our study of this subject, let us be sure that our ears are open to receive the teachings of God's word, and that we are not blinded by any ideas that we may have received, or by any theory we may have held in regard to it.

The question of the disciples was evidently twofold: first, When will the destruction of Jerusalem take place? and, second, What shall be the sign of the second coming of Christ, and of the end of the world? The Saviour's instruction, found in the twenty-fourth chapter of Matthew, deals with both these important questions.

The destruction of Jerusalem, the signs preceding it, the terrors accompanying it, and the relation which the followers of Jesus should sustain toward it, were fully explained to the listening disciples.

But to those living in the last days, the instructions given at this time are of the most vital importance. Plainly laid down and carefully explained are the waymarks and milestones which mark the approaching end of this world's history. And clearly are we told of the changeless nature of these evidences.

"Heaven and earth shall pass away, but My words shall not pass away." Matthew 24: 35.

"Watch ye therefore: . . . lest coming suddenly He find you sleeping. And what I say unto you I say unto all, Watch." Mark 13: 35-37.

Destruction *of* Jerusalem

ANCIENT Jerusalem was spoken of by David as "beautiful for situation, the joy of the whole earth, . . . the city of the great King." Psalm 48: 2. Its greatest attraction was the temple. Situated upon the hill of Zion, more anciently called Mount Moriah, it could be seen at a great distance. Built of great blocks of the whitest marble, finished with the most precious woods, and garnished with the most costly metals, the temple was regarded with wonder and awe by both Jew and Gentile.

Not only was Jerusalem the capital city of the nation, but Jehovah had chosen it as the center of worship for all people. "For the Lord hath chosen Zion; He hath desired it for His habitation." Psalm 132: 13.

At the feast of the Passover and other national memorials, the tribes gathered to Jerusalem from all the land of Palestine. There those who had sin-offerings to make brought to the Lord their sacrifices. "There, for ages, holy prophets had uttered their messages of warning. There, priests had waved their censers, and the cloud of incense, with the prayers of the worshipers, had ascended before God. There, daily the blood of slain lambs had been offered, pointing forward to the Lamb of God. There, Jehovah had revealed His presence in the cloud of glory above the mercy-seat."

But Israel had been a rebellious nation. God's messages of warning had been disregarded, His prophets had been imprisoned and slain, and His holy law that might have been their bulwark had been perverted and made "of none effect" by their "traditions."

Jesus loved Jerusalem and would have saved the city and the nation, but they had rejected His mission, despised His

Autotype Fine Art Co., Ltd.
Christ curses the fig-tree.

warnings, and both were doomed. Hence, shortly before His crucifixion, while denouncing the Pharisees, He closes with the sorrowful exclamation:

"O Jerusalem, Jerusalem, thou that killest the prophets, and stonest them which are sent unto thee, how often would I have gathered thy children together, even as a hen gathereth her chickens under her wings, and ye would not. Behold, your house is left unto you desolate." Matthew 23: 37, 38.

Shortly before this time occurred the incident of the withered fig-tree. One author has aptly said, "The cursing of the fig-tree was an acted parable."

Immediately after His triumphant entry into Jerusalem, Jesus quietly withdrew from the temple, and, with His disciples went to Bethany. "Now in the morning as He returned into the city, He hungered. And when He saw a fig-tree in the way, He came to it, and found nothing thereon, but leaves only." Matthew 21: 18, 19.

The Levitical law permitted any one in need of food to take from the growing grain, or the fruit of the trees, that which was necessary to satisfy hunger. It would have been perfectly lawful for the Saviour to take of the fruit of the fig-tree to supply His need, if there had been fruit upon it.

In the highlands about Jerusalem, it was true that "the time of figs was not yet." (Mark 11: 13.) But in that orchard of bare trees there was one tree covered with leaves.

Now the fig-tree is peculiar, in that the fruit develops before the leaves appear. Whenever the leaves were fully grown there should be ripened fruit. Hence, when Jesus saw a fig-tree covered with leaves He had a right to expect figs upon it. But when He came to it, He "found nothing thereon, but leaves only, and said unto it, Let no fruit grow on thee henceforward forever. And presently the fig-tree withered away." (Matthew 21: 19.)

The lesson from this "acted parable" is obvious. One

tree in the orchard made great pretentions to thrift. It was covered with leaves, while the others were bare. Christ made it and its pretentions a symbol of the Jewish nation.

The Jews were different from the nations around them. God had chosen them as His peculiar people, they laid great stress upon their birthright, and claimed righteousness above all others. But they had lost the characteristics of true godliness, and had become proud, hypocritical, greedy of gain, and cruel to those less successful than they. Their religion had degenerated to formal service in their synagogues and in the temple.

Their outward claims to holiness were symbolized by the great show of leaves on the fig-tree of the parable, and like this tree they bore no fruit toward God. The graces of humility, love, and benevolence, which to God are of great price, were lacking.

The other trees in the orchard were yet bare and made no pretentions to fruit-bearing. They represented the Gentiles, who laid no claim to righteousness, made no pretentions to holiness. Their "time was not yet." They were waiting for the season that would bring them the light of the gospel and hope in God.

"And in the morning, as they passed by, they saw the fig-tree dried up from the roots." Mark 11:20. This circumstance fitly represented the doom of the Jewish nation.

The lesson contained in this parable of the fig-tree was not given for the Jews alone. It stands as a warning to all professors of godliness, to all Christians, to all churches, and for all time. This application is well expressed in the following words:

> "In this generation there are many who are treading on the same ground as were the unbelieving Jews. They have witnessed the manifestation of the power of God; the Holy Spirit has spoken to their hearts; but they cling to

their unbelief and resistance. God sends them warnings and reproof, but they are not willing to confess their errors, and they reject His message and His messenger. The very means He uses for their recovery becomes to them a stone of stumbling.

"The prophets of God were hated by apostate Israel because through them their hidden sins were brought to light. Ahab regarded Elijah as his enemy because the prophet was faithful to rebuke the king's secret iniquities. So today the servant of Christ, the reprover of sin, meets with scorn and rebuffs.

"Bible truth, the religion of Christ, struggles against a strong current of moral impurity. Prejudice is even stronger in the hearts of men now than in Christ's day. Christ did not fulfill men's expectations; His life was a rebuke to their sins, and they rejected Him.

"So now the truth of God's word does not harmonize with men's practices and their normal inclinations, and thousands reject this light. Men prompted by Satan cast doubt upon God's word, and choose to exercise their independent judgment. They choose darkness rather than light, but they do it at the peril of their souls.

"Those who caviled at the words of Christ, found ever-increased cause for cavil, until they turned from the Truth and the Life. So it is now. God does not propose to remove every objection which the carnal heart may bring against His truth. To those who refuse the precious rays of light which would illuminate the darkness, the mysteries of God's word remain such forever. From them the truth is hidden. They walk blindly, and know not the ruin before them."—*"Desire of Ages," 587, 588.*

Higher criticism seeks to take from us our faith in God and in the definiteness and reliability of the Bible. The open infidelity which is honeycombing even denominational colleges and theological seminaries is turning upon the religious world a ministry of theological dreamers and speculators. The old gospel is at a discount. The congregations do not want the plain truths of the Scriptures. The prediction of Paul is being fulfilled in our day:

Autotype Fine Art Co., Ltd. Christ driving the money changers out of the temple

"For the time will come when they will not endure sound doctrine; but after their own lusts shall they heap to themselves teachers, having itching ears; and they shall turn away their ears from the truth, and shall be turned unto fables." 2 Timothy 4: 3, 4.

Like the Athenians of old, many of the modern churchgoers desire little but "to tell, or to hear some new thing." To this class the Old Testament is obsolete, the Ten Commandments are abolished, the prophets are out of date, the Revelation something hidden, and the teachings of Christ and the apostles mere parables and figments of speech.

For a moment let us consider another fig-tree parable given by our Saviour, which lends emphasis to the foregoing lessons:

"A certain man had a fig-tree planted in his vineyard; and he came and sought fruit thereon, and found none. Then said he unto the dresser of his vineyard, Behold, these three years I come seeking fruit on this fig-tree, and find none: cut it down; why cumbereth it the ground?

"And he answering said unto him, Lord, let it alone this year also, till I shall dig about it, and dung it: and if it bear fruit, well: and if not, then after that thou shalt cut it down." Luke 13: 6-9.

For three years Jesus had labored for His people, the house of Abraham. But each year brought little or no fruit. Of His mission it is said, "He came unto His own, and His own received Him not." John 1: 11. The great heart of Israel did not respond. Their religion remained mere outward show. There was no fruit,—"nothing but leaves." The test and waiting had not availed to save them, and their coming doom was prefigured by the withered, blasted fig-tree of Bethany.

Jesus loved His people with an unchanging love. It was with the deepest sorrow and agony of soul that He realized that they were, by the hardness of their impenitent hearts, sealing the doom of Jerusalem and their nation.

At the time of the triumphant entry into Jerusalem, the joyous throng supposed they were escorting the Messiah to His seat on the throne of David,— that He would then take His place as king, deliverer, and temporal ruler of Israel.

As the procession arrived at the brow of the hill overlooking Jerusalem, "the joy of the whole earth," its great beauty came into full view, bathed in the rays of the setting sun. The stately grandeur of the temple attracted all eyes. The shouts of the multitude were hushed, and they turned their eyes upon the Saviour, expecting to see Him, too, wrapped in admiration for the beauties of the city and the glories of the temple. But they were surprised and dismayed to see Him swayed by an agony of sorrow and weeping. And in anguish He exclaimed:

"If thou hadst known, even thou, at least in this thy day, the things which belong unto thy peace —" He did not conclude the sentence, but in sorrowful tones added, "but now they are hid from thine eyes." Luke 19: 42.

"Had her people walked in the counsel of God, Jerusalem would have 'stood forever.' She might have become the queen of kingdoms, free in the strength of her God-given power. There would then have been no armed soldiers waiting at her gates, no Roman banners waving from her walls. From Jerusalem the dove of peace would have gone to all nations. She would have been the crowning glory of the world.

"But the Jews had rejected their Saviour; they were about to crucify their King. And when the sun should set that night the doom of Jerusalem would be forever sealed."—*"Christ Our Saviour," p. 91.*

Forty years afterward, the Roman army, under Titus, after a prolonged siege, took Jerusalem, slaughtered its inhabitants, laid low the temple, and destroyed the city.

Destruction of Jerusalem

As Jesus left the temple for the last time, His closing words to the multitude were, "Behold, your house is left unto you desolate." Mathew 23: 38.

Our Saviour's last discourse in the temple was one of stern rebuke to the scribes and Pharisees. For three years He had labored earnestly and untiringly to arouse the leaders of Israel to repentance.

But at this time the utter hopelessness of the effort seemed pressed upon Him with a crushing force. He knew that this was the last opportunity He would have to bring these truths to the people. He said, "Ye shall not see Me henceforth, till ye shall say, Blessed is He that cometh in the name of the Lord." Matthew 23: 39. His voice would never again be heard in the temple.

He realized that in a few days would be enacted the disgraceful scenes of His arrest, condemnation, and crucifixion. Yet He promised that after His voice should no more be heard among them, He would still send faithful witnesses to instruct and warn them. Yet they would pursue toward them the same course that they had toward Him.

"Behold," He said, "I send unto you prophets, and wise men, and scribes: and some of them ye shall kill and crucify; and some of them shall ye scourge in your synagogues, and persecute them from city to city: that upon you may come all the righteous blood shed upon the earth, from the blood of righteous Abel unto the blood of Zacharias son of Barachias, whom ye slew between the temple and the altar." Matthew 23: 34, 35.

The spirit of the impenitent persecutors of old was actuating the people of that day. In the face of all the light of the past, they, by their present course gave sanction to all the evil work of the past, and would thus be held accountable.

As the Master was departing, the disciples came to show Him the wonders, and strength, and beauty of the temple.

The Roman army taking Jerusalem

Destruction of Jerusalem

"And Jesus said unto them, See ye not all these things? Verily I say unto you, There shall not be left here one stone upon another, that shall not be thrown down." Matthew 24: 2.

This prediction was fulfilled when the Romans destroyed Jerusalem in A.D. 70. The Talmud records that the Roman officer left in charge after the city fell "did with a plowshare tear up the foundation of the temple."

Josephus testifies:

"As soon as the army had no more people to slay, . . . Cæsar gave orders that they should demolish the entire city and temple, but should leave as many of the towers standing as were of the greatest eminency,—namely, Phasaelus, Hippicus, and Mariamne, and so much of the wall as inclosed the city on the west side. This wall was spared in order to afford a camp for such as were to lie in garrison: as were the towers also spared in order to denominate to posterity what kind of city it was, and how well fortified, which the Roman valor had subdued. But for all the rest of the wall, it was so completely leveled with the ground, by those that dug it up to the foundation, that there was left nothing to make those who came thither believe it had ever been inhabited."—*"Wars of the Jews," Whiston's Translation, Book 7, chap. 1, page 1.*

The iniquity of Israel and the utter destruction to come upon the nation for their sins were foretold in Micah 3: 10-12: "They build up Zion with blood, and Jerusalem with iniquity. The heads thereof judge for reward, and the priests thereof teach for hire, and the prophets thereof divine for money: yet will they lean upon the Lord, and say, Is not the Lord among us? None evil can come upon us. Therefore shall Zion for your sake be plowed as a field, and Jerusalem shall become heaps, and the mountain of the house as the high places of the forest."

But the disciples could not understand how those massive walls could be thrown down. Portions of this wall were very ancient, and had withstood the siege of Nebuchadnezzar. And they had been so added to and strengthened that they seemed impregnable to any weapons of siege and warfare known at that day. This foretold destruction was a hard saying to them. They could not comprehend it.

Soon after Jesus' departure from the temple, "as He sat upon the mount of Olives, the disciples came unto Him privately, saying, Tell us, when shall these things be? And what shall be the sign of Thy coming, and of the end of the world?" (Matthew 24: 3.)

"With the overthrow of Jerusalem the disciples associated the events of Christ's personal coming in temporal glory to take the throne of universal empire, to punish the impenitent Jews, and to break from off the nation the Roman yoke." —"*Great Controversy,*" *p. 25.* The Lord had told them of His second coming, and they associated this with the foretold destruction of Jerusalem.

From the form of their question, and the logic of subsequent events, it is evident that the disciples had but a vague conception of the nature of either event. It is a fact that they did not understand the true mission of Christ to earth until taught by the Holy Spirit after His ascension. They could not divest themselves of the popular opinion that Christ would soon set up a kingdom upon earth, as shown by the following references:

Shortly before the triumphant entry of Jesus into Jerusalem, James and John, through their mother Salome, asked that when His kingdom should be set up (referring to His supposed temporal kingdom on earth) one might have the seat of authority on His right hand, and the other on His left. (See Matthew 20: 20; Mark 10: 35-38.)

Although at this time such a spirit was rebuked by our Lord, yet at the institution of the Lord's supper, this ambition still possessed the disciples. "And there was also a strife

Destruction of Jerusalem

among them, which of them should be accounted the greatest." Luke 22: 24.

At the end of the forty days in which Jesus was with His disciples after the resurrection, the establishment of an earthly kingdom was still their paramount thought. As He stood with them on the mount of Olives, they asked the very last question they ever addressed to Him on earth: "Lord, wilt thou at this time restore again the kingdom to Israel?" Acts 1: 6.

So strong a hold did the early education of the disciples have upon them that it was not possible for Jesus to give them all the important truths which He desired them to receive. This condition is expressed in the words of His memorable talk with them at the Passover Supper: "I have yet many things to say unto you, but ye cannot bear them now." John 16: 12.

For this reason He was cautious in His answer to the question, "When shall these things be? And what shall be the sign of Thy coming, and of the end of the world?" Matthew 24: 3.

Their minds were still clouded, and He did not answer their question by considering separately the destruction of Jerusalem and His second coming. Had He told them fully of the impending destruction of Jerusalem, the utter ruin of their nation, and the terrible events accompanying, they could not have endured it. Hence, in His instruction, He blended the two events, leaving them to study out the application. But to them as to us He sent the infallible guide, the Holy Spirit, so that no error need be made. "Howbeit when He, the Spirit of truth, is come, He will guide you into all truth." John 16: 13.

In the same manner He has left us to grasp the truths of His great prophecy which meet their fulfillment down through the intervening years to the end of time.

As we study our Saviour's words we can but conclude that much of this chapter is twofold in its application. Dire calamities to the Jews were foretold, and startling events were to warn them of the impending destruction of the nation. To us the Jewish nation is a type. God's dealing with them is an object lesson to us. All these things prophesied of the Jews are to have a broader and more complete fulfillment as we near the end of time, in which all the earth will be involved. This method of interpretation is aptly expressed in the words of another:

"When He referred to the destruction of Jerusalem, His prophetic words reached beyond that event to the final conflagration in that day when the Lord shall rise out of His place to punish the world for their iniquity, when the earth shall disclose her blood, and shall no more cover her slain. This entire discourse was given, not for the disciples only, but for those who should live in the last scenes of the earth's history."—*"Desire of Ages," p. 628.*

"The experience of the people of that generation who rejected the message concerning His first advent, and were then led on step by step to crucify the Lord of glory, and who thus brought the end of their nation in their own time, was typical of the experience of the generation who should reject the message of the second advent, and thus crucify the Lord afresh, and bring the end of the world in their time. The prophecy concerning these two generations, connected by a very brief outline of the ecclesiastical history of the intervening centuries, constitutes what is usually designated our Lord's great prophecy. Viewed from this standpoint, it will be seen that the answer of Jesus to the inquiry of His disciples is a continuous prophecy covering step by step, in consecutive order, the whole period of time until He should be manifested in glory; but that it gives a more full outline of the experiences of those two generations, one of which rejected His first advent and as a consequence witnessed the end of their nation, while the other should reject His second advent

Destruction of Jerusalem

and in consequence witness the end of the world. So closely related are the experiences of these two generations, that the prophecy which leads up to the destruction of Jerusalem has a secondary fulfillment in those events in the last generation which lead up to the destruction of the world."—"*Two Great Crises,*" *by W. W. Prescott, in Review and Herald, April 15, 1909.*

In both these great events Satan was to come in with all the powers of cunning and deception in which his centuries of evil had made him the master. "Take heed," said Jesus, "that no man deceive you," and, "Behold, I have told you before." Matthew 24: 4, 25.

He also said, "Many shall come in My name, saying, I am Christ; and shall deceive many." V. 5. Between the time of these words and the destruction of Jerusalem many false messiahs appeared, claiming to work miracles, and proclaiming that the deliverance of the Jewish nation was at hand.

Many historians have recorded the claims of these false christs. Ridpath says of the Jewish people after the days of Christ:

"Never was a people so turbulent, so excited with expectation of a deliverer who should restore the ancient kingdom, so fired with bigotry and fanaticism, as were the wretched Jews of this period. One christ came after another. Revolt was succeeded by revolt, instigated by some pseudo-prophet or pretended king."—*Ridpath's "History of the World," Vol. I, p. 840.*

"Very soon after our Saviour's decease appeared Simon Magus (Acts 8: 9, 10), 'and bewitched the people of Samaria.' . . . He boasted himself likewise among the Jews, as the Son of God. Of the same stamp and character was also Dositheus the Samaritan, who pretended that he was the Christ foretold by Moses."—*"Dissertations on the Prophecies," Bishop Newton, London, 1840, p. 375.*

Josephus states that in A.D. 46, a magician named Theudas "persuaded a great part of the people to take their effects

Keystone View Co.
[94] The wailing wall at Jerusalem ever reminds the Jews of the loss of their holy city.

with them, and follow him to the River Jordan. For he told them he was a prophet; and that he would, by his own command, divide the river, and afford them an easy passage over it." But the Roman soldiers fell upon the company, and slew many of them. "They also took Theudas alive, and cut off his head, and carried it to Jerusalem."—*"Antiquities of the Jews," Book 20, chap. 5.*

At a later date an Egyptian false prophet arose who gathered in the wilderness a body of thirty thousand men. Josephus stamps him as a cheat, but his professed object was to take Jerusalem by force of arms, and so relieve the Jews from the Roman yoke.—*See Josephus' "Wars of the Jews," Book 2, chap. 13.*

"Then if any man shall say unto you, Lo, here is Christ, or there; believe it not." Matthew 24: 23-26. From the secret seances of Spiritualism, from the temples of Christian Science, from the Mormon desert, and through many other manifestations already extant do we now see such open and blasphemous fulfillment of this prophecy as was never dreamed of in the days of the Jewish nation, and greater deceptions are to follow.

"And ye shall hear of wars and rumors of wars: see that ye be not troubled: for all these things must come to pass, but the end is not yet. For nation shall rise against nation, and kingdom against kingdom." Matthew 24: 6, 7.

After the ascension of Christ, and before the destruction of Jerusalem, there was a period of unrest among the nations. There were plots and counterplots, there were preparations for, and rumors of, wars. But "the end is not yet." Not until the armies of Rome were actually encamped before Jerusalem were the disciples to realize that the time was at hand for the fulfillment of the Saviour's prophecy concerning the destruction of the city. Then, in response to the warning given them, they forsook the city and fled to the mountains.

The Coming King

But these "wars and rumors of wars" were largely confined to conflicts between insurgent Jews and their enemies. The condition of the nations which fulfill this feature of prophecy is thus stated by Bishop Newton:

"It is said, moreover, that 'nation shall rise against nation, and kingdom against kingdom.' Here, as Grotius well observes, 'Christ declares that greater disturbances than those which happened under Caligula, should fall out in the latter times of Claudius and in the reign of Nero.' That of 'nation against nation' [or race against race] portended the dissensions, insurrections, and mutual slaughter of the Jews and those of other nations who dwelt in the same cities together; as particularly at Cæsarea, where the Jews and Syrians contended about the right of the city, which contention at length proceeded so far that above twenty thousand Jews were slain, and the city was cleared of the Jewish inhabitants.

"At this blow the whole nation of the Jews were exasperated; and dividing themselves into parties, they burned and plundered the neighboring cities and villages of the Syrians, and made an immense slaughter of the people. The Syrians, in revenge, destroyed not a less number of the Jews, 'and every city,' as Josephus expresseth it, 'was divided into armies.'

"At Scythopolis the inhabitants compelled the Jews who resided among them to fight against their own countrymen, and after the victory, basely setting upon them by night, murdered about thirteen thousand of them, and spoiled their goods.

"At Ascalon they killed two thousand and five hundred, at Ptolemais two thousand, and made not a few prisoners. The Tyrians put many to death, and imprisoned more. The people of Gadara did likewise, and all the other cities of Syria, in proportion as they hated or feared the Jews.

"At Alexandria the old enmity was revived between the Jews and heathen, and many fell on both sides, but of the Jews to the number of fifty thousand. The people of Damascus, too, conspired against the Jews of the same

Destruction of Jerusalem

city, and assaulting them unarmed, killed ten thousand of them."—*"Dissertations," pp. 377, 378.*

During this time there were factional troubles at Rome. Albert Barnes, in his notes on this text, states that "four emperors, Nero, Galba, Otho, and Vitellius, suffered violent deaths in the short space of eighteen months." These assassinations resulted for a time in violent wars and much bloodshed.

"And there shall be famines, and pestilences, and earthquakes, in divers places." Matthew 24:7.

In Jerusalem a great store of provision had been laid up against the time of siege for which the Jews were preparing. But in their internal dissensions these stores were destroyed. The city was, in consequence, not well provisioned when the armies of Rome besieged it. A terrible famine ensued, which was more disastrous from the fact that the city was at that time filled with people from all parts of Judea who had come up to celebrate the Feast of Tabernacles. So fierce was the famine that battles for bread were common, and the eating of human flesh was resorted to.

Other famines occurred during this time of stress for the Jewish nation, but they were confined to narrow limits, and were insignificant when compared with the recent famines in India, Russia, China, etc. More died in the famine of India in 1897 than perished from war, famine, earthquake, and pestilence in all the world during the forty years preceding the destruction of Jerusalem.

Grim pestilence, which always accompanies famine, stalked abroad in the sorely smitten Jerusalem. But this visitation is not to be compared with the more recent epidemics of the black plague, the cholera, yellow fever, etc., among some of the crowded nations of today.

Wonderful signs were seen in Jerusalem before its overthrow, and "the earth trembled."

"Signs and wonders appeared, foreboding disaster and doom. In the midst of the night an unnatural light shone over the temple and the altar. Upon the clouds at sunset were pictured chariots and men of war gathering for battle. The priests ministering by night in the sanctuary were terrified by mysterious sounds; the earth trembled, and a multitude of voices were heard crying, 'Let us depart hence.' The great eastern gate, which was so heavy that it could hardly be shut by a score of men, and which was secured by immense bars of iron fastened deep in the pavement of solid stone, opened at midnight, without visible agency.

"For seven years a man continued to go up and down the streets of Jerusalem, declaring the woes that were to come upon the city. By day and by night he chanted the wild dirge, 'A voice from the east; a voice from the west; a voice from the four winds; a voice against Jerusalem and the temple; a voice against the bridegroom and the bride; and a voice against all the people.' This strange being was imprisoned and scourged; but no complaint escaped his lips. To insult and abuse he answered only, 'Woe to Jerusalem! woe, woe to the inhabitants thereof!' His warning cry ceased not until he was slain in the siege he had foretold."—*"Great Controversy," p. 30. See Josephus' "Wars of the Jews," Book 6, chap. 5.*

There were earthquakes at various places. Newton says of them:

"'Particularly that in Crete in the reign of Claudius, mentioned by Philostratus in the life of Apollonius, and those also mentioned by Philostratus at Smyrna, Miletus, Chios, Samos,' in all which places some Jews inhabited; and those at Rome mentioned by Tacitus; and that at Laodicea, in the reign of Nero, mentioned by Tacitus, which city was overthrown, as were likewise Hierapolis and Colosse; and that in Campania, mentioned by Seneca; and that at Rome in the reign of Galba, mentioned by Suetonius."—*"Dissertations," page 379.*

Another earthquake, which occurred in Judea, is thus described by Josephus:

Destruction of Jerusalem

"For there broke out a prodigious storm in the night, with the utmost violence, and very strong winds, with the largest showers of rain, with continued lightnings, terrible thunderings, and amazing concussions and bellowings of the earth. These things were a manifest indication that some destruction was coming upon men, when the system of the world was put into this disorder; and any one would guess that these wonders foreshadowed some great calamities that were coming."—*"Wars of the Jews," Book 4, chap. 4.*

But these disturbances of nature before the destruction of Jerusalem were as the rocking of a cradle compared with the earthquakes at Lisbon, San Francisco, Messina, and other recent seismic convulsions, and more especially the great coming earthquake in which the whole earth is to be involved. (See Revelation 16: 18.)

The more complete fulfillment of this prophecy is well set forth in the following forcible language:

"The Saviour's prophecy concerning the visitation of judgments upon Jerusalem is to have another fulfillment, of which that terrible desolation was but a faint shadow. In the fate of the chosen city we may behold the doom of a world that has rejected God's mercy and trampled upon His law. Dark are the records of human misery that earth has witnessed during its long centuries of crime. The heart sickens and the mind grows faint in contemplation. Terrible have been the results of rejecting the authority of heaven. But a scene yet darker is presented in the revelations of the future. The records of the past,— the long procession of tumults, conflicts, and revolutions, the 'battle of the warrior, with confused noise, and garments rolled in blood' (Isaiah 9: 5),— what are these, in contrast with the terrors of that day when the restraining Spirit of God shall be wholly withdrawn from the wicked, no longer to hold in check the outburst of human passion and Satanic wrath. The world will then behold, as never before, the results of Satan's rule."—*"Great Controversy," page 37.*

In the twenty-fourth chapter of Matthew the apostle gives our Saviour's account of a series of events to occur from the days of the apostles on through to the end of time. To the student of God's word, these scenes are to be waymarks to show where we stand in this world's history, and we should give them careful consideration.

The first event predicted is the destruction of Jerusalem and the temple. That His followers might be prepared to meet this dire calamity, the Saviour gave them warning and instruction:

"When ye therefore shall see the abomination of desolation, spoken of by Daniel the prophet [see Daniel 9: 26, 27], stand in the holy place, (whoso readeth, let him understand,) then let them which be in Judea flee into the mountains: let him which is on the housetop not come down to take anything out of his house: neither let him which is in the field return back to take his clothes." Matthew 24: 15-18.

Luke in his account of this same prophecy says: "When ye shall see Jerusalem compassed with armies, then know that the desolation thereof is nigh. Then let them which are in Judea flee to the mountains; and let them which are in the midst of it depart out; and let not them that are in the countries enter thereinto." Luke 21: 20, 21.

This quotation from Luke shows conclusively that the "abomination of desolation," spoken of by Daniel and Matthew was the armies of some enemy that would surround the city, besiege it, and finally destroy it.

Dr. Adam Clarke writes:

"This 'abomination of desolation' refers to the Roman army; and this abomination standing 'in the holy place' is the Roman army besieging Jerusalem; this, our Lord says, is what was spoken of by Daniel the prophet, in the ninth and eleventh chapters of his prophecy; and so let every one who reads these prophecies understand them; and in reference to this very event they are understood by the Rabbins. The Roman army is called an 'abomination,' for its ensigns and images, which were so to the Jews."—*Commentary on Matthew 24.* (*All references from the commentary of Dr. Adam Clarke are taken from the original edition published in 1836.*)

Josephus says, "The Romans brought their ensigns into the temple, and placed them over against the eastern gate, and sacrificed to them there."—"*Wars,*" *Book vi, chap. 6.*

The Saviour tells His followers what to do when the armies of Rome shall invest Jerusalem: "Then let them which are in Judea flee to the mountains." But how can the Christians escape after being completely surrounded by the enemies of their people? At first glance this would seem impossible, but the Lord made no mistake.

In the twelfth year of the reign of Nero, Jerusalem was surrounded by a powerful army led by Cestius Gallus, the president of Syria. But in God's mercy the siege was abandoned for a time, and the investing army was withdrawn.

Upon this point Josephus says, "He [Cestius Gallus] might have assaulted and taken the city, and thereby put an end to the war; but without any just reason, and contrary to the expectation of all, he raised the siege and departed." —"*Wars,*" *Book ii, chap. 19.*

Upon the authority of Eusebius, Clarke, in his commentary on verses 13 and 16 says that "at this juncture, after Cestius Gallus had raised the siege, and Vespasian was approaching with his army, all who believed in Christ left Jerusalem and fled to Pella, and other places beyond the river Jordan; and so they all marvelously escaped the general shipwreck of their country." "It is very remarkable that not a single Christian perished in the destruction of Jerusalem, though there were many there when Cestius Gallus invested the city; and, had he persevered in the siege, he would soon have rendered himself master of it; but, when he unexpectedly and unaccountably raised the siege, the Christians took that opportunity to escape."—*See Eusebius, Hist. Eccles. lib. iii, chap. 5.*

The Saviour further says, "Let him which is on the housetop not come down to take anything out of his house: neither let him which is in the field return back to take his clothes." Matthew 24: 17, 18. Like Lot in leaving Sodom, their flight must be hurried, or it would be too late, and they would be overwhelmed in the destruction coming upon the doomed city.

In the walled cities of the East, the roofs of the houses were usually flat, and of such a uniform height as to make possible a continuous passage to the very gates of the city.

It was customary to walk and sleep on these housetops. When the time came for God's people to escape, the need of haste was so great that if any were on the housetop or in the field, they must not take time to secure anything from their houses, but must flee immediately to a place of safety.

"But pray ye that your flight be not in the winter, neither on the Sabbath day." Matthew 24: 20. This instruction was given forty years before the Romans overran Judea. In view of the coming desolation, the followers of Christ were to pray earnestly for two great mercies:

1. That they be not compelled to flee in the winter, for the cold of that season would bring great suffering to the refugees from Judea.

2. That God would so overrule events that they would not be compelled to flee upon the Sabbath day, or else be overtaken in the destruction which was to follow.

For forty years this prayer was to go up to God. It shows the regard Christ had for the Sabbath. In this we find a fitting rebuke for the little respect that is paid to this institution,—an institution which had its birth at creation, and which was given to commemorate that event.

Soon after the flight of the Christians, the army of Vespasian, under Titus, entered Judea, and besieged Jerusalem, until the city was destroyed and the temple burned with fire.

Terrible distress and calamity came to the Jews as the result of this siege. Moses foretold this one thousand five hundred years before. He said:

"The Lord shall bring a nation against thee from far, from the end of the earth, as swift as the eagle flieth; a nation whose tongue thou shalt not understand. . . . And he shall besiege thee in all thy gates, until thy high and fenced walls come down, wherein thou trustedst, throughout all thy land: and he shall besiege thee in all thy gates, throughout all thy land, which the Lord thy God hath given thee. And thou shalt eat the fruit of thine own body, the flesh of thy sons and of thy daughters, which the Lord thy God hath given thee, in the siege, and in the straitness, wherewith thine enemies shall distress thee." Deuteronomy 28: 49, 52, 53.

The Roman ensign was an eagle, and the Romans spoke the Latin language, which the Jews did not understand, thus fulfilling the first part of the above prophecy to the letter. To the other horrors of war was added that of famine. Josephus says that mothers would snatch the food from their children in their distress, and that many houses were found full of women and children who had died of starvation. Human flesh was sometimes eaten; and the same author tells of a lady of rank who killed, roasted, and ate her own son, thus fulfilling the latter part of the prophecy of Moses. —See "Wars," Book v, chap. 10; Book vi, chap. 3.

Christ had said: "The days shall come upon thee, that thine enemies shall cast a trench about thee, and compass thee round, and keep thee in on every side. . . . And they shall fall by the edge of the sword, and shall be led away captive into all nations." Luke 19: 43; 21: 24.

The siege of Jerusalem was protracted for months. When finally taken, the inhabitants were butchered without regard to age or sex. Josephus states that eleven hundred thousand perished at this time, and that ninety-seven thousand were carried away captive. How accurately this fulfills the Saviour's prophecy, quoted from Luke 21:24.— *See "Wars," Book vi, chap. 9.*

We also read that "Jerusalem shall be trodden down of the Gentiles, until the times of the Gentiles be fulfilled." Luke 21:24. This will be when the work of the gospel is finished.

Great Tribulation

TO HIS followers Christ gave no promise of a life of ease. "If they have persecuted Me," He said, "they will also persecute you." John 15: 20. "Ye shall be hated of all men for My name's sake: but he that endureth to the end shall be saved." Matthew 10: 22. To His opposers He said, "Behold, I send unto you prophets, and wise men, and scribes: and some of them ye shall kill and crucify; and some of them shall ye scourge in your synagogues, and persecute them from city to city." Matthew 23: 34.

Christ declared to His disciples that following the destruction of Jerusalem, the elect were to pass through a period of terrible persecution. "For then shall be great tribulation, such as was not since the beginning of the world to this time, no, nor ever shall be. And except those days should be shortened, there should no flesh be saved; but for the elect's sake those days shall be shortened." Matthew 24: 21, 22. This prediction began to meet its fulfillment very early. With the exception of John the Revelator, all the apostles died for their faith. And even he endured painful tortures and banishment, and addressed the persecuted church as their "companion in tribulation, and in the kingdom and patience of Jesus Christ." (Revelation 1: 9.)

Paul's description of the trials endured by the church before his day, fitly illustrates what a later church was to meet. Thus he writes:

"And others had trial of cruel mockings and scourgings, yea, moreover of bonds and imprisonment: they were stoned, they were sawn asunder, were tempted, were slain with the sword: they wandered about in sheepskins and goatskins; being destitute, afflicted, tormented." Hebrews 11: 36, 37.

At the time of the establishment of the Christian church, idolatrous Rome had extended its rule over the greater portion of the civilized world. The emperor of Rome was the supreme pontiff of paganism, and in the Roman Pantheon were statues of the recognized gods of the empire. It was

Autotype Fine Art Co., Ltd.
The stoning of Stephen

inevitable that at that critical period there should be conflict between paganism and Christianity. In such a struggle, the followers of Christ could employ only the invisible weapons of spiritual power. Against them was arrayed the mightiest empire the world had ever known.

In those days of pagan supremacy, it was a crime against the government for any one to worship gods, other than those recognized by Rome. The penalty for such worship was severe, as indicated by the following statute: "Whoever introduces new religions, the tendency and character of which are unknown, whereby the minds of men may be disturbed, shall, if belonging to the higher rank, be banished, if to the lower, punished with death."

As most of the Christians were from the lower walks of life, and as they advocated a new religion,—a religion uncompromisingly opposed to the corrupt and licentious practices of paganism,—the death penalty was often inflicted on them.

During the reign of Nero, the Christians suffered severe persecutions, and many were hunted down and cruelly tormented. The most terrible of the pagan persecutions, however, was waged during the reign of Dioceletian. In A.D. 303 he "issued a decree that every church should be burned, that every copy of the Scripture should be consigned to the flames, and that every Christian, of whatever rank, sex, or age, should be tortured, and thus compelled to renounce Christianity. No pen can describe the horrors of this persecution, the dismay with which it crushed all Christian hearts, or the fortitude with which the disciples of Jesus bore the scourgings, fire, and death."— *Dr. J. C. Abbott, "History of Christianity," p. 298.*

"Among the authentic records of pagan persecutions there are histories which display, perhaps more vividly than any other, both the depth of cruelty to which human nature may sink, and the heroism of resistance it may attain. . . . The most horrible recorded instances of torture were usually inflicted, either by the populace, or in their presence, in the arena. We read of Christians bound in chairs of red-hot iron, while the stench of their half-consumed flesh rose in a suffocating cloud to heaven; of others who were torn to the very bone by shells, or hooks of iron; . . . of two hundred and twenty-seven converts sent on one occasion to the mines, each with the sinews of one leg severed by a red-hot iron, and with

an eye scooped from its socket; of fires so slow that the victims writhed for hours in their agonies; of bodies torn limb from limb, or sprinkled with burning lead; of mingled salt and vinegar poured over the flesh that was bleeding from the rack; of tortures prolonged and varied through entire days. For the love of their divine Master, for the cause they believed to be true, men, and even weak girls, endured these things without flinching, when one word would have freed them from their sufferings."
—*W. E. H. Leckey, "History of European Morals," Chapter III, 1877 edition, Vol. 1, pp. 467, 468.*

Terrible as these accounts may seem, the church was overtaken by a danger graver than persecution. Enlarged by numerous accessions of only partially converted heathen, its religion espoused by high officials and finally even by the emperor himself, the church at length rode high on a wave of popular favor. The strength of the church of Christ is a spiritual strength, dependent on the purity of its teachings and practices. Only the purest of motives usually actuate men when they choose to suffer in behalf of an unpopular truth. But when a church becomes popular and numerically powerful, there will flock around its standard many who have no true conception of Christian humility.

In later years, the church that had been persecuted rose to a height of importance that led political leaders to seek the favor of its support. At length, this support having been granted, the State was obliged to perform the dictates of the Church. Thus the power of civil government was placed in the hands of a church in which the purity of Christ's teachings had been corrupted. Believing that they held the true and pure doctrine, and that those who did not believe as they did would be eternally lost, those in responsible positions in the church came to regard it as their duty to compel all, so far as was possible, to accept the tenets of their faith; and these same religious leaders often sought to punish and even to destroy those who dared oppose them; bigotry destroyed love.

Jesus had foretold what would come. After telling His disciples of the hatred and opposition they would encounter in the world, He said: "These things have I spoken unto you, that ye should not be offended. They shall put you out of the synagogues: yea, the time cometh, that whosoever killeth you will think that he doeth God service." John 16:1, 2.

The great apostle Paul testified regarding his motives in persecuting the Christians prior to his conversion: "I verily thought with myself, that I ought to do many things contrary to the name of Jesus of Nazareth. Which thing I also did in Jerusalem: and many of the saints did I shut up in prison, having received authority from the chief priests [the religious leaders]; and when they were put to death, I gave my voice against them." Acts 26: 9, 10.

As the church lost the power of its early purity, schisms began to appear. Various factions arose, differing on matters of but minor importance. Early in the fourth century there began the famous controversy over the nature of the Trinity. Two great parties arose, known respectively as the Arians and the Athanasians. Other controversies characterized that troublous period. Councils were held to determine which party was orthodox, and to pass decisions on what was heresy. In the settlement of these disputes, both sides at times resorted to violence, even to the shedding of blood.

By the thirteenth century the power of the church had so risen that she was able to force sovereigns to use the arms of their nations, in repeated attempts to extirpate so-called heresy. Under the threatened penalty of excommunication, of deposition, and of confiscation of their kingdoms, unhappy sovereigns were forced to march their armies against cities and villages where lived those who were branded as heretics. Often, rulers were compelled to lay waste their own territories and to massacre thousands of their loyal subjects, because of

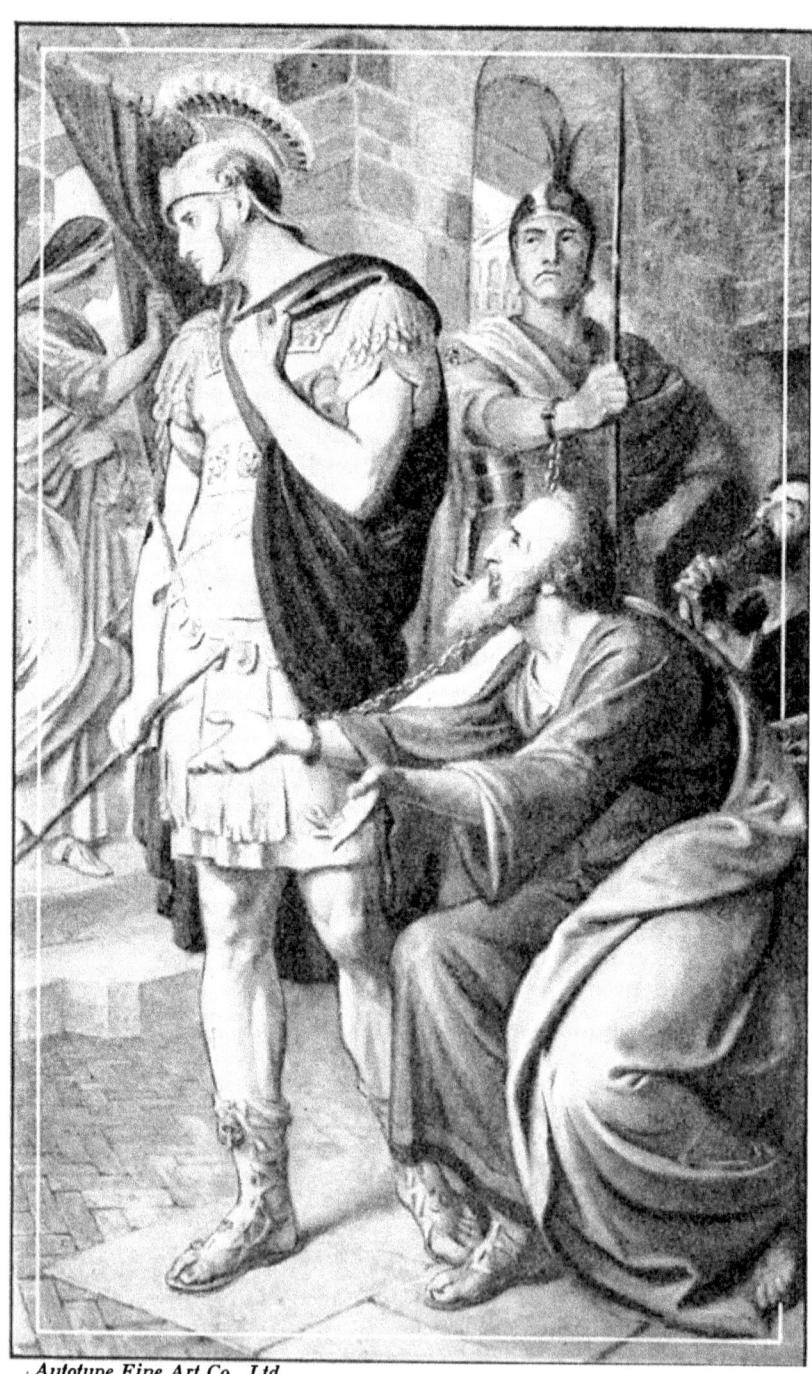
Paul in chains preaches the gospel to a Roman officer.

differences of religious belief and practice. In some lands, instruments of torture were invented to use in attempting to induce men, women, and even children under suspicion of heresy, to declare their faith in all the dogmas of the dominant church.

During the centuries of "great tribulation" it is estimated that many millions of people were put to death for no other reason than that they held tenaciously to doctrines that they firmly believed to be right. Fittingly has this period been termed the "Dark Ages." Religious intolerance was the spirit of the times. When one religious party was in the ascendancy, it oppressed all others, and when one of the oppressed parties gained the supremacy, too often it in turn persecuted all who disagreed with it.

Inasmuch as the elect — the true followers of Him who bade the impetuous Peter to sheathe his sword—cannot make use of carnal weapons to propagate His doctrines, it follows that they must have been among those who were hunted and oppressed. Had these conditions continued indefinitely, the true believers would in time have all perished. "Except those days should be shortened," said our Saviour, "there should no flesh be saved." But He gave assurance that "for the elect's sake those days shall be shortened." Matthew 24: 22.

About the middle of the eighteenth century, there came about a general change of sentiment, and an era of religious toleration began. Thus it is evident that this portion of the Saviour's prediction has been accurately fulfilled.

Among those whom the apostle John in prophetic vision saw with the redeemed, were those "that were beheaded for the witness of Jesus, and for the word of God." (Revelation 20: 4.) Though reviled and despised during their lifetime on earth, these noble martyrs in the cause of Jesus will have an eternal reward.

Darkening *of the* Sun

"IMMEDIATELY after the tribulation of those days shall the sun be darkened, and the moon shall not give her light." Matthew 24: 29.

This prophecy met a remarkable fulfillment in the mysterious dark day of May 19, 1780. The unprecedented darkness of that day extended through all New England and the Atlantic Coast, from the South to unknown regions of the North. It brought great alarm and distress to many people, who thought that the day of judgment had come. The fear produced by this phenomenon was shared alike by man and beast.

No better account of this day can be given than found in the statements of eye witnesses as recorded in many of the libraries of the East.

"The 19th day of May, 1780, was unprecedented in New England for its great darkness. . . . The darkness extended over several thousand square miles, though differing much in intensity in different places. Nowhere, perhaps, was it greater than in this vicinity. The day was appropriately called and is still known, as The Dark Day."—*From "History of the Town of Hampton, New Hampshire," by Joseph Dorr, Salem, Mass. Vol. I, page 217. Printed by the Salem Press and Printing Co., 1893. (Boston Pub. Library.)*

"There appears to have been an absence of clouds for the most part, though light rain occurred. Though known as the 'Black Friday of New England,' the area covered by darkness also extended west of that section."—*"Encyclopedia Americana," The Americana Company, New York, 1903, Art. "Dark Day."*

"This strange darkness increased until by noon the people had to light candles to eat their dinners by! Lights

Darkening of the Sun

were seen in every window, and out of doors people carried torches to light their steps. Everything took a different color from what it had by sunlight, and consequently the strange reflections of the torchlights were in keeping with the marvelous and changed appearance of everything.

"Hosts of people believed the end of the world had begun to come; men dropped to their knees to pray in the field; many ran to their neighbors to confess wrongs and ask forgiveness; multitudes rushed into the meetinghouses in towns where they had such, where pious and aged ministers, pleading repentance, interceded with God in their behalf; and everywhere, throughout this day of wonder and alarm, the once careless thought of their sins and their Maker!

"At this time the legislature of Connecticut was in session, and when the growing darkness became so deep that at midday they could not see each other, most of them were so alarmed as to be unfit for service. At this juncture, Mr. Davenport arose and said:

"'Mr. Speaker, it is either the day of judgment or it is not. If it is not, there is no need of adjourning. If it is, I desire to be found doing my duty. I move that candles be brought and that we proceed to business.'

"The darkness somewhat increased all day, and before time of sunset was so intense that no object whatever could be distinguished. Anxiously and tremblingly, people waited for the full moon to rise at nine o'clock, and even little children with strained eyes, sat silently watching for its beautiful beams to appear. But they were disappointed, the darkness being unaffected by the moon. The most feeling prayers ever prayed in Antrim were at the family altars that night. Children never had more tender blessing than these mothers gave them that night. They slept soundly for the most part, but the parents chiefly sat up all night to wait and see if the glorious sun would rise again. Never dawned a lovelier morning than that 20th of May! Never were hearts more thankful on the earth! Even thoughtless people praised God!

"So much were the whole population affected by this event, that, at the succeeding March meeting, the town voted, March 9, 1781, to keep the next 19th of May as a day of fasting and prayer."—*"History of the Town of Antrim, New Hampshire," Rev. W. R. Cochrane, pages 58, 59. Published by the Town. Manchester, N. H.: Mirror Steam Printing Press. 1880. (N. H. State Library.)*

"May 19th, 1780 Was a Thunder shower in the morning and was followed by an uncommon darkness such as is not remembered it was so dark That one could not known a man but at a small distance, and Were obliged to keep a light in the chimney to see to go about and the night was Extraordinary dark until one oClock, that a person could not see their hand when held up nor even a white sheet of paper the day and night was cloudy the clouds in the day did not seem thick and was of a lightening up couler our almanack makers have given no account of the matter the cause unknown The works of the Lord are great and marvellous past finding out untill he Graciously pleases to Reveal them."—*"The Diary of Matthew Patten of Bedford," N. H. From 1754 to 1788, p. 414 (verbatim et literatim). Published by the Town. Concord, N. H. The Rumford Printing Company, 1903. (N. H. State Library.)*

The effect on both domestic and wild animals was the same as if night had come. An eyewitness says of it:

"Fowls retired to their roosts, mounted them, tucked their heads under their wings, going to sleep as quietly and assuredly as if it had been sunset rather than noon. As the appearance of twilight prematurely came on, cattle lowed and gathered at the pasture bars, waiting to be let out that they might return to their barns and make ready for another night's repose, apparently forgetful of the short lapse of time since they had gone out to their daily feeding. Sheep huddled by the fences, or in the open fields in circles. Frogs peeped as they were accustomed to do as soon as the sun went down. The day birds sang their evening songs, as their habit was, woodchucks whistled and bats came out of their hiding places and flew about. Near fences and buildings many birds were found dead, probably having flown against these objects in the darkness and been killed by the contact.

"The time of the commencement of this extraordinary darkness was between the hours of ten and eleven in the forenoon of Friday, . . . and it continued until the middle of the following night, but with different appearances at different places. As to the manner of its approach, it seemed to appear first of all in the south-

The dark day of 1780

west. The wind came from that quarter, and the darkness appeared to come on with the clouds that came in that direction. . . .

"The extent of the darkness was also very remarkable. It was observed at the most easterly parts of New England; westward to the furthest part of Connecticut, and at Albany; to the southward, it was observed all along the seacoasts; and to the north as far as the American settlements extended. It probably far exceeded these boundaries, but the exact limits were never positively known."—"*Our First Century (1776-1876), Great and Memorable Events,*" *pp. 89, 90. (Boston Pub. Library.)*

It was the impression with many of the people that the day of judgment had come. Special services were held in churches, sins were confessed and wrongs righted, and an effort made to prepare, so far as possible, for the great event which was felt to be impending. The poet Whittier thus speaks of this memorable day:

> "'Twas on a May-day of the fair old year
> Seventeen hundred eighty, that there fell
> Over the bloom and sweet life of the spring,
> Over the fresh earth, and the heaven of noon,
> A horror of great darkness.
>
> "Men prayed and women wept; all ears grew sharp
> To hear the doom-blast of the trumpet shatter
> The black sky, that the dreadful face of Christ
> Might look from the rent clouds, not as He looked
> A loving guest at Bethany, but stern
> As Justice and inexorable Law."

"Dark Day: refers especially to May 19, 1780, which was very dark in Connecticut, New York, and New Jersey, causing great alarm."—"*The Universal Cyclopedia,*" *New York, D. Appleton & Co., 1900; Art., Dark Day.*

"'The dark day of New England,' so familiar to old and young, came May 19, 1780. . . . Near eleven o'clock, it began to grow dark, as if night were coming. Men ceased their work; the lowing cattle came to the barns, the bleating sheep huddled by the fences, the wild birds screamed and flew to their nests, the fowls went to their roosts. . . .

"Men, ordinarily cool, were filled with awe and alarm. Excitable people believed the end of the world had come; some ran about saying the day of judgment was at hand; the wicked hurried to their neighbors to confess wrongs and ask forgiveness; the superstitious dropped on their knees to pray in the fields, or rushed into meetinghouses to call on God to preserve them. . . .

"At night it was so inky dark that a person could not see his hand when held up, nor even a white sheet of paper."—*From "History of Weare, New Hampshire," 1735-1888. By Wm. Little, Lowell. Mass., page 276.*

Printed by S. W. Huse & Co., 1888. (Boston Pub. Library.)
"Friday, May 19, 1780, will go down in history as 'the dark day.' . . . Fear, anxiety, and awe gradually filled the minds of the people. Women stood at the door looking out upon the dark landscape; men returned from their labor in the fields; the carpenter left his tools, the blacksmith his forge, the tradesman his counter. Schools were dismissed, and tremblingly the children fled homeward. Travelers put up at the nearest farmhouse. 'What is coming?' queried every lip and heart. It seemed as if a hurricane was about to dash across the land, or as if it was the day of the consummation of all things. . . .

"Dr. Nathanael Whittaker, pastor of the Tabernacle church in Salem, held religious services in the meetinghouse, and preached a sermon in which he maintained that the darkness was supernatural. Congregations came together in many other places. The texts for the extemporaneous sermons were invariably those that seemed to indicate that the darkness was consonant with Scriptural prophecy.

"Such texts as these were used: Isa. 13: 10; Eze. 32: 7, 8; Joel 2: 31; Matt. 24: 29, 30; Rev. 6: 12.

"Devout fathers gathered their families around them in their homes and conducted religious services; and for a few hours Christians were stirred to activity, and non-professors earnestly sought for salvation, expecting 'To hear the thunder of the wrath of God break from the hollow trumpet of the cloud.'"—*From "The Essex Antiquarian," Vol. III, No. 4, pp. 53, 45. Salem, Mass., April, 1899. (Boston Pub. Library.)*

Efforts have been made to explain the cause of this extraordinary dark day, but none of them have been able to stand the test of scientific investigation. We can only conclude that, like the great darkness which enshrouded Egypt, it was "an act of God" in fulfillment of our Saviour's prophecy. The explanation is simple when we treat it from that standpoint. Our Lord said that "the sun shall be darkened and the moon shall not give her light." This was to be an evidence that the end is near. Jesus foretold it, and on May 19, 1780, the prophecy was fulfilled.

"On the 19th of May, 1780, an uncommon darkness took place all over New England, and extended to Canada. It continued about fourteen hours, or from ten o'clock in the morning till midnight. The darkness was so great, that people were unable to read common print, or tell the time of the day by their watches, or to dine, or transact their ordinary business without the light of candles. They became dull and gloomy, and some were excessively frightened. The fowls retired to their roosts. Objects could not be distinguished but at a very little distance, and everything bore the appearance of gloom and night.

"The causes of these phenomena are unknown. They certainly were not the result of eclipses."—*"The Guide to Knowledge, or Repertory of Facts,"* edited by Robert Sears, *page 428. New York, 1845. (Astor Library.)*

"The primary cause must be imputed to Him that walketh through the circuit of heaven, who stretcheth out the heaven like a curtain, who maketh the clouds His chariots, who walketh upon the wings of the wind. It was He at whose voice the stormy winds are obedient — that commandeth these exhalations to be collected and condensed together, that with them He might darken both the day and the night — which darkness was, perhaps, not only a token of His indignation against the crying iniquities and abominations of the people, but an omen of some future destruction that may overtake this land like a deluge, unless a speedy repentance and reformation should immediately take place."—*Dr. Samuel Stearns in an article addressed "To the Public," in the Worcester Spy of June 29, 1780.*

This dark day was not caused by an eclipse, as may be understood by considering what causes an eclipse. It is caused by the shadow of the moon falling upon the earth, and in order to do that the moon must be between the earth and the sun. But upon this day the position was almost reversed, the earth being nearly between the sun and the moon. But if an eclipse at that time had been possible, it would have remained for a short period only, while this darkness continued through half a day and half a night.

"An eclipse of the sun can occur only at new moon. The reason is obvious. To produce it the sun, the moon, and the earth must be in a straight line, the moon being in the center."—"*American Encyclopedic Dictionary*," *Art.* "*Eclipse.*"

"That this darkness was not caused by an eclipse, is manifest by the various positions of the planetary bodies at that time, for the moon was more than one hundred and fifty degrees from the sun all that day, and, according to the accurate calculations made by the most celebrated astronomers, there could not, in the order of nature, be any transit of the planet Venus or Mercury upon the disc of the sun that year; nor could it be a blazing star— much less a mountain — that darkened the atmosphere, for this would still leave unexplained the deep darkness of the following night.

"Nor would such excessive nocturnal darkness follow an eclipse of the sun; and as to the moon, she was at that time more than forty hours' motion past her opposition." —*Article by R. M. Devens, "Our First Century," 1776-1876. "Great and Memorable Events," pp. 89-96. (Boston Pub. Library.*)

"That the smoke of burning forests cannot be the cause may be rendered very certain. . . . Had the woods from the 40th degree of latitude in America to the 50th been all consumed in a day, the smoke would not have been sufficient to cloud the sun over the territory covered by the darkness on the 19th of May (1780). Any person can judge of this who has seen large tracts of forest on fire. That thirty or forty miles of burning forest, should cover five hundred miles with impenetrable darkness, is too absurd to deserve a serious refutation."—"*A Brief History of Epidemic and Pestilential Diseases; With the Principal Phenomena of the Physical World, Which Precede and Accompany Them." In two Volumes. Pages*

91-93, Vol. II. By Noah Webster. Hartford. Printed by Hudson and Goodwin, 1799. (Lenox Library, New York.)

"The moon shall not give her light." Although the moon was in the full, the first half of the following night was remarkable for the density of its darkness.

"The darkness of the following night was so intense that many who were but a little way from home, on well-known roads, could not, without extreme difficulty, retrace the way to their own dwellings."—"*Sketches of the History of New Hampshire,*" *by John W. Whiton, p. 144. 1834. (N. H. State Library.*)

"The darkness of the following evening was probably as deep and dense as ever had been observed since the Almighty fiat gave birth to light; it wanted only palpability to render it as extraordinary as that which overspread the land of Egypt in the days of Moses. . . . If every luminous body in the Universe had been shrouded in impenetrable shades, or struck out of existence, the darkness could not have been more complete. A sheet of white paper, held within a few inches of the eyes, was equally invisible with the blackest velvet."—*Letter of Dr. Samuel Tenney, dated Exeter, N. H., December, 1785; cited in "Collections of Massachusetts Historical Society," Vol. 1, 1792.*

John the Revelator was given a view, in vision, of some of the scenes foretold by our Saviour as signs of His soon coming. He says, "The sun became black as sackcloth of hair, and the moon became as blood." Revelation 6: 12. Upon this feature Milo Bostwick writes:

"My father and mother, who were pious, thought the day of judgment was near. They sat up all night, during the latter part of which they said the darkness disappeared, and then the sky seemed as usual; but the moon which was at the full, *had the appearance of blood.*"

"What shall be the sign of Thy coming, and of the end of the world?" Matthew 24: 3. This was the question asked by the disciples on the Mount of Olives. It was this question which Jesus answered in succeeding verses. His answer considered:

First, the destruction of Jerusalem with its accompanying signs and horrors.

Second, a long period of "great tribulation" to, and persecution of, the church of Christ, commonly called the Dark Ages, in which the "mystery of godliness" was to be largely supplanted by the "mystery of iniquity," which Paul said was already working in his day.

Third, a group of signs of the end which were to immediately follow the period of persecution of the church of Christ, and which were to usher in the coming of the Lord of glory. Jesus said:

"Immediately after the tribulation of those days shall the sun be darkened, and the moon shall not give her light, and the stars shall fall from heaven, and the powers of the heavens shall be shaken: and then shall appear the sign of the Son of man in heaven." Matthew 24: 29, 30.

And to His true followers He says, "When these things begin to come to pass, then look up, and lift up your heads; for your redemption draweth nigh." Luke 21: 28.

The "great tribulation," brought about by the persecution of the church of Christ, practically ceased in the middle of the eighteenth century. The dark day, the first of the signs given by our Lord to foretell His soon coming, occurred in 1780, so it comes in the proper order of events as foretold.

In infinite mercy our Saviour has seen fit to draw aside the curtain which hides the future. The disciples asked, "When shall these things be?" and what "signs" shall precede them? In His answer He describes the road His followers must travel and sets signboards at the parting of the ways. He plants milestones by the side of the road so that we may know how near we are to our journey's end.

Are these things real? Are they important to us? Ancient Israel received warnings by the hands of the prophets of God, but they rejected the warnings and persecuted the prophets. Hence God could not work for them, could not protect and save them. They were afflicted by nations around them, they were taken captive to Babylon, and at last Jerusalem was utterly destroyed, and they were obliterated as a nation.

Now God calls upon the true Israel to fall into line for the closing scenes of earth. He has clearly marked out the way, defined the time when "it is near," and warned us regarding the dangers to be met. He says, "Take heed that no man deceive you."

There is no truth of the Bible which Satan hates with such vindictiveness as he does that pertaining to the second coming of Christ. Hence he employs every ingenuity of men and evil angels to destroy the faith of mankind in the reality and nearness of this event. At the coming of Christ the reign of Satan ends. Jesus will come when the number of His people who are watching and waiting for Him is made up. It is Satan's master work of the ages so to distract and deceive the world that God's plan may be delayed as long as possible. But the delay cannot long continue. The forces of the world are lining up. On which side will you stand?

The Falling Stars

THE next sign foretold by our Saviour was that of the falling stars. "And the stars shall fall from heaven." Matthew 24:29. This was literally fulfilled in the great meteoric shower which occurred November 13, 1833. This wonderful exhibition of celestial fireworks began between two and four o'clock in the morning, and continued until daylight. It extended over North America, and as far south as Mexico and the island of Jamaica. No better description can be given of this phenomenon than found in the publications of the time in which it occurred:

"About half-past 4 o'clock on the morning of Wednesday the 13th Nov. inst., brilliant objects were seen to pass by the window, at first taken to be sparks from the chimney or some building perhaps on fire, but on further examination, they were found to be what are commonly called *shooting stars*.

"On going into the street, where the prospect was bounded only with horizon, the heavens presented one of the most extraordinary, sublime, and beautiful prospects ever beheld by man. Imagination can picture nothing to exceed it. These luminous substances, numberless as the stars themselves, were seen flying in every possible direction, through a clear, unclouded sky, leaving long luminous trains behind.

"In any direction, the scene could not be compared more aptly to anything than a distant shower of fire, whose particles were falling sparsely to the earth. Frequently one larger and more luminous than the rest would shoot across the heavens, producing a flash like vivid lightning. Towards the approach of daylight the sky began to be obscured with clouds, and these substances appeared less frequent, but did not disappear till long after the light of the morning had arisen, and were seen as long as stars were visible."—*New Hampshire Patriot and State Gazatte (semi-weekly), Vol. I, No. 104; Concord, Saturday, November 16, 1833. (State Library.)*

"But the year 1833 is memorable for the most magnificent display [of falling meteors] on record. This was on the same night of November [13] also, and was visible over all the United States, and over a part of Mexico, and the West India Islands. Together with the smaller shooting stars, which fell like snowflakes and produced phosphorescent lines along their course, there were intermingled large fireballs, which darted forth at intervals, describing in a few seconds an arc of 30 or 40 degrees.

"These left behind luminous trains, which remained in view several minutes, and sometimes half an hour or more. One of them seen in North Carolina appeared of larger size and greater brilliancy than the moon. Some of the luminous bodies were of irregular form, and remained stationary for a considerable time, emitting streams of light.

"At Niagara the exhibition was especially brilliant, and probably no spectacle so terribly grand and sublime was ever before beheld by man as that of the firmament descending in fiery torrents over the dark and roaring cataract."—*"The American Cyclopedia," art. "Meteors." New York. D. Appleton and Company, 1881.*

"All our exchange papers, from every direction, contain accounts of the splendid exhibition in the atmosphere witnessed on Wednesday morning last."—*Dover Gazette and Strafford Advertiser, Vol. VIII, No. 51, Tuesday morning, Nov. 19, 1833. Dover, N. H. (State Library.)*

"The Meteoric Phenomenon witnessed in this country on the 13th instant, was also seen at Halifax the same morning. Many persons rose from their beds supposing there was a fire near their dwellings."—*Portland Evening Advertiser, Nov. 27, 1833. (Portland Pub. Library.)*

"Having been engaged in running the standard lines for the general survey of the Chickasaw Nation in Mississippi, I was at the house of Major Allen, on the night of the falling stars. Major Allen is the government agent, and resides nearly in the center of the Nation. About an hour before daylight, I was called up to see the falling meteors. It was the most sublime and brilliant sight I had ever witnessed. The largest of the falling bodies appeared about the size of Jupiter or Venus, when brightest. Some persons present affirmed that they heard a hissing noise on the fall of some of the largest. The sky presented the appearance of a shower of stars, which many thought were real stars, and an omen of dreadful events."—*Extract from a letter to Prof. Denison Olmstead, of Yale College, from Prof. Thomson, "formerly of the University of Nashville, Tenn." Printed in a pamphlet and bound in a volume with the title "Bowditch Pamphlets." (Boston Pub. Library.)*

MICHILIMACKINAC, Jan. 6, 1834.

TO PROF. OLMSTEAD:—

Sir:—The Meteoric display described in your letter of the 13th November, was observed, at the same time, on this island, and the adjacent shores of Lake Huron. The appearances coincided, generally, with these you mention. The sentinels at post in the garrison, which is situated on a cliff, saw the lake illuminated, as it were, with falling stars.

I am, Sir, very respectfully your obedient servant,

HENRY R. SCHOOLCRAFT.

"We have been informed by Capt. Jackson, who was at sea that night, at the distance of nine miles from land, that the heavens were illuminated with the meteors, during nearly the whole night, as far as the eye could reach, in every direction, presenting a spectacle of uncommon magnificence and sublimity, attended with frequent explosions resembling the discharge of small arms. We learn also that a meteor of extraordinary size was observed at sea to course the heavens for a great length of time, and then exploded with the noise of a cannon."—*Charleston Courier. (Portland Pub. Library.)*

The course of this meteoric shower was foretold in prophecy: "The stars of heaven fell unto the earth, even as a fig-tree casteth her untimely [unripe] figs, when she is shaken of a mighty wind." Revelation 6:13.

The falling of the stars in 1833

Professor Olmstead, of Yale College, says that "the meteors . . . appeared to emanate from a point in the constellation Leo, near a star called Gamma Leonis, in the bend of the sickle."

Of the literal fulfillment of the foregoing text, Henry Dana Ward writes:

> "Here is the exactness of the prophet. . . . They fell not as *ripe* fruit falls; far from it; but they flew, they were *cast*, like the unripe fig, which at first refuses to leave the branch, and when, under a violent pressure, it does break its hold, flies swiftly, straight off, descending; and in the multitude falling, some cross the track of others, as they are thrown with more or less force, but each one falls on its own side of the tree."

"Compared with the splendors of this celestial exhibition, the most brilliant rockets and fireworks of art bore less relation than the twinkling of the most tiny star to the broad glare of the sun. The whole heavens seemed in motion, and little need have been borrowed from a morbid sensibility, to imagine that the opening of the sixth seal was indeed at hand, when the stars of heaven fell unto the earth, even as a fig-tree casteth her untimely figs, when she is shaken of a mighty wind. Never before has it fallen to our lot to observe a phenomenon so magnificent and sublime."—*New York Commercial Advertiser. Quoted in the Eastern Argus of Nov. 18, 1833.*

"Scientific study of the orbits of shooting stars began after the occurrence of the most brilliant meteoric shower of record,— that of Nov. 13, 1833. This spectacle, which excited the greatest interest among all beholders, and was looked upon with consternation by the ignorant, many of whom thought that the end of the world had come, was witnessed generally throughout North America, which happened to be the part of the earth facing the meteoric storm. Hundreds of thousands of shooting stars fell in the course of two or three hours. Some observers compared their number to the flakes of a snow storm, or to the rain drops in a shower."—"*The Encyclopedia Americana," The Americana Company, New York, 1903. Article, "Meteors or Shooting Stars."*

"We pronounce the Raining Fire which we saw on Wednesday morning last an awful *type* — a sure forerunner — a merciful sign of that great and dreadful day which the inhabitants of the earth will witness when the *sixth seal shall be opened.*

"That time is just at hand described not only in the New Testament but in the Old; and a more correct picture of a fig-tree casting its leaves [figs] when blown by a mighty wind it was not possible to behold.

"Many things *now* occurring upon the earth tend to convince us that we are in the "latter days." This exhibition we deem to be a type of an awful day fast hurrying upon us. This is our sincere opinion; and what we think, we are not ashamed to tell."—"*The Old Countryman,"*

New York, printed in the *New York Star* and quoted in the *Portland Evening Advertiser*, Nov. 26, 1833. (*Portland Pub. Library.*)

"During the three hours of its continuance, the day of judgment was believed to be only waiting for sunrise, and long after the shower had ceased, the morbid and superstitious were still impressed with the idea that the final day was at least only a week ahead.

"Meetings for prayer were held in many places, and many other scenes of religious devotion, or terror, or abandonment of worldly affairs, transpired under the influence of fear occasioned by so sudden and awful a display."—"*Great Events of the Greatest Century,*" *p. 229.*

The great fall of meteoric stars upon Nov. 13, 1833, was so remarkable as to attract the attention of many thousands of people of all classes, from the scientist to the humblest tiller of the soil. Some persons of world-wide fame have described the scene and the impression it made upon them. Among them was the famous colored orator, Frederick A. Douglas. In his book, "My Bondage and Freedom," he describes the falling of the stars in the following manner:

"I witnessed this gorgeous spectacle, and was awestruck. The air seemed filled with bright descending messengers from the sky. It was about daybreak when I saw this sublime scene. It was not without the suggestion at that moment that it might be the *harbinger of the coming of the Son of man;* and in my state of mind I was prepared to hail Him as my friend and deliverer. I had read that the stars shall fall from heaven, and they were now falling. I was suffering much in my mind, and I was beginning to look away to heaven for the rest denied me on earth."

Lucy Reese lived at Point Lookout, Ga., Nov. 13, 1833. She says:

"I was fourteen years of age at the time the stars fell. It seemed to me like a shower of rain. The people were greatly frightened, and there was much reading of the Bible because they thought the judgment had come."

To the student of prophecy there can be no question as to this event forming another link in the chain of prophecy already fulfilled. It is another milestone to tell us where we are in the rapidly passing events of this world's history.

"Heaven and earth shall pass away, but My word shall not pass away."

The Days *of* Noah

THE people living before the flood were a long-lived, clear-headed race; but they had departed from God, and their ability to work iniquity was very great.

So far did they go in sin, that "God saw that the wickedness of man was great in the earth, and that every imagination of the thoughts of his heart was only evil continually. . . . The earth also was corrupt before God, and the earth was filled with violence." (Genesis 6: 5, 11.)

Finally the Lord declared, "My Spirit shall not always strive with man," and the fiat went forth, "I will destroy man whom I have created from the face of the earth." Genesis 6: 3, 7.

Still He gave them opportunity to repent. For one hundred and twenty years Noah gave God's warning to the world. Without doubt many at first believed the teachings of Noah; but as the years rolled on, and no change came, they joined those who were scoffing at his big boat on dry land. They could see no change in the earth to indicate that its destruction was impending, and so put the matter out of their minds.

But when the world had been warned, and the ark was finished,— when the great procession of beasts and birds, led by the angels of God, had taken their proper places in the ark,— the angel shut the door, and mercy departed from the unbelieving, wicked people.

Noah and his family were all that were safe,— shut in by the power of God. The rain fell,— something which had never occurred on the earth before. The lightnings flashed, and the thunders rolled. The fountains of the great deep were broken up. All outside perished; but the ark rode the stormy billows in safety, protected by powerful angels of God.

The Days of Noah

In Matthew 24: 38, 39 the Saviour declares that the scenes of wickedness and the condition of the earth will be the same just prior to the second coming of Christ as they were before the flood.

"For as in the days that were before the flood they were eating and drinking, marrying and giving in marriage, until the day that Noe entered into the ark, and knew not until the flood came, and took them all away; so shall also the coming of the Son of man be." Matthew 24: 38, 39.

As the hopes, cares, and busy activities of life filled all the heart and claimed all the attention of the world before the flood, so will it be when the end is near. As wickedness, strife, and violence filled the earth then, so also will they increase as we near the time for the coming of the Lord.

We have only to look abroad in the land to see these specifications fulfilling everywhere. The eager chase for wealth, and the mad hurry and rush of worldly and business enterprises, were never before seen as now, while the increase of wickedness and crime on all hands is appalling.

God sent Noah to warn the world of its impending doom. He is now sending His servants throughout all the world with warnings of the last great calamity in store for it.

But as in the days of Noah they "knew not" that the flood was coming, so those who refuse the light at the present time will know not of the great destruction by fire which is near.

Speaking of this time, Peter says: "Knowing this first, that there shall come in the last days scoffers, walking after their own lusts, and saying, Where is the promise of His coming? For since the fathers fell asleep, all things continue as they were from the beginning of the creation." 2 Peter 3: 3, 4.

The people before the flood walked in their own way and scoffed at Noah. In the last days they will be pursuing the

Russ Photo
132]   Modern, atheistic Russians scoff at the Christian religion.

same course, and scoffing at the message of the final overthrow. "Where is there anything in nature to show that these terrible things are coming?" "Day and night, summer and winter, seedtime and harvest, come and go just as they always have since creation."

No; they have not. "For this they willingly are ignorant of, that by the word of God the heavens were of old, and the earth standing out of the water and in the water: whereby the world that then was, being overflowed with water, perished: but the heavens and the earth, which are now, by the same word are kept in store, reserved unto fire against the day of judgment and perdition of ungodly men." 2 Peter 3: 5-7.

A few more days, and the cup of iniquity of the world will be filled to the brim, and the angel of mercy will again leave the earth. Finally the fires of the great day of God will break forth, and destroy the earth by fire, as it was destroyed by water over four thousand years ago.

False Christs *and* False Prophets

CHRIST not only foretold what He would do in the future, but He also forewarned His disciples of what the enemy would do to deceive them and cause their destruction. False christs and false prophets were to arise, and by the use of miraculous powers, which they possessed, and which were of satanic origin, would deceive the people. "For there shall arise false christs, and false prophets, and shall show great signs and wonders; insomuch that, if it were possible, they shall deceive the very elect." Matthew 24:24.

In every age since the ascension of Christ there have arisen men, who, either as false christs or as false prophets, have deceived the people. Said Christ, "Take heed that ye be not deceived: for many shall come in My name, saying, I am Christ; and the time draweth near: go ye not therefore after them." Luke 21:8.

Many false christs and false prophets arose among the Jews, between Christ's ascension and the destruction of Jerusalem. (See chapter, "Destruction of Jerusalem.")

Mohammed, though not pretending to be a christ, was, nevertheless, a "false prophet." He was the originator of the Mohammedan religion. This religion has been established both by persuasion and by the sword, and twice did the followers of Mohammed almost sweep Christianity from the earth. They now number about two hundred millions, and a high authority declares that "no other faith offers so stubborn a resistance to the spread of Christianity."

The prophecy of Christ, however, makes these words of warning in regard to false christs and false prophets apply with peculiar force just at the time when His second coming is near. The prophecy shows that as the attention of the world will be called to the nearness of the Lord's coming, Satan will bestir himself to furnish false teachers who will claim that their work is the coming of Christ. Hence, the doctrine is widely taught that Christ will never literally come again, that His coming is only a spiritual coming. Others teach that the world is to be converted before the coming of the Lord.

The Mormons, who established themselves in the desert of Utah, come within the compass of Christ's warning words: "Wherefore if they shall say unto you, Behold, He is in the desert; go not forth." Matthew 24: 26.

Modern Spiritualism is evidently the work of lying, seducing spirits. Many of the devotees of this great delusion claim that the second coming of Christ is seen in the dissemination of the doctrines of Spiritualism.

Spiritualists, almost universally, deny the atonement of Christ, and teach that every man is his own savior. Of these the apostle says: "There shall be false teachers among you, who privily shall bring in damnable heresies, even denying the Lord that bought them, and bring upon themselves swift destruction." 2 Peter 2: 1. Spiritualists have claimed that they were Christ,— that all good men are Christ. They invite us to their secret seances, but Christ has told us if they say, "He is in the secret chambers, believe it not."

Christian Science is presented to us as the coming of Christ. A writer in the *Christian Science Journal* of October, 1897, referring to the fact that there was an expectation in the minds of many person that Christ would come in 1866, asks: "Was it a coincidence that Christian Science should have been discovered in the year 1866? . . . There is no reason for expecting that the beginning of the new dispensation should be so very different from the years preceding it, that is, from the standpoint of mortal man. Are not all God's works performed through the still, small voice? It was in this manner, and in this year of 1866, that Rev. Mary Baker Eddy discovered Christian Science, which, from the testimony of Jesus and the apostles, we feel sure is the second coming of Christ."

But Christian Science is not the second coming of Christ. It will be more than a still, small voice, for "the Lord Himself shall descend from heaven with a shout, with the voice of the archangel, and with the trump of God." (1 Thessalonians 4: 16.) Christ will then be "revealed from heaven with His mighty angels, in flaming fire taking vengeance on them that know not God, and that obey not the gospel of our Lord Jesus Christ." (2 Thessalonians 1: 7, 8.)

Christ has Himself declared that He will come as He went away, in the clouds of heaven; that "every eye shall see Him"; that His brightness and glory shall be like the lightning shining from the eastern to the western horizon. If we believe His words, we shall not be deceived by the numerous cries of "Lo, here," or "Lo, there."

Parable *of the* Fig-Tree

IN MATTHEW 24:3, the disciples asked the question, "What shall be the sign of Thy coming, and of the end of the world?" Most carefully does the Lord answer this question. He first reviews the great events which were to take place on the earth. Jerusalem was to be destroyed; the elect, or true people of God, were to pass through the most terrible period of persecution which had ever come upon God's people. The nations of the earth were to be rent with wars, and perplexed and distressed with the rumors and alarms of war. Great calamities were to come upon the earth, such as famines, pestilences, and earthquakes. These were to become more frequent and desolating until the final plagues of God should end in its destruction.

As the days of this world's history should draw to a close, our Saviour promised that unmistakable and striking signs would appear in the heavens. The sun would be darkened; the moon would refuse to give her light; and the stars would fall from heaven.

These were to be tokens of Christ's coming; for He says: "Then shall appear the sign of the Son of man in heaven: and then shall all the tribes of the earth mourn, and they shall see the Son of man coming in the clouds of heaven with power and great glory." Matthew 24:30.

Within the lifetime of people now living, the heavens have been ablaze with the glory of these very signs and marvels which were to immediately precede the second coming of Christ.

But it is Satan's chief purpose to lull the world to sleep, so that these signs and the warning message of God's servants will have no effect.

The Saviour knew that this would be the case, and so He sounded the warning: "Take heed that no man deceive you." Verse 4. There are two ways in which we may be deceived in regard to the coming of the Lord. One is to believe that He has come when He has not, and the other is to deny the signs that He has given to show that His coming is near, and so be found unbelieving and unprepared at His coming.

The signs foretold by our Saviour were given that men might know of His coming. He says, "Now learn a parable of the fig-tree; When his branch is yet tender, and putteth forth leaves, ye know that summer is nigh: so likewise ye, when ye shall see all these things, know that it [margin, He] is near, even at the door." Matthew 24: 32, 33.

When the trees begin to bud and put forth leaves, we *know* that summer is near. No one will presume to deny it. It is a sign that never fails. To those who will heed this warning, Christ states that the signs He has given are just as positive evidence that His coming is "even at the doors."

"These things" to which Christ refers as signs of His near coming, are given in Luke 21: 25, 26: "And there shall be signs in the sun, and in the moon, and in the stars; and upon the earth distress of nations, with perplexity; the sea and the waves roaring; men's hearts failing them for fear, and for looking after those things which are coming on the earth."

We are living in an age when "all these things" have been fulfilled, or are happening around us. Let history respond to the great prophecy of our Saviour, as found in the 24th chapter of Matthew.

Jerusalem was destroyed within forty years of the giving of this prophecy. See Luke 21: 20, 21. The great tribulation of Matthew 24: 21, 22, is in the past. The sun was darkened May 19, 1780. The falling of the stars occurred Nov. 13, 1833. Wars and rumors of wars are becoming more frequent and startling. Distress and perplexity are spread upon all nations, and the enormous standing armies are taxing the resources of the world.

The awful tidal waves, and the more frequently recurring cyclones and earthquakes, show that God's restraining hand is being removed, and the prince of the power of the air is permitted to work out his evil purposes in the destructive elements of wind and water. Famine and pestilence are abroad in the land. Says Christ:

"Now learn a parable of the fig-tree; When his branch is yet tender, and putteth forth leaves, ye know that summer is nigh: so likewise ye when ye shall see all these things, know that it is near, even at the doors. Verily I say unto you, This generation shall not pass, till all these things be fulfilled." Matthew 24: 32-34.

Iniquity Shall Abound

ONE of the signs given by our Saviour of the approaching end of the gospel age is that "iniquity shall abound." (Matthew 24: 12.) To the same intent the apostle Paul wrote to his son in the gospel, "Evil men and seducers shall wax worse and worse." 2 Timothy 3: 13.

That these two latter-day predictions are being fulfilled today surely needs no extended argument. Lawlessness (that is the real meaning of the Greek word rendered "iniquity" in Matthew 24: 12) and crime are rampant on every hand. Corruption has stalked boldly into the high places, and sin and lasciviousness have become popular with great segments of society. Evil has become so prevalent that multitudes mistake it for good. And, as Paul says, this condition is getting "worse and worse."

In a recent book by Judge Marcus Kavanagh of Chicago, he makes this challenging statement:

> "However much it hurts to hear the truth, the situation obliges its utterance. Within twenty-five years the United States has become the richest and most powerful, the most lawless and the most law-ridden country on earth."

And then he goes on to give us a glimpse of the awfulness of the tide of crime and iniquity to which we are subjected today:

> "In spite of all these laws and the uncounted fortunes spent for the protection of our citizens, twelve thousand unshielded inhabitants perished last year at the hands of assassins. Stay a moment!... Unless the national mind becomes saturated with the realization that under the dreadful pall of these figures lie stretched twelve thousand stark, pathetic bodies, and that above them weep at

International Newsreel
The arrest of women communists. They shake their fists in the face of government as now organized.

least sixty thousand agonized kindred; and unless the man on the street and the woman at her task are made to feel that for all this crime and suffering, they themselves bear a part of the responsibility, there will fall twelve thousand more next year and a like number every year after. Thirty-nine thousand people were robbed last year; thirty-two thousand others had their homes or other premises broken into. . . . There is no crime wave, merely a constantly rising tide. It is sinful to minimize the situation."

In an endeavor to impress upon us the enormity of the situation, and to give us a graphic portrayal of the army of 350,000 criminals in our land, he says:

"At this moment the country is being attacked by an army of three hundred fifty thousand, who form an invisible foe; hosts of the air, whose stroke is sudden, remorseless, and unspeakably cruel. In other words, American soil is occupied by an invading hostile army more formidable in size and efficiency than any that before the World War ever invaded civilized country. It is twice the size of the armies that fought at Waterloo. In the Battle of Gravelotte, which decided the Franco-Prussian War, French and Prussians combined had thirty thousand soldiers less than the number we have of dangerous women and men who constitute a never-ceasing threat and menace to our lives and property. Our Black Army is twice the size of the Union and Confederate Armies that fought at Gettysburg. No story of atrocities told against the Germans by the newspapers of the Allied countries during the World War, no inflammatory tale of French cruelty published by German writers at that time, half equals in savagery the actual deeds this advancing army is sure to inflict on the patient, law-abiding American citizen during the coming twelve months."

Professor Joseph Mayer, teacher of economics and sociology in Tufts College, in a recent issue of the *Scientific Monthly*, says that the money loss due to crime is at least $4,000,000,000 annually, and may amount to as much as $10,000,000,000. He observes:

"That the economic and financial loss involved in criminal activities in the commercial field is considerable will readily be conceded. The exact extent of the annual loss cannot, of course, be accurately computed. However, authorities are fairly well agreed that a figure somewhere between two thousand and ten thousand millions represents it. If we take the higher figure of this estimate, our commercial crime cost is three times as much as is now appropriated each year for the running expenses of our government, and represents fifteen per cent of the total annual national income. It is just about equal to the sum total of the war debts owed to the United States as a result of the late war. William J. Burns, former head of the Bureau of Investigation of the Department of Justice, and Mr. James E. Baum, manager of the protective department of the American Bankers Association, are

Iniquity Shall Abound 143

practically agreed on setting the present yearly loss due to commercial crime at something like four thousand millions."

Calvin Coolidge, in one of his syndicated daily newspaper articles, has declared that the American people are forced to pay one eighth of their total income each year for crime. In some of the large cities the proportion is much higher. In Chicago, for example, the various "rackets" extract $15,000,000 a year from the building trades alone, and another $5,000,000 from the laundries. Scarcely any branch of legitimate business is not preyed upon to the tune of hundreds of thousands of dollars by the "rackets." As the *World's Work* has said:

"Racketeering is one of the newest words added to the vocabulary of the daily press. It is rapidly becoming one of the commonest. Scarcely a day passes without a report of some new manifestation of this latest device of America's new-rich gangsters. . . . Under threat of violence, the gangster extorts money which is paid to him for 'protection' against the gun he carries. We may as well admit that this is nothing less than the system of *maffia* which ruled Sicily for so many years."

In view of such distressing conditions, the description of the antediluvian world certainly fits our day. Of that time it was said: "The earth also was corrupt before God, and the earth was filled with violence." Genesis 6: 11. And Christ said of the days just before His return, "As it was in the days of Noe, so shall it be also in the days of the Son of man." Luke 17: 26.

That we are living in an age that duplicates that of the world before it was destroyed by a flood of waters, and that we are today seeing the fulfillment of Christ's prediction, cannot be doubted when one reads such a description of our time as the following from an editorial writer on a large metropolitan daily:

"However calloused one may have become to human suffering, he cannot fail to be impressed by the increasing volume of frightful crimes of violence which are sweeping over the country like a strange mental malady. They are startling alike in their number and variety. There are automobile killings that are nothing short of murder; there are holdups, crimes against chastity, burglaries, bank robberies, murderous assaults of husbands upon wives; mothers kill children newborn and yet unborn; wives and children are killed by husbands and fathers; addicts kill to secure money to buy prohibited drugs and liquors; defaulters kill to cover traces of their crimes; radicals burn and slay, cloaking their murders under the guise of patriotism. Daughters accuse their fathers, and nieces accuse their uncles.

"There seems to be an irrepressible mania for shedding blood and experimenting with vice and the illicit. The laws of God and man are alike helpless to prevent this Saturnalia of crime. A whole generation is seeing red. Some of the killings are from mere wantonness. Cults of reds commit murder in search of a new sensation. Often a crisis of nerves is deemed sufficient justification for taking human life. The inhibition, 'Thou shalt not kill,' is as much out of date in certain social and unsocial circles as the other nine commandments. . . .

"The deeds of violence are greater in number and more horrible in detail than ever before. . . . We are in the midst of a storm and whirlwind of insurrection."

Another one of the outstanding characteristics of Noah's day, and one that hastened the destruction of that generation, was vice. So impure was the society of that time that Moses described it thus: "God saw that the wickedness of man was great in the earth, *and that every imagination of the thoughts of his heart was only evil continually.*" Genesis 6:5.

Our day and generation closely parallels Noah's in immorality and impurity; we are fast reverting to the standards that rule the pagan world. If you doubt this statement, read the following paragraphs from an editor of a great magazine:

"Study the crowds on the great thoroughfares of our cities, especially in the districts where the places of amusement are found; look into the faces of the people you find jostling each other in their mad scramble for amusement. You will see all the types that were found in Ephesus in her wickedest days. They are the peacocks that strut, the wolves and hyenas that prowl, the apes that mimic, the serpents that crawl — a whole menagerie of beastly things in human form. It is a well-known fact among doctors that millions of our young men and women are utterly unfit to enter the marriage state and rear children, while the number of the married who are becoming divorced is ever on the increase.

"How can anyone face these ominous facts without serious misgivings as to the future of American civilization? It is high time for the church to awake from her sleep, to put on her *whole* armor instead of a third of it, and wage her warfare against the world, the flesh, and the devil. Our riotous living must give place to something entirely different unless we are to repeat the history of the pagan nations of antiquity and go down in a welter of moral and spiritual ruin."

One of the startling developments of the last decade or two has been the increasing smuttiness and rottenness of popular literature. Our news stands are stacked with magazines and books that a few years ago would have been debarred from the mail under the heading of "obscene literature." Young and old are devouring pages that reek with sexual excitement. One of the well-known book reviewers of the land has recently said that "five out of twenty books that I have reviewed the past month are built around prostitution, an extensive and unnecessary vocabulary of profanity, adultery, Bacchanalian orgies, and immature sex consciousness." He says further:

"The trend of modern literature is way to the left in salaciousness, pornography, and *risque* characterizations. Among the *intelligentzia* a generous mixture of sex, color differentiation, sprinkled with sufficient blasphemous utterances to add piquancy and racy zest — a sort of sophistication, as it were — together with a garnishing of satire, insulting humor, and a general cynic philosophy — all these are the ingredients of three fourths of the popular, high-class fiction of today."

All this flood of obscenity in literature and theater has so lowered the standards of morality that Dean W. R. Inge of London says that commercial prostitution has actually declined, not because of a lack of demand for such things, but because tens of thousands of girls and women who are not regular prostitutes have driven many of the regulars out of business, — "the competition of the amateurs," he calls it. Some idea of the frightful extent of immorality may be gained from figures telling us of the appalling amount of venereal diseases.

The office of the surgeon-general of the United States Public Health Service has recently announced that there are 1,000,000 persons in this country under medical care for venereal diseases at the present time. This is approximately one out of every 120 of our population.

The report further states that the loss occasioned by these diseases in earning power to males alone between the ages of 15 and 45 amounts to $229,000,000 a year. The cost of medical care, of course, is to be added to this total.

Perhaps the greatest contributor to the vice of the age is the motion picture. Its graphic and realistic portrayal of all forms of licentiousness, as eagerly looked upon by twenty million people each day in this country, has stirred up the lower instincts of the masses and incited millions to sex promiscuity. Not long ago at the special assignment of the *Christian Century* magazine, a trained investigator made a thorough study of the motion picture industry and its

The character of many of the movies is a menace to morals.

influence on the fast-mounting vice and crime of the nation. This investigator, Dr. Fred Eastman, says:

"Their character is shady. Their morals are a mess. Their pull is downward. . . . But, worst of all, they are educating millions of young people daily in false standards of taste and conduct, false conceptions of human relationship."

His indictment of the movies is:

"The movies are so occupied with crime and sex stuff and are so saturating the minds of children the world over with social sewage that they have become a menace to the mental and moral life of the coming generation."

An analysis of what our modern motion pictures are made up of is most enlightening:

"The Child Welfare Committee of the League of Nations analyzed 250 films in 1926 and found in them '97 murders, 51 cases of adultery, 19 seductions, 22 abductions, and 45 suicides. Among the principal characters in these 250 pictures were 176 thieves, 25 prostitutes, 35 drunkards, etc.'

"The Chicago Censorship Board in 1924 is said to have made the following eliminations from 788 pictures: 1,811 scenes of assault with guns, with intent to kill; 175 scenes of assault with knives, with intent to kill; 129 scenes of assault with other weapons; 231 scenes of hanging; 173 scenes of horror (as clawing out eyes, biting off ears, etc.); 757 scenes of attacks on women for immoral purposes; 929 scenes of nudity and seminudity; 31 scenes of jail breaking."

When one takes into consideration the fact that thousands of communities, outside the few large cities that have boards of censors, see all these movies with nothing eliminated, one can easily appreciate the incitement toward crime and immorality the movies constitute. They are the chief debaucher of our present-day civilization.

Dr. Eastman interrogated scores of young boys and girls as to their impression of the movies. Here are two characteristic replies:

"A sixteen-year-old girl: 'Those pictures with hot love-making in them, they make girls and boys sitting together get up and walk out, go off somewhere, you know.'"

"A young delinquent: 'Movies make most anything seem all right. Things that look bad on the outside don't seem to be bad at all in the movies.'"

That is perhaps the greatest single charge that could be made against the movies, — they make bad seem good. In other words, they dull the moral perceptions. They blur the distinction between right and wrong. They obscure the line of demarcation between righteousness and iniquity. They so educate the young that they do not differentiate between honesty and dishonesty, purity and impurity, uprightness and degradation, integrity and moral obliqueness. They make sin and sinning attractive, and point the finger of scorn at the high standards of morality and religion.

It is no wonder that vice and crime are rampant when such education as the movies give is being poured into the impressionable minds of our youth day by day. That it is having its baleful effect is evident from the statistics of juvenile delinquency and crime. Statisticians tell us that the age of criminals committed to the penal institutions has rapidly lowered during the past ten years, that whereas the criminals convicted of major crimes used to run around 35 to 40 years in age, that now they average between 20 and 25.

Another one of the distressing and ominous signs of the times in the world today is the dissolution of the marriage tie and the break-up of the home. The *Western Watchman* says that in this respect we are even worse than pagan Rome:

> "No institution is more vital to the well-being of society, and on the other hand, none is more viciously assailed in our days than matrimony. The world is fast going back to the paganism and immorality from which our divine Saviour reclaimed it nineteen hundred years ago. Indeed, it is only in the worst days of pagan Rome that matrimony was so lightly regarded as it is today."

Bishop Charles Fiske calls our stream of frequent divorce "consecutive polygamy," and so it is. There have been one million divorces in the past five years in the United States. At the beginning of this century we had but one divorce to every fifteen weddings. Now the ratio stands at approximately one divorce to every six marriages. Of this trend the *Ladies' Home Journal* says:

"There will be one marriage dissolved for every marriage made in the United States during 1938 if divorces continue to increase at their present rate. Barring a checking of the rising tide by some moral, religious, or legal agency, not yet discovered, the annual matings and unmatings will equalize each other by, or before, then.

"The divorce habit, urge, frenzy — call it what you will — gathers additional momentum with each year. In 1924 one marriage was broken for every 6.89 contracted. In 1925 one couple was legally parted for each 6.33 who were wed. This was an increase in divorces over marriages of .56. Continue this rate for twelve years, and you reach the balance point in or about 1938.

"It may come earlier. The proportion of canceled marriages to matings is increasing like the speed of a barrel rolling downhill. In 1906 there was one divorce to every 11.84 weddings; in 1916, one to every 9.11. During this decade the divorce rate gained 2.73 on matrimony. In the subsequent ten years, just completed, it increased about 3.00. Mathematically the day when, in America, the divorce decrees of a year excel in number the marriage licenses issued is not far away."

One of the most lamentable features of the situation is that many molders of public opinion are today actually condoning and defending the divorce rate and marital infidelity. We have had such men as Judge Ben Lindsey who advocate "companionate" or trial marriage, and who openly declare that men and women should be free to separate and remarry at will and caprice. Indeed, if the world should take some of these men at their word and follow their reasoning to the end, we would have nothing but "free love" left. To show the lengths to which some thinkers and writers are going, the *Century Magazine* has thus summed up what some leading men and women of Great Britain have been teaching along this very line:

"From England has come recently a chorus of voices, listened to with as much interest here as there, advocating theories, schemes of life, in whose atmosphere the family would quickly perish. Says Bertrand Russell, famous philosopher and scientist, in 'What I Believe': 'It should be recognized that, in the absence of children, sexual relations are a purely private matter which does not concern either the state or the neighbors,' a theory the

"Without natural affection" is the cause of many a swift journey from the marriage altar to the divorce court.

general acceptance of which would soon disrupt every home, whether or not it contained children, and leave nothing whatever of the social institution or the family. Anthony M. Ludovici, in 'Lysistrata: or, Woman's Future and Future Woman,' and also in a previous book entitled 'Woman: A Vindication,' advocates what he calls 'legalized concubinage,' which is, quite frankly, polygamy. He foresees this as a development likely to come about and one which, he asserts, would greatly increase human welfare and happiness. Mrs. Bertrand Russell argues for a sexual promiscuity that would throw down every bar to the satisfaction of individual desire in both men and women. 'Grant each man and woman,' she says, in 'Hypatia; or, Woman and Knowledge,' 'the right to seek his or her own solution [of the sex question] without fear of public censure. It would not be wrong for a man to have six wives, provided he and they all found mutual happiness in the arrangement; nor for a woman to have six husbands and a child by each, if she and they found such a life satisfactory.' C. E. M. Joad, a popular British author who has gained a considerable audience for his writings on ethics and religion, discusses, in 'Thrasymachus; or, The Future of Morals,' the influence that the economic independence of women and general knowledge concerning birth control are destined to have on social institutions. He foresees the general acceptance of 'irregular unions' and of 'the right to sexual experience' and 'the right to motherhood' among women without marriage, and advocates what he calls 'a day of conjugal amnesty at recurring intervals' of every few years, wherein any married couple that wished might dissolve their union and each member of it seek another mate. In every one of these and similar proposals — whose advocates are many — there is latent or open hostility to the family and contempt for it as a factor of civilization. Not one of them but would inevitably disrupt it, destroy its foundations, send it to the rubbish heap."

It is a notorious fact that Russia under the communistic regime has demolished the old Christian standards of marriage, and has made both divorce and marriage trivial things to be taken on or thrown off at a moment's notice.

In morals the world is fast reverting to the low standards that prevailed in old Sodom and Gomorrah. All this is in direct fulfillment of the Saviour's words that in the days just prior to His second coming "iniquity shall abound," and that the extreme wickedness that brought destruction to the antediluvian world would be re-enacted.

Another startling development in modern times, and one that bodes only ill for the future, is the prodigious amount

Iniquity Shall Abound 153

of liquor, tobacco, and narcotic drugs being consumed in the world today.

Of course, it must be noted that in the United States the consumption of alcoholic liquors as beverages has been prohibited since 1920. In many ways this has been a great boon to the nation. It has diverted many billions of dollars that formerly went into the saloon's coffers into useful channels. It has helped the health of the nation greatly. It has aided in retarding the moral corruption of the age. But the world at large has gone right on drinking oceans of liquor. England, for example, in a recent year spent $200,000,000 on education and $1,500,000,000 on drink. In a recent seven-year period the total cost of the "dole system" and other relief for the poor and unemployed in the British Isles was less than the amount spent on drink in a single year. These astounding figures could be duplicated in France, Germany, Italy, and other nations. The world is saturated with alcohol, and much of the prevailing low moral standards can be laid at the door of drink.

When it comes to tobacco the world is enveloped in a huge cloud of nicotine-filled smoke. America alone spends more than two and a half billion dollars annually on tobacco. In a recent year 123,000,000,000 cigarettes were produced in the United States. This means on the average that each man, woman, and child in the United States used more than 1,000 cigarettes in that year. These cigarettes, if placed end to end, making a line 5,338,542 miles long, would reach to the moon and back 11 times; and would girdle the world at the equator 213½ times. The amount of money spent on cigarettes alone each year would build 2½ Panama Canals, and 5½ Boulder Dams.

One of the most significant and ominous developments of the postwar years has been in the astounding increase in woman and girl smokers. It used to be that no one but women of ill repute smoked, but now hosts of high school and college girls, "society" women, women employed in the business world, smoke. So prevalent has the habit become that theaters have provided special smoking rooms for women, and in trains, hotels, and restaurants one sees smoking on the part of women a very commonplace thing.

International Newsreel
One million dollars' worth of demoralizing drugs destroyed by the New York police.

In England and France the habit is even more universal among the women than in America.

Public health authorities of the entire world are deeply alarmed over the great increase in the use of narcotic drugs since the World War. The illicit international traffic in morphine, heroin, cocaine, and other forms of "dope" is of alarming proportions. The figures run up into several billions of dollars each year, and despite many laws against it, this diabolical trade flourishes everywhere, even apparently fostered, or sheltered, by some governments.

It has been estimated by British colonial authorities in Egypt that one out of every twenty-five people in that country is a dope addict, hopelessly enmeshed in the toils of narcotics. It is said that there are 1,000,000 illicit users of these drugs in the United States. Every country of the world, Occidental and Oriental, is likewise beset by this terrible thing.

There is no vice that mankind is heir to that breaks down a man physically and morally faster and more completely than does the use of narcotic drugs. It is the greatest single factor in the making of desperate criminals. Gerhard Kuhne, chief of the Bureau of Criminal Identification of New York City, asserts that "drugs are the cause of from 50 to 75 per cent of our crimes in New York City today, and throughout the state."

Eighty per cent of the known addicts of New York have criminal records, affirms Dr. Carleton Simon of New York, who reports that he was constantly in touch with 25,000 addicts.

The New York Department of Correction, through its chief, Frederick A. Wallis, announced that 60 per cent of the inmates of the jails and penitentiaries of New York State are narcotic addicts.

The U. S. District Attorney in Southern California says that sixty per cent of the time of the two Federal Grand Juries in Los Angeles and Fresno is taken up with narcotic cases.

One turns almost sickened with despair from all the sordid facts recorded in this chapter to the word of God for some ray of comfort and hope in the world's present undone condition. Will our world be swallowed up in the mire of evil? Will it be submerged in a veritable cesspool of iniquity? Is there no hope and no salvation and no succor from these abominations done in the land?

Paul, speaking of our very day, gave this dark prophecy: "This know also, that in the last days perilous times shall come. For men shall be lovers of their own selves, covetous, boasters, proud, blasphemers, disobedient to parents, unthankful, unholy, without natural affection, truce-breakers, false accusers, incontinent, fierce, despisers of those that are good, traitors, heady, highminded, lovers of pleasures more than lovers of God; having a form of godliness, but denying the power thereof." 2 Timothy 3: 1-5.

This catalogue of sins fits our very day as precisely as if Paul were alive now and writing from actual observation rather than by prophetic inspiration nineteen hundred years ago. But the great cheering thought to us is that Paul says these conditions will be found "in the last days." In other words, Paul saw that when the world should become so dissolute and abandoned and criminal, it would not then be long until the second appearing of Christ, who would bring to an end the age of sin and iniquity and lawlessness. What an encouragement it is to know that we do not have to look forward to centuries of this dreadful state of things, but that soon Jesus will be revealed in the clouds of heaven to rid the earth of sin and sinners, and to establish His kingdom of righteousness and peace.

The Church Apostatizing

THE New Testament Scriptures, especially the prophetic portions, tell us that in the generation before Christ's return to earth a great apostasy will take place in the Christian church. Jesus himself foretold it in the form of a question: "When the Son of man cometh, shall He find faith on the earth?" Luke 18: 8. Peter predicted that "among you also there shall be false teachers, who shall privily bring in destructive heresies, denying even the Master that bought them." 2 Peter 2: 1, A. R. V. Of like tenor are the words of Paul concerning these last days:

"Preach the word; be urgent in season, out of season; reprove, rebuke, exhort, with all longsuffering and teaching. For the time will come when they will not endure the sound doctrine; but, having itching ears, will heap to themselves teachers after their own lusts; and will turn away their ears from the truth, and turn aside unto fables." 2 Timothy 4: 2-4, A. R. V.

These prophetic utterances are being fulfilled before our very eyes. If such men as the Wesleys, Spurgeon, and Moody were to come to life today, they would not recognize great portions of their own churches. Christians by the millions have gone whoring after strange gods. They have been told that science has discovered a new god, and they fain would worship him and discard Jehovah of old. Through the almost universal teaching of the theory of evolution in the school system of many states, through the capture of the theological seminaries, the pulpits, the denominational schools, and the publishing houses of the various bodies, by the Liberals and the Modernists, multitudes have been constantly educated to the idea that the tenets of Christianity that our fathers believed are wholly out of date and in error today.

From a thousand pulpits every Sunday, congregations are assured by those who purport to be ambassadors of God that the Bible is a good book and in many respects the world's greatest book, but that we must not regard it as the inspired

Kadel & Herbert, N. Y.
The theory that man ascended from an ape is undermining belief in God and the Bible.

and infallible word of God — that when the great men of to-day disagree with the Bible, we must take their word rather than that of Scripture. We are told that the Genesis record is either a myth, or just a beautiful Hebrew poem; that it is in no case to be accepted as a literal statement of the origin of the earth and of the animal and human life upon it. We are told that Christ was the world's greatest man, but that the Bible record of His virgin birth, His miracles, His vicarious atonement on Calvary's tree, His bodily resurrection from the dead, etc., are not to be taken as literal, that they merely reflect the too credulous belief in supernaturalism that was extant when the Bible was written. We are told by these "divines" that the old idea of the blood atonement was all right for the untutored Hebrews in the days of their bloody sanctuary services, but that modern man cannot accept the idea of substitution in the matter of atonement for sin; that sin, after all, is not something to be too much concerned about anyway, that it is merely a "hangover" from our prehistoric animal ancestry, which will be automatically sloughed off with the passing of a few more millenniums.

When the creation of man and the world by God is taken away, when the fall of man is rejected, when the redemption through the blood of Christ is discredited, when the Bible as man's guide and source of authority is derided, what have we left of evangelical Christianity? Nothing but the husk. And yet this denatured and emasculated Christianity is what is capturing the popular churches of Christendom today. The utter incompatibility between the evangelical view of the Christian religion and the new Modernist view has been set forth very ably by one of the leading Modernist periodicals, the *Christian Century:*

"Two worlds have crashed. . . . There is a clash here as profound and as grim as that between Christianity and Confucianism. Amiable words cannot hide the differences. 'Blest be the tie' may be sung until doomsday but it cannot bind these two worlds together. The God of the Fundamentalist is one God; the God of the Modernist is another. The Christ of the Fundamentalist is one Christ; the Christ of Modernism is another. The Bible of Fundamentalism is one Bible; the Bible of Modernism is another. The church, the kingdom, the salvation, the consummation of all things — these are one thing to Fundamentalists and another thing to Modernists. Which God is the Christian God, which Christ is the Christian Christ, which Bible is the Christian Bible, which church, which kingdom, which salvation, which consummation are the Christian church, the Christian kingdom, the Christian salvation, the Christian consummation? The future will tell. But that the issue is clear and that the inherent incompatibility of the two worlds has passed the stage of mutual tolerance is a fact concerning which there hardly seems room for anyone to doubt."

Another issue of this same journal reiterates:

"The two groups represent a divergence and dissimilarity so deep-going and distinct as to suggest two distinct religions. There is hardly a greater disparity between Christianity and Confucianism than between Modernism and Fundamentalism."

And again:

"The church of this hour is undergoing a more fundamental change than that which occurred in Martin Luther's day."

Several polls and questionnaires conducted among the ministers of the great Protestant denominations have shown this estimate of the wide divergence in views on the very basic principles of Christianity to be none too harsh. Thousands of ministers have replied that Christ's death on the cross was not necessary for the remission of man's sins; that the question of whether or not Christ was literally resurrected is inconsequential; that the doctrine of His second appearing is too visionary and uncertain for modern men to put faith in; that prayer has little or no effect on anything except a man's own state of mind; that the doctrine of a personal God is quite unbelievable today; that the idea of God as the Creator of the world harks back to the pre-scientific era, etc.

The Church Apostatizing 161

Skepticism, agnosticism, and rank infidelity, stalk openly in the churches and denominational schools of the land today, and in many quarters are received with open arms and applauded by teachers and preachers alike. Whereas the devil used to attack Christian doctrine and belief from outside the church, through such men as Paine and Ingersoll, now, by insidious doctrine, by subtle logic and by covert teaching, the same work is done within the church itself by those who are sworn to defend it. Men have substituted science for God, and themselves for the Saviour.

To be sure, there are "seven thousand" who have not yet bowed their knee to Baal. There are still tens of thousands who adhere to the Bible and its teachings, but in all too many cases the leaders and those in control of denominational interests have sold out to religious liberalism. If Christ himself were to return to earth today and sit in the church pews and in the classrooms of our seminaries and denominational schools, He would not recognize as Christian more than one half of that which parades under His name. Many churches are teachers of morals and ethics, many are centers of pleasure and society, many are forums for philosophical and scientific discussion, but all too few are really Christian in the sense of Bible and evangelical Christianity. It is no wonder that a great English writer has said:

> "Everywhere today men are breathing a spiritual atmosphere that is heavy and oppressive with the deadly vapors of unbelief. They are living in days of spiritual darkness, 'darkness that may be felt.'"

In view of the awful apostasy within the church today, certainly the prophecies quoted at the beginning of this chapter are faithful and true. They are being fulfilled today to the very letter. There can be no mistake but that we are living "in the last days"; the apostasy within Christendom would prove that, if there were no other sign of Christ's coming to be seen.

In such an age as this the two following Scriptural passages are most appropriate: "Beloved, while I was giving all diligence to write unto you of our common salvation, I was constrained to write unto you exhorting you to contend earnestly for the faith which was once for all delivered unto the saints. For there are certain men crept in privily, even they who were of old written of beforehand unto this condemnation, ungodly men, turning the grace of our God into lasciviousness, and denying our only Master and Lord, Jesus Christ." Jude 3, 4, A. R. V.

"But thou, O man of God, flee these things; and follow after righteousness, godliness, faith, love, patience, meekness. Fight the good fight of the faith, lay hold on the life eternal, whereunto thou wast called, and didst confess the good confession in the sight of many witnesses. I charge thee in the sight of God, who giveth life to all things, and of Christ Jesus, who before Pontius Pilate witnessed the good confession; that thou keep the commandment, without spot, without reproach, until the appearing of our Lord Jesus Christ: which in its own times He shall show, who is the blessed and only Potentate, the King of kings, and Lord of lords; who only hath immortality, dwelling in light unapproachable; whom no man hath seen, nor can see: to whom be honor and power eternal. Amen." 1 Timothy 6: 11-16, A. R. V.

Famines

PERIODICALLY for millenniums the pages of history have recorded the tragic inroads of famine upon the inhabitants of the earth. Scarcely any part of the world, especially in its more crowded areas, has escaped. However, for famine severity and for the number of famine victims, our very recent times have exceeded the grim record of former generations. This may seem strange at first, for with our rapid means of transportation these days, it would seem to be almost impossible for any one part of the world to suffer greatly from lack of food. But Christ said that famine would be one of the portents in the generation that would see His return to earth; and so it is. (Matthew 24: 7.)

The famine in China in 1919 is no doubt one of the most dreadful the human race has ever suffered. The exact number of victims will perhaps never be accurately known, but it is certain that at least a half million — some say two millions — were wiped out by starvation within a few months. In three provinces alone there were at one time 13,000,000 absolutely destitute of food, many of whom subsequently died. Whole tribes turned cannibal, devouring one another, mothers eating their children, and children attacking their parents in the death throes of that terrible death, — starvation.

And then there followed the great Russian famine, which the London *Times* described as "a spectacle that is apocalyptic in its awful suggestion of collapse." The archbishop of Canterbury declared that "never in the history of the world has a condition of things existed comparable to the ghastly death by famine of whole millions of men, women, and children." The Norwegian explorer and scientist,

Fridtjof Nansen, said, "The famine is beyond all doubt the most appalling that has ever happened in the recorded history of man."

Besides these two monster famines, there have been the famines of Armenia and India, both of which would have loomed much larger had they not been dwarfed for the moment by those in China and Russia. There have been food shortages also in unusual places.

Within very recent years and as late as 1929 and 1930,

Paul Thompson
Famine victims in Russia soon after the World War.

several hundreds of thousands have died of starvation in distant provinces of China. In fact, famine in China has become so common a story that the newspapers give but scant space to the story nowadays. The *Christian Century* says that six millions have perished there for lack of food since the World War. Surely such figures as these are ample fulfillment of Christ's prophecy that devastating famines would constitute a sign to the last generation of His coming.

Famines

We must not pass by, either, some manifestations in nature that are akin to famine, and that are often its cause. In the summer of 1930 the severest drought on record swept much of the eastern and southern portions of the United States. For months not a drop of rain fell. Crops scorched under intolerable heat and dried up in the fields. Live stock died for lack of food and water. Thousands of families were reduced to a scant living, and Congress and the Red Cross appropriated tens of millions of dollars to care for the sufferers.

In the same year a great plague of locusts swept across northern Africa and up through the Arabian lands, — Palestine, Trans-Jordania, — and Irak, eating every green thing before them. Such a plague had not been seen on so great a scale for many decades.

All over the world man is battling for food against the great and increasing hordes of insects. Indeed, Dr. L. O. Howard, who was for thirty-three years chief of the Bureau of Entomology of the United States Department of Agriculture, has said:

> "It has become strikingly obvious that insects are collectively the most important enemies and rivals of humanity on the earth. It has also become perfectly plain that if human beings are to maintain their hold on this globe, if they are to continue to exist, they must learn to control insects."

The *Saturday Evening Post* in comment upon this statement of Dr. Howard's has declared:

> "America has become a stupendous battlefield. Throughout the length and breadth of this broad land, from the Golden Gate to New York Harbor, from the Great Lakes to the Gulf, an implacable conflict is raging, the importance and magnitude of which have escaped general attention simply because of the insignificant stature of our Lilliputian foes. It is a war without quarter between mankind and the insect race as to which shall

possess the food supplies of the world. Man, the dominant type on this terrestrial body, who has subdued or turned to his own use nearly all kinds of living creatures, has laid claim to the food supplies, most of which — in the civilized world at least — he has created by his own toil. The insects, the dominant type within their own series, which in many ways are better fitted for existence on this earth than man, do not even bother to dispute that claim; they simply take possession of the food supply, dig in— and the whole proposition is reduced to a Diet of Worms.

"In America, on one side of the line-up stand the embattled farmers with their poison sprays, the citrus growers, the cotton planters, the corn and wheat and alfalfa producers, the deciduous fruit and truck farmers; and on the opposing side are assembled millions upon millions of destructive pests, hundreds of different species, and most of them hailing from Europe."

The destruction of the citrus fruits in Florida by the Mediterranean fruit fly is still fresh in our minds. Millions of dollars' worth of fruit and trees were destroyed within a few weeks, and an army of 5,000 men were mobilized to repel the advance of this insect enemy. This particular fly takes thirty-five per cent of the citrus fruit crop in Africa annually. So serious are its depredations in Hawaii that resistance has been virtually given up. In Brazil and Spain it also lays waste the fields and orchards every year. No part of the world is immune from insect attack, and year by year the situation is becoming more serious. Science with all its advancement has not proved equal to coping with the bug menace.

Some idea of the situation may be gained from the awful toll bugs are taking in America each year. Bugs hold up the American farmer to the pretty tune of $1,500,000,000 annually. Some would even put the figure at $2,000,000,000. Insect depredations steadily mount, despite the vigilance of the Bureau of Entomology, which has hundreds of scientists working all the time, devising new methods to fight new and old bugs. About the time the enemy is vanquished in one part of the land, a new one crawls out of the ground or from a tree.

The boll weevil, the bollworm, the chinch bug, and the

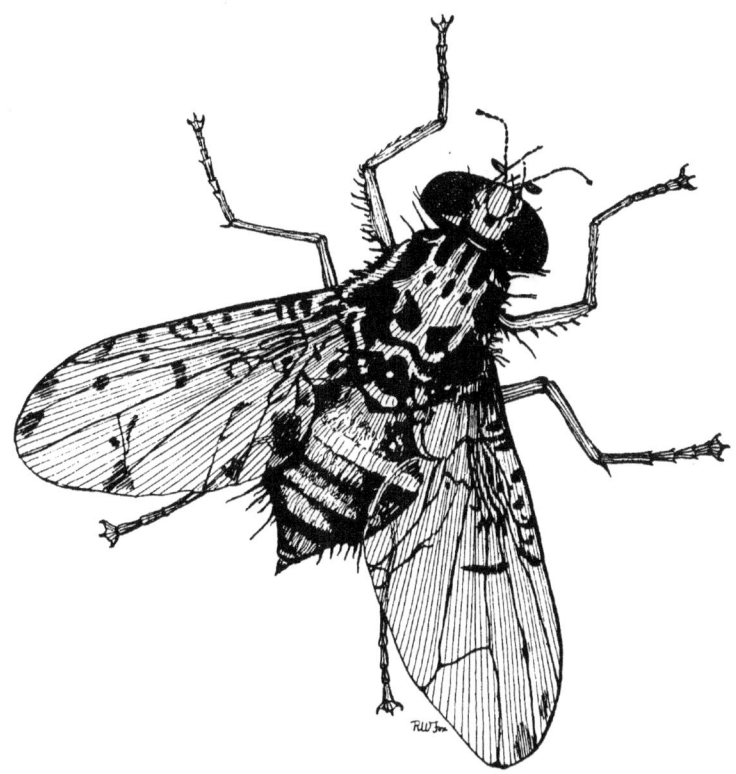

The destructive fruit fly

Hessian fly are the "four horsemen" of the American insect pest world. These pests in a single year damage the cotton and cereal crops of the United States to the extent of more than $366,000,000.

Other pests that do considerable damage in the aggregate are the codling moth, which annually renders unfit for food apples valued at $13,000,000; the plum curculio, whose appetite for peaches and apples costs the orchard men $14,000,000 annually; the potato leaf hopper, which takes $11,000,000 out of the pockets of the potato growers; the pea aphid, with its $2,082,000 appetite; the stripped cucumber beetle, which destroys $2,000,000 worth of cucumbers and melons each year; the cabbage worm, which takes $3,000,000 yearly from the truck farmers; the bark beetles, which do $15,000,000 damage to the fir and spruce forests; the sugar-cane borer, whose forays cost the sugar-cane planters about $4,500,000 every year; the spruce bud worm, which destroys pulp wood to the sum of $71,000,000.

Dr. Charles L. Marlatt, now the chief entomologist of the United States Department of Agriculture, sums up the insect damage bill as follows:

Farm Crops:

Cereals	$430,204,600
Hay	116,230,500
Cotton	165,000,000
Tobacco	16,900,800
Vegetables	199,412,600
Sugar crops	8,436,800
Fruits	141,264,300
Farm-forest products	22,138,900
Other crops	29,649,700
Total	$1,129,238,200
Natural forests and forest products	100,000,000
Products in storage	100,000,000
Insect-borne diseases of man	150,000,000
Direct or indirect damage to domestic animals	100,000,000
Grand Total	$1,579,238,200

Famines

Joel the prophet foresaw this insect destruction, and he likened it to an advancing army. "A nation is come up upon my land, strong, and without number; his teeth are the teeth of a lion, and he hath the jaw teeth of a lioness. He hath laid my vine waste, and barked my fig-tree: he hath made it clean bare, and cast it away; the branches thereof are made white. . . . The field is laid waste, the land mourneth; for the grain is destroyed, the new wine is dried up, the

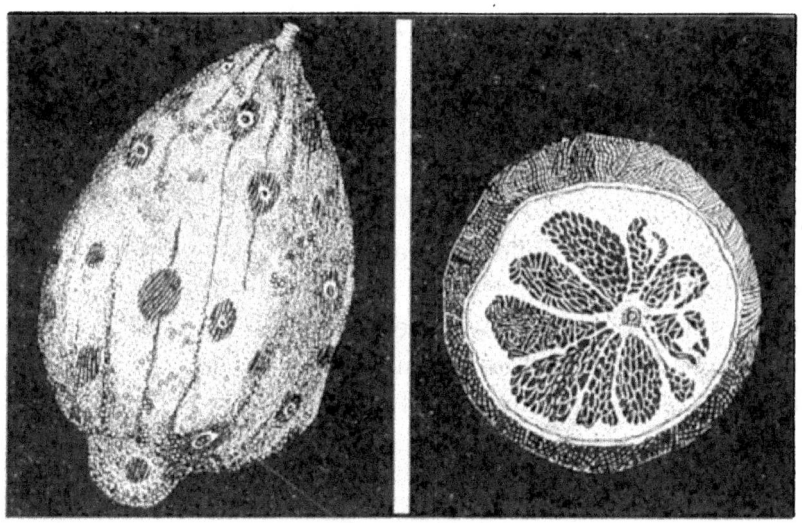

A lemon and an orange after being attacked by the fruit fly.

oil languisheth. Be confounded, O ye husbandmen, wail, O ye vinedressers, for the wheat and for the barley; for the harvest of the field is perished. The vine is withered, and the fig-tree languisheth; the pomegranate-tree, the palm-tree also, the apple-tree, even all the trees of the field are withered: for joy is withered away from the sons of men. . . .

"The seeds rot under their clods; the garners are laid desolate, the barns are broken down; for the grain is withered. How do the beasts groan! the herds of cattle are perplexed, because they have no pasture; yea, the flocks of sheep are made desolate." Joel 1: 6-12, 17, 18, A. R. V.

That these statements must apply to a day just prior to the day of the Lord as well as to Joel's time is evident from these verses: "Alas for the day! For the day of Jehovah is at hand, and as a destruction shall it come from the Almighty. . . . Blow ye the trumpet in Zion, and sound an alarm in My holy mountain; let all the inhabitants of the land tremble: for the day of Jehovah cometh, for it is nigh at hand." Joel 1: 15; 2: 1, A. R. V.

These insect plagues are therefore another token that the earth is growing old and is groaning for its latter end. This is but one of the signs that the end of the age is approaching with its promise of a new world re-created by the power of God.

To the Bible student the events occurring around us are significant, and point to the day near at hand when the earth and the things that are therein have waxed "old as doth a garment; and as a vesture shalt Thou fold them up, and they shall be changed." Hebrews 1: 11, 12.

Pestilence *and* Earthquake

AS CHRIST sat upon the Mount of Olives the disciples asked Him the direct question, "What shall be the sign of Thy coming, and of the end of the world?" A part of the Master's reply was: "And there shall be famines, and pestilences, and earthquakes in divers places." Matthew 24:7. Surely then, pestilences and earthquakes in outstanding manifestations can be looked for in this generation, if this is the one that is to witness the second coming of Christ.

A pestilence in this era when medical science and sanitation have made such unparalleled progress would seem wellnigh impossible. We naturally would think that medieval times, before the germ theory of disease was known, and before serums and anti-toxins were discovered, would be the time when the most virulent pestilences would be experienced. To be sure, they did have their plagues then that swept away tens of thousands of lives. Within the memory of men now living, bubonic plague, cholera, smallpox, yellow fever, etc., swept across whole continents. But it has remained for very modern times to furnish the most decimating pestilence of all history in the influenza epidemic of 1918 and 1919. Almost before men were aware of its presence, thousands fell its victims; and in the course of a few months, millions had succumbed. Deaths were so numerous in the army camps of the United States that in some instances the usual custom of burial in separate graves was abandoned, and instead, great trenches were dug with tractors, and the bodies buried *en masse*. It is estimated that in India alone, 12,000,000 people died of "flu"; and some would place the number even higher. Statistics of course vary, and are meager at best, because the nations were engaged in war and had little time for keeping such figures; but conservative students place the number of deaths in all the world due to influenza, and its concomitant, pneumonia, at 15,000,000 to 20,000,000. And the effects of this disease are not to be reckoned in the number of deaths alone; for hundreds of thousands of persons who suffered of influenza were left so weakened in constitution or in particular organs of the body, that they afterwards died of diseases which otherwise would not have proved fatal.

Severe earthquakes have been a tragic mark of the twentieth century. Indeed, more severe earthquakes have happened in the past quarter of a century than in any five-hundred-year period up to this time. Beginning with 1905 here is a list of the major earthquakes that have occurred,—earthquakes in which from 1,500 to 200,000 people have perished:

1905 Kangra	1913 Guatemala
1906 San Francisco	1914 Japan
1906 Valparaiso	1914 Italy
1907 Jamaica	1915 Italy
1907 Turkestan	1920 China
1908 Messina-Reggio	1922 Chile
1910 Costa Rica	1923 Japan
1911 Turkestan	1927 Japan
1911 Luzon	1928 Dutch East Indies
1912 Turkey	1930 Italy
1912 Mexico	1930 Japan

The two greatest earthquakes of all history were those of the Kansu province, China, in December, 1920, and that of Japan in September, 1923. That the Kansu earthquake killed only 200,000 people is owing to the fact that it occurred in one of the sparsely settled sections of China. That earthquake changed the surface of the earth more than any

Pestilence and Earthquake 173

Scene after the great earthquake in Japan

earthquake on record. A special observer who visited the region soon after said, "Likely no other earthquake in scientific annals ever changed the physical geography of the affected region to the extent of the Kansu cataclysm."

This observer, writing in the *National Geographic Magazine*, said that "mountains that moved in the night, landslides that eddied like waterfalls, crevasses that swallowed houses and camel trains, and villages that were swept away under a rising sea of loose earth, were a few of the subsidiary occurrences that made the earthquake in Kansu one of the most appalling catastrophes in history."

But great as was the Kansu disaster, it was surpassed by the destruction of Tokyo, Yokohama, and other Japanese cities, by earthquake on September 1, 1923. The earthquake in China caused the greatest physical changes ever known, but the one in Japan destroyed the most property. The figures given out by the Japanese government as authentic are:

Refugees by the thousand after the Japan earthquake

[174]

Killed - - - - - - 99,331
Wounded - - - - - 103,733
Missing - - - - - - 43,476

Total casualties - - 246,540
Houses totally destroyed:
By fire - - - - - - 447,128
By collapse - - - - - 128,266
By tidal waves - - - - 868

Total - - 576,262
Houses partially destroyed - - 126,233

Grand total - - 702,495

"The greatest single disaster since the Flood," is the appraisal of one writer; and another, an eyewitness, penned this graphic description for *McClure's Magazine:*

"The gates of hell swung open for Central Japan two minutes before the noon hour on Saturday, September the first, and for two days the demons of destruction worked their will with all the elements of earth, fire, and water. Death in a hundred forms stalked abroad. The solid earth turned fluid. The sea invaded the land. Fire, unleashed and uncontrollable, fed upon the wreckage of half a hundred cities and villages, and drowned the shrieks of perishing thousands in its on-rushing roar.

"Without one second of warning the blow fell that swept at least two hundred thousand people over the brink of eternity; that destroyed a majority of the buildings over three thousand square miles of one of the most densely populated sections of the world; that reduced one of the five Great Powers from a mighty, proud, and powerful nation to a people forced to turn abroad for many of the necessities of life."

Of recent years we must mention the earthquake of 1930 in the Izu Peninsula, Japan. This temblor lasted 30 minutes and razed the towns to the ground all over that peninsula. It was Japan's worst since 1923.

In the summer of 1930 southern Italy was visited by an earthquake that was the worst since the Messina catastrophe of 1908. In the recent quake 2,000 lives were snuffed out in a moment, and 5,000 injured. The whole city of Melfi was leveled to the ground, and other towns had almost every building so wrecked that they had to be rebuilt from the ground up.

The year 1931 was introduced by a disastrous earthquake in New Zealand. The resort seaport town of Napier was added to the "divers places." A cliff 300 feet high was cast into the sea, private dwellings and the General Hospital were buried in the landslide; the harbor bottom was raised; and death and destruction visited all the surrounding region.

Jesus says: "All these things are the beginning of sorrows."

The sure word of prophecy informs us that just before the coming of our Lord from heaven, there will be an earthquake more awful than any that has been experienced since the "fountains of the deep were broken up" at the Flood. In this calamity the whole earth will be involved. "The foundations of the earth do shake. The earth is utterly broken down, the earth is clean dissolved, the earth is moved exceedingly. The earth shall reel to and fro like a drunkard, and shall be removed like a cottage." Isaiah 24: 18-20.

The apostle-prophet John says of this earthquake: "There was a great earthquake, such as was not since men were upon the earth, so mighty an earthquake, and so great. . . . And every island fled away, and the mountains were not found." Revelation 16: 18, 20.

Very many texts in the Bible refer to this terrific convulsion which takes place in connection with the great day. Here is one passage: "The Lord also shall roar out of Zion, and utter His voice from Jerusalem; and the heavens and the earth shall shake: but the Lord will be the hope of His people, and the strength of the children of Israel." Joel 3: 16. On this point read carefully Ezekiel 38: 19, 20.

May we have made our peace with God so that we may be "hid in the day of the Lord's anger." May ours be the experience foretold by David of this time: "A thousand shall fall at thy side, and ten thousand at thy right hand; but it shall not come nigh thee. Only with thine eyes shalt thou behold and see the reward of the wicked." Psalm 91: 7, 8.

Storms *and* Tidal Waves

ALONG with the other calamities that are coming upon the earth as the "day of the Lord" draws near, we may naturally expect, according to the prophecy of Luke 21: 25, to see disastrous storms by land and sea. "Stormy wind fulfilling His word." Psalm 148: 8. "And there shall be signs in the sun, and in the moon, and in the stars; and upon the earth distress of nations, with perplexity; the sea and the waves roaring." Luke 21: 25.

We have only to look at the long list of terrible tornadoes and the awful tidal waves, as reported in the public press from time to time, to see that we are already in a period of disaster from these causes, such as the history of the world has never before known.

That this type of disaster is increasing is evident from the recent statement of one of the great newspapers of the land:

> "Never before have the papers of this country had to record such a series of disasters due to tornado as have marked the present seasons. Day after day additions have had to be made to a somber list already large beyond known precedent.
>
> "Man has done much to make life more safe and comfortable. He may protect himself against cold and heat, and in some measure even against the fury of the elements. But when the winds are loosed in all their fierceness, they represent an energy beyond human control, a force that no strength of steel or timber may resist.
>
> "Life is destroyed and property swept away. There seems nothing to be done about it save to aid the impoverished and suffering, and hope for the best."

The New York *Tribune* in similar vein reflects that man "remains at the mercy of endless giant forces, and his wisdom

The awful hurricane in Miami, Florida

thereof, if one looks to the whole area of the universe, is as a candle blown by winds in the night."

Colonel John P. Finley of the Signal Corps of the United States Army has been keeping tornado statistics since 1879, when he was but a private in the ranks. Early in his career, says the New York *Times* of April 21, 1929, he organized a corps of 2,500 tornado observers at various points throughout the country. At the present time he has the aid of 5,000 trained observers in the climatological division of the Weather Bureau. "A particularly high degree of accuracy is believed to have been maintained during the past thirteen years." Note the following:

"The record shows for the period 1916-1928 inclusive, a total of 1,400 tornadoes, with property losses aggregating $173,000,000 and an aggregate loss of 3,861 lives."

Surely, such astounding totals of lives snuffed out and of property razed, is an irrefutable attestation to the fact that our world is growing old "like a garment."

Within recent years we have witnessed several storms of unusual ferocity. On September 18, 1926, southern Florida was laid waste by one of the terrific hurricanes off the Caribbean. Miami received the brunt of the maelstrom of wind and water. The Atlantic was driven back into Biscayne Bay by the force of the wind until the water rose eight feet. Boats and barges were beached and wrecked by the hundreds. For hours the air was filled with flying debris as great buildings and dwellings houses were torn apart and hurled hither and yon. Five hundred people were killed in and around Miami, and the property loss ran into the tens of millions.

In the later summer of 1930 another one of these Caribbean hurricanes struck Santo Domingo. When it had done its fearful work of destruction scarcely a building stood intact in that great city, and 4,000 lay dead, and 20,000 injured. So great was the force of the hurricane that great modern

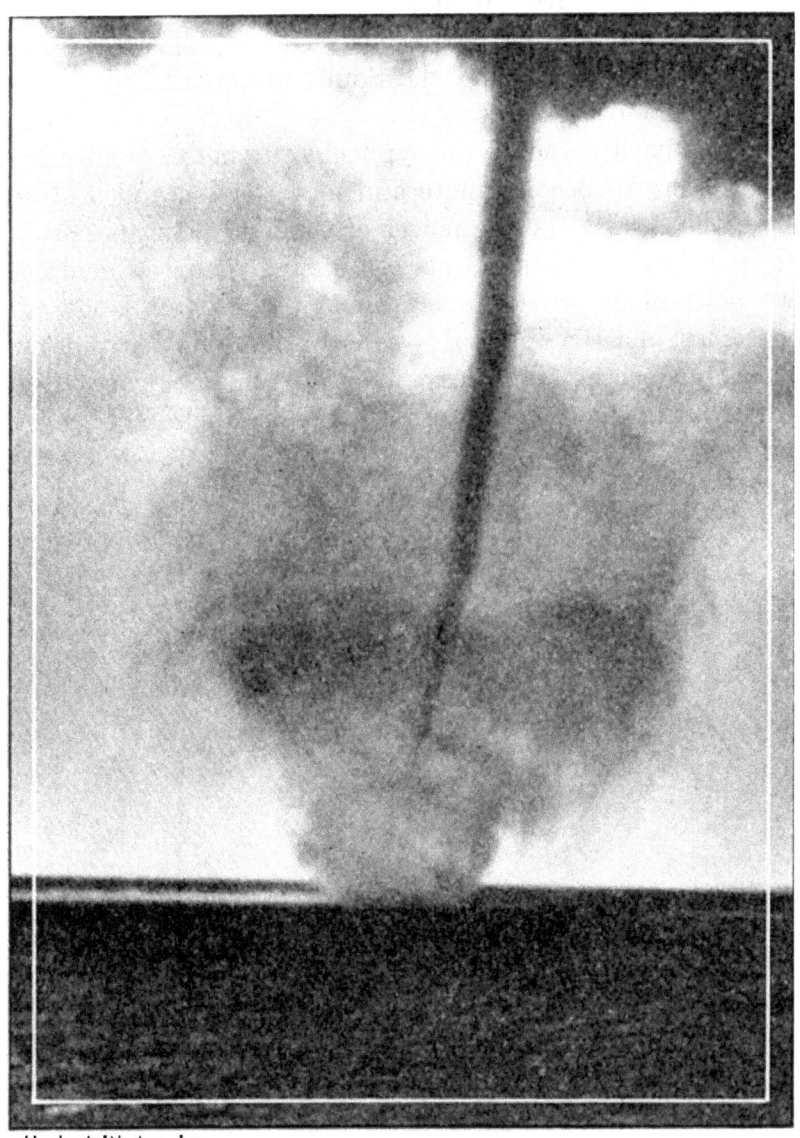

Herbert Photos, Inc.

A tornado in the distance

steel bridges were broken in two and flung into the water as if they had been cardboard.

Time and space would fail us to tell of the tornadoes that have swept their besom of destruction across sections of the Middle West and the South in the United States, as well as in other lands.

With each passing year typhoons, tornadoes, and hurricanes seem to become more and more terrific and destructive, the "prince of the power of the air" being permitted to marshal, more and more forcibly, these elements as weapons of destruction, as "the great day of God" approaches, and the Spirit of the Lord is more fully withdrawn from the earth. This leaves Satan almost unchecked to carry out his plans and desires for the destruction of life and property.

Capital *and* Labor

"COME now, ye rich, weep and howl for your miseries that are coming upon you. Your riches are corrupted, and your garments are moth-eaten. Your gold and your silver are rusted; and their rust shall be for a testimony against you, and shall eat your flesh as fire. Ye have laid up your treasure in the last days. Behold, the hire of the laborers who mowed your fields, which is of you kept back by fraud, crieth out: and the cries of them that reaped have entered into the ears of the Lord of Sabaoth. Ye have lived delicately on the earth, and taken your pleasure; ye have nourished your hearts in a day of slaughter. Ye have condemned, ye have killed the righteous one; he doth not resist you. Be patient, therefore, brethren, until the coming of the Lord. Behold, the husbandman waiteth for the precious fruit of the earth, being patient over it, until it receive the early and latter rain." James 5: 1-7, A. R. V.

It is clear that this prophecy and denunciation applies to our times, for the Scripture explicity says, "in the last days." And it is likewise evident that God's judgment will be executed against the rich who have made their riches at the expense of the poor, who have stepped upon the bodies and souls of the poor to reach for gold, and who have lived in luxury and ease while around them men and women suffered for the necessities of life.

Now it is commonly thought that in America the laboring class no longer suffer injustice or deprivation. We often read statistics as to the number of automobiles driven to the shop or job by employees, the number of radios purchased by them, etc. It is true that some classes of labor in the United States are much better off than the world has ever before witnessed. At the same time it must be borne in mind that these favored ones are but a small part of the world's laboring classes, and that even right here in our own country there is still much injustice done those who must toil for others.

From 1916-1930 there were some 30,000 strikes, lockouts, and other forms of conflict between capital and labor in the United States alone. This averages more than 2,000 annually. In some instances the disturbance was relatively small. In others, such as the serious labor troubles in the textile centers of the Virginias and the Carolinas, the situation has been most acute. Great mobs of laborers have attacked the factories, and company men and policemen have repelled them with tear gas, clubs, and even guns.

When it comes to some of the other nations, we find the strife between capital and labor very serious. In England, the coal miners, the railway workers, the textile workers, and other classes have frequent strikes, and several times within the last decade the whole future of the British Isles has hung in the balance when a great nation-wide strike has been called. The situation there is far from settled, and may flare up into serious proportions at any time.

Japan, too, now that she has become industrialized to such a great extent, is continually beset by labor troubles. The capitalists there, or at least many of them, try to make their swollen profits at the expense of very low wages to the factory workers. The workers rebel and demand their due. Australia has experienced some of the most severe disputes between the forces of capital and labor that the world has ever seen. At times within recent years not a ship could leave the ports for weeks because of strikes. Great industries were paralyzed, exports were detained on the wharves. And so we might go on around the world.

In our own country trouble brews in the capital and labor world because of five factors: (1) too low wages for certain

Capital and Labor

classes, (2) the unbalance of the economic structure of the nation, (3) increasing technological unemployment, (4) centralization of money control in the hands of a few, (5) wanton luxury on the part of the rich. Let us take a hasty glance at these trouble-filled elements.

While it is true that "skilled labor" is paid a good wage today when employment is to be had, there are several million men and women who are classed as "unskilled" workers who do not receive a living wage. They cannot support and educate their families upon the $1,000 or $1,500 a year they receive when they are employed the year around. When long periods of unemployment come, they are absolutely down and out, and their families must suffer.

We prate much about our great economic system in the United States, our Federal Reserve banks, etc. We have heard it declared only a few years ago that "hard times" could never again come, that "panics" and long periods of depression had been done away with forever. But with the crash of the stock market in the fall of 1929 there was ushered in a period of business depression that was one of the most trying in the history of the nation. The very magnitude of our economic and industrial structure threw the nation off stride as never before. So intricate and complex has our business system become that when it is thrown off balance ever so little the reaction is felt the nation over.

During the winter of 1930-31, from 3,000,000 to 5,000,000 were out of work in this country alone. Great bread lines were formed. Millions upon millions of dollars had to be appropriated to keep people from actual starvation. Huge factories were closed down, or forced to employ only a few hundred men instead of thousands as before. Those with money became frightened and would not invest it in business enterprises or in new construction. One wave of economic depression created another and another, until the whole nation was in the slough of despond. This reacted on other nations, and practically the whole world suffered as a result.

In such a time the rich of course have their savings and investments to fall back on and they suffer only disappointments that their earnings are not greater. On the other

International Newsreel
A parade of labor to denounce oppressive capitalism.

hand, the laboring classes who have no great margin of earnings are brought to despair when the pay checks stop. In such a time the seeds of revolution, communism, and Bolshevism grow fast, and trouble portends.

The unbalance of the economic structure of Great Britain has been marked since the War. Due to loss of export trade, Britain's industries have suffered acutely. As a consequence they have put in a "dole" system by which those permanently unemployed receive a small weekly pittance at the hands of the government. For year upon year from 1,500,000 to

3,000,000 have existed only at the expense of the government, and the worst of it is that there is no sign that the dole system can ever be done away with. There is a great body of honest men and women who are forced to live on a few shillings a week with no hope of ever getting enough money properly to house, care for, and educate their families.

Another very serious phase of the capital-labor problem is the unemployment due to the mechanization of industry; "technological unemployment," it is termed. Our age glories in its fast-multiplying machines that seem to have human brains as they uncannily turn out their perfected products at lightning speed. But every one of these machines displaces human labor, and this is growing to such gigantic proportions that it has become a most serious matter.

For example, one automatic brick-making machine now turns out as many bricks in one hour with one operator as 55 men used to turn out by hand. Consequently 54 men are out of work.

A newly perfected rubber heel-making machine with eight men now turns out a million rubber heels a day, the amount it used to take 500 men to make. As a consequence 492 men lose their jobs.

In every industry we could cite similar instances. Every month sees the perfection of new time-saving and labor-saving machinery, all of which are exceedingly wonderful, but which displace men and women who are dependent upon their daily toil for their daily bread. As science and efficiency advance, more people will be turned away from our factories. This is a problem already bad, which will become worse and worse, and which eventually will wreck the nations.

Perhaps one of the most ominous phases of the capital and labor issue in this fourth decade of the twentieth century is the centralization of money power in the hands of a few. This is done through control of the mammoth corporations and investment trusts by a few powerful men. Here is a statement from one of the well-known financiers of the land that appeared in the *Atlantic Monthly* for December, 1930:

"We are now in a new phase of capitalism. We have had, since the war, an enormous increase in the direct participation of small investors in common stock, largely of American corporations. Nothing like it ever has happened in the world. If it be true that we have, in America, some 20,000 persons who have invested their savings in American industrial corporations, this fact should make advisable a reconsideration of the safety features of the corporate structure.

"At the same time that this program has steadily proceeded, we also have had an enormous increase in concentration of financial control of American industries by the concentration in relatively small hands of the control of credit. When the Pujo investigation of banks was made years ago, we refused to be alarmed sufficiently at the concentration of credit then obtained by the interlocking of directors of financial groups. Nothing was done to stop this concentration, which has become more extreme during the past few years by the merger of banks into enormous banking systems — a concentration which in other fields, and with banking assistance, has resulted in great mergers in the industrial and public utility fields.

"On April 1 of this year, there were reported two hundred and seventy of these so-called investment trusts handling over four and one-half billion dollars of other people's money and controlled in large part by bankers who by a modest investment of their own money, have obtained voting control over this vast amount of investment money — a control which has been too frequently exercised by the bankers in selling to the investment trusts which they operate securities which they themselves have issued. The tendency to consolidate control in organizations of this kind over the vast amount of sound securities available for investment goes on apace.

"Today we are told that, out of nine billion dollars' worth of railroad stocks now outstanding, all but two billion dollars' worth are held by corporate stockholders, insurance companies, investment trusts, and the like, rather than by individuals. How much this tendency has been accelerated by the feeling of helplessness of the average stockholder as to his own incapacity to watch over his own money, it is, of course, impossible to say."

Another phase of this same question is the marked trend toward mergers and chains today. Hundreds of banks merge in one gigantic system. This means concentrated money control. Then we have chain systems of grocery stores, drug stores, restaurants, dry goods stores, hardware stores, butcher shops, candy stores, and what not. One great corporation controlled by a few men may own three thousand retail stores the nation over, and all the profits flow from the smaller communities to a large money center. Some have declared these chains and mergers capital's latest and most successful attempt to get an absolute corner on the manufacture, transportation, and distribution of every commodity necessary for man's existence in our modern civilization. Instead of business being spread out among thousands and thousands of smaller merchants the nation over, now a few super-corporations controlled by a few super-financiers in New York City hold the business world in the palm of their hands.

Likewise we have the huge power trusts controlling the manufacture, distribution, and sale of electric power, natural gas, water, etc. Undoubtedly a show-down will some day have to be had in the United States over the question of the colossal power of the power trust. Through watered stock many of these huge concerns boost their financial sheets upon which prices to the consumer are based, and thereby charge exorbitantly for their service and make unjustified profits at the expense of the consumer.

Thus goes on in ever-increasing figures the concentration of money and power in the hands of the few. A short time ago there was widespread discussion throughout America over the publication of a list in the public press of some "sixty men who control America." With the exception of two or three publishers and labor leaders, the entire list was made up of bankers, financiers, and industrialists. These men are rarely heard of by the general public. Though they do not hold public office they determine who will, when and how, and what their policies shall be. It is no exaggeration to say that no more than one hundred men control the entire economic structure of this great nation at the present time.

Not only is the control of money vested in a very few, but the actual wealth of the country is not so widely distributed as sometimes we hear it alleged to be. In a recent year .29 of 1 per cent of the population paid more than 95 per cent of the income tax of the entire nation. There were 511 persons that year who each had an income of at least one million dollars. This does not mean they owned but one million apiece, but their income on investments was one million. In that year there were 11,000 millionaires in the land.

Now it is not surprising if the great mass who "have not" feel envious and jealous of those that "have," especially when those that have are so wanton and pagan in their luxury. On December 29, 1930, at the very height of that hard winter when hundreds of thousands of unemployed men were walking the streets of such cities as New York, hungry and cold, this news story appeared in the newspapers from the pen of Lemuel F. Parton, one of the best newspaper writers in the country:

"Henry L. Doherty's $50,000 party for his debutante daughter in Washington caused no gasping or eye-rolling among the more *orchidaceous* elements of New York's *haut monde*. That's just run-of-the-mill entertainment for the 3,750 millionaires and multi-millionaires of Manhattan, Westchester, and Long Island.

Capital and Labor 191

"This decrepit old year limps off stage with a flourish of ermine and a glitter of jewels. There have been several $50,000 parties here and hereabouts during the last eventful twelve-month; there have been $60,000 and $70,000 parties and at least one glittering $80,000 'bust.'"

All available evidence is that around Park Avenue and the manorial estates of Long Island, where life has a satin lining, spending has increased rather than diminished since the start of the business depression.

"Over the New Year season it is indicated that expenditures in the top hat and champagne zones will reach a higher total than last year. This is the estimate of *maitres d'hotel*, caterers, *couturiers*, costumers, florists, and veteran head waiters who have watched the annual ebb and flow of the dollar tides since away back in the day of Harry Lehr and James Hazen Hyde. There isn't a single gilded hotel in the town that isn't booked right up to the roof for the big New Year's doings, and furthermore, they are booked for months to come for exclusive dinner dances and several coming-out parties where 'l'addition' of $50,000 is scarcely worth footing up.

"Estimates by a woman who makes a specialty of organizing coming-out parties — formerly of the *noblesse* — are that it costs New York about $6,000,000 for the string of big splashes which bring in the debs."

And all this when unemployment and its consequent suffering were at their height!

What do you think is the natural reaction of the man who has a wife and children shivering and starving for the bare necessities of life who walks past a hotel where a bloated millionaire is throwing away $50,000 on a "big party" for his pampered daughter who is about to make her debut in society?

Would you not think it unjust if your family had nothing but rags on their backs and you would see coming from one of the fashionable shops on Fifth Avenue some rich man's darling with a $40,000 ermine coat on?

If your own blood relations faced burial in the potter's field, how would you feel to see the family of a rich man following a hearse to a cemetery, and in the hearse was a pet poodle being given a $1,500 funeral?

It is no wonder that men like Harry Emerson Fosdick have declared:

"Unless we adapt our capitalistic society to the needs of the present age and adapt it to social planning and control, some form of communism will inevitably be thrust upon our children. Meanwhile verbal attacks on communism will avail us nothing."

Dr. Leslie A. White, a professor in the University of Michigan, declared at a recent meeting of the American Anthropological Association, that "capitalism will soon be fighting for its life. It was created by the machine and by the machine it will be destroyed."

More than one great thinker has declared the day coming when the strife between capital and labor will break out in a great world-revolution, when the employed will demand at the point of the gun justice and equality from the capitalists. Now the rich depend upon their possession and their control of the world's money to keep things in hand with those that would rebel, but the time is near when the very hoards of gold on which the rich have trusted will be their undoing. How aptly is this time described by the apostle: "Your gold and silver is cankered; and the rust of them shall be a witness against you, and shall eat your flesh as it were fire." James 5: 3.

How vivid are the words of the prophet as he sees the last act of the drama when those who have hoarded wealth shall seek to purchase a little respite by a lavish scattering of the treasures on which they have relied: "They shall cast their silver in the streets, and their gold shall be removed: their silver and their gold shall not be able to deliver them in the day of the wrath of the Lord: they shall not satisfy their souls, neither fill their bowels: because it is the stumblingblock of their iniquity." Ezekiel 7: 19.

Grenell Photo
A racing auto capable of running over three hundred miles an hour. Speed is the craze of our age.

Wars *and* Rumors *of* Wars

THE Saviour, describing the condition of the world previous to His second coming, declared: "And ye shall hear of wars and rumors of wars." Matthew 24: 6. "And upon the earth distress of nations with perplexity." Luke 21: 25. This would indicate that, as the time draws near for the return of the Lord, the nations of earth will be making unusually great preparations for war.

The world has been a great battlefield, where the strong and the weak have contended for the mastery. Nations have arisen by battle and blood, held sway by the sword, and gone down the same way they arose. Time has not changed the hearts of men, and as nations have done in the past, so they are doing and preparing to do with greater intensity than ever before. As we look upon the world today, we cannot but be impressed with the remarkable preparations for war that are in progress, which far exceed anything ever before known in the history of the race.

It seems passing strange that such a condition as this could actually exist after the terrible lesson in the utter uselessness and the stark tragedy of war that the world went through in the years 1914-1918. It appears as one great thinker, Schopenhauer, has phrased it, that "the only teaching of history is that we have learned nothing from history." We were so often assured during the last conflict that that was "the war to end war," and have heard so much since of peace and disarmament conferences that it seems a great anomaly that the nations should be so earnest in preparing for "the next war." But as summed up by the *Sunday Star*, of Washington, D. C., not long ago, we face this situation today:

International Newsreel
The glare and shadow of war stalks everywhere.

"In the last few months, dark clouds have been gathering on the political horizon of Europe.

"In spite of the economic depression which exists in almost every country in Europe, there has been lately a good deal of saber rattling, and hundreds of millions of dollars are being spent just now on naval, military, and air armaments. Various reports describing the feverish military preparations of the European countries, seem to indicate that the European nations have already forgotten the terrific lessons of the last war, and are getting ready for a new mad venture.

"The most ardent pacifists and the most inveterate optimists will admit in private conversations that the situation in Europe today is at least as bad as in the years preceding the World War, if not worse. Many are inclined to think that it is much worse."

In a late book, "That Next War," by one of Europe's geniuses in military strategy, Major K. A. Bratt, he declares that in Europe "everywhere there is a feeling that the ground is rocking as if by an earthquake."

Sir Philip Gibbs, the noted English writer, has said in a recent book:

"Europe is haunted by a thousand fears. Its statesmen know that they are building upon volcanic ground. There is not an intelligent observer of political conditions today who does not admit, privately, that the present map of Europe cannot remain unchanged as it was drawn after the War, and that if it is not redrawn by general consent its boundaries between one nation and another will be upheaved by violent eruptions. On the other hand, the first attempt at revision may precipitate the explosion."

At the beginning of the year 1931, David Lloyd George, one of England's greatest statesmen, painted this picture, which is gloomy but not overdone:

"Since the signing of the peace treaties the general outlook has not been so disquieting as it is now. During the disturbed conditions that unavoidably followed war, there was no danger of any general conflagration. The war spirit had burnt itself out. But it is welling up again, especially amongst the young men who saw nothing of war. On the continent of Europe wherever you go 'the next war' is being freely discussed, and groupings in that impending war are convassed.

"It seems too foolish to be credible. But there it undoubtedly is — a caldron of suspicions, hatreds, and fears. The disarmament discussions have been an elaborate sham. No country contemplates a serious reduction in its armaments. When the Soviet representative at the meetings of the disarmament commission proposed a resolution in favor of reducing military forces and of destroying great accumulated reserves of war material, a foolish chairman actually ruled him out of order and refused to allow the proposal to be recorded on the minutes. A worthy chairman for a fatuous commission!

"Europe is already dividing into two camps — those who stand for the revision of the peace treaties and those who are opposed to any revision. This is how they stand today: Revisionists, Italy, Germany, Austria, Hungary, Bulgaria; Anti-revisionists, France, Belgium, Poland, Czechoslovakia, Jugoslavia, Roumania."

Frank Simonds, that astute observer of European conditions, likewise sees Europe breaking up into two armed camps again, a thing that was one of the great factors leading on to the World War of 1914-1918. He outlines the future "balance of power" in these words:

"Europe is likely to divide into two great coalitions, as it did in the years preceding the World War, — France, Belgium, Poland, Czechoslovakia, Roumania, and Jugoslavia in one camp; Italy, Germany, Hungary, Austria, and Bulgaria in the other, with Russia inclining to the German orientation, but actually working for the ruin of both democratic and Fascist systems and the triumph of Communism.

"This unmistakable tendency represents the obvious peril to all conceptions of co-operation and association. In a word, it is the antithesis of the principle and spirit of Locarno. It is a push away from the internationalism of the years since the War, and particularly since 1925; an abandonment of the League of Nations, and a frank and unrestrained pursuit of national aims. Beyond all else, it is a direct turning away from the ideal of a new Europe to the forms of the old."

Perhaps the most danger-filled situation in Europe today is the intense rivalry between France and Italy. For many years after the war France was practically master upon the Continent, but with Mussolini's growing power and ambitions, and Italy's need for expansion, the Fascist chief has seen fit to develop his national policy along lines that run absolutely counter to the ambitions of France. France has large colonial possessions. Italy has few. France controls practically all of northern Africa across the Mediterranean from Italy, but Mussolini has long had an envious eye on a section of that territory. France has tried to build up a paramount influence in the Balkans. Mussolini has challenged France in that field. France has had her stakes set on a bigger army, air force, and navy than any other continental power. Mussolini says that Italy, not France, must be first. And so the dragon's teeth are being sown thick and recklessly on both sides of the Alps, and more than one European observer believes that a future world conflict will grow out of an explosion between France and Italy.

If the two nations were the only ones to be involved that would be quite serious enough, but each has friends and allies who are ready to jump into the fray with them. This is especially true of the Balkans, that troubled region whence have come so many of the world's wars.

Inasmuch as much of the ferment for another world war is being generated in the Balkans, we will cite the opinion of R. H. Markham, Balkan correspondent for the Chicago *Tribune*, as to what the future holds for humanity as a result of the Balkan tangle and its portentous ramifications:

"The Balkan peninsula, situated in the extreme southeastern corner of Europe, though a rich land and one of the most beautiful in the world, is notorious for its wars, violent tribal hatred, and general backwardness. It is divided among six states, and is inhabited by an extremely intricate mixture of races with different religions, cultures, and traditions. In little Albania, with less than a million inhabitants, there are three different religions and two different tribes. In Jugoslavia there are four religions and ten tribal or racial groups; in Roumania, even more religions and a greater variety of races.

"All this heterogeneity has led to much violence, intense national fanaticism, frequent conflicts, and a network of boundaries very difficult to cross. For almost a year the Jugoslav boundary has been closed to most Bulgarians. There is not a single bridge across the Danube between Bulgaria and Roumania. There is no direct route between Bulgaria and the chief cities in Greece. Sofia has no telephonic connection with the other Balkan capitals. Bulgarians have recently been condemned to death in Greece, Albania, and Jugoslavia as political murderers. To cross almost any Balkan boundary in an ordinary train requires two hours. Generally speaking, the press of one Balkan capital is inclined to be scurrilously bitter toward the neighboring countries. Political conditions in the Balkans have acquired such specific characteristics that the division of a given area into small hostile states is known as 'Balkanization.'

"All the evil, hatred, and violence of the Balkans, however, is not due exclusively to the races that inhabit the peninsula. Rival groups of the great powers preserve and accentuate Balkan strife. They build their strength on Balkan weakness, their prosperity on Balkan misery, and their security on Balkan insincerity, although it eventually turns out that the insecurity and wretchedness of the Balkans always destroy the security and prosperity of the rest of Europe.

"Formerly the two rival European groups, stirring up strife and violence in the Balkan peninsula, were led by Russia on one hand and Austria-Hungary on the other. Russia was supported by France and encouraged by Great Britain; Austria-Hungary was spurred on by Germany with the approval of Italy.

"Since the war the line-up of the great European teams on the Balkan field is somewhat different in appearance but essentially very similar. Russia has temporarily been eliminated as a dominant power from European combinations. The Austro-Hungarian empire has been broken up, and Germany weakened. So now the leaders in the European conflicts over the Balkans are Italy and France. Italy is the aggressor, and France is on the defensive.

"The political goals for which the great powers are now contending in the Balkans are not the same as they were before the war. Then Austria and Germany wanted to push through the Balkans into Asia Minor. This was one of the most powerful of all the European imperialistic drives. It was a gigantic trend, supported by a hundred million capable and vigorous people who felt the impulsion of an imperative need to expand, coupled with the call of a self-imposed 'cultural' mission. To attain this goal it was necessary for Central Europe to dominate the Balkans. And it was very close to the Balkans. Austria-Hungary was just across the river from Belgrade, and actually bordered on European Turkey.

"A similar terrific nationalistic push toward the Balkans came from the northeast, and was supported by over a hundred and fifty million Russians and related Slavs of tremendous expansive capacity. The Balkans constitute Russia's road to the open sea. And the peninsula was inhabited chiefly by Slavs of the same racial stock as the Russians. Furthermore, Russia was really almost as near to the Balkans as was Austria-Hungary. Thus two extremely powerful and exceedingly vital political drives met in the Balkan peninsula, and for decades succeeded in keeping the Balkan States separated, mutually antagonistic, and impotent.

"Now a similar historic process is being carried on. The aggressor is Italy, and she seeks both expansion and power. Italy has reached a stage in her nationalistic or imperialistic development similar to that attained by Germany and Russia before the war. She has completed her process of liberation and unification, which are always the first steps in a nationalistic movement, and now presses vigorously on to win her 'place in the sun' and fulfill her 'spiritual mission.'

"Italy is one of the great powers. At present only one other state on the Continent is more powerful, and that is France. Italy sits in that small council of great states that dictates the fate of humanity. She is one of the determining factors in affairs of the greatest import. Her chief takes his place proudly among the greatest in the world. However, some other states still have her out-distanced in many ways, and especially in the amount of territory controlled. The space governed by England and France and Russia and America are enormous in comparison with the area dominated in Italy. The Italians are squeezed up. They have an important state that hasn't enough real estate to show for its greatness. All Italy is only slightly larger than the state of Nevada. So as a matter of necessity and of prestige she must expand. . . .

"Therefore, in order to succeed in her attempt to penetrate into the Balkans, Italy must overcome Jugoslavia only. And there are circumstances that make this appear comparatively easy. One is that Jugoslavia is unstable. It is a new state, not yet ten years old, and made up of contending factions. . . .

"Then, besides, Jugoslavia has bitter external enemies. The Bulgarians fiercely hate the Serbs, the Greeks are afraid of them, the Albanians have grievances against them, the Austrians are their age-old antagonists, and the Hungarians are eager to help bring about the collapse of Jugoslavia that they may recover lost territory.

"So Italy is trying to unite these powers and weave her net about Jugoslavia. She is forming alliances with Greece and Turkey. Her influence is rapidly growing in Bulgaria. It is believed that the Macedonian revolutionists are in her service and in her pay. She is altogether at home in Albania, which is her base of operations against Jugoslavia. She has recently improved her relations with Austria, and is considered a great champion of treaty revision by the Hungarians. She is even winning friends among the Roumanians, who are formal allies of Jugoslavia. So she has almost encircled Jugoslavia.

"This, of course, does not mean immediate war. Mussolini is most experienced and prudent, and does not care to precipitate an immediate conflict. However, this encircling does show very plain tendencies, and foreshadows future events. Nationalism is growing in Bulgaria. It is rampant in Hungary. Some day Austria and Germany will probably unite. If a violent internal conflict should break out in Jugoslavia, encircled by enemies, Italy would probably act. She is waiting her chance, and her diplomatic position is strong. . . .

"Of course, Jugoslavia has powerful allies; namely, France, and the French satellites, Czechoslovakia, Poland, Roumania. France helps Jugoslavia so as to prevent Italy from becoming too powerful.

"Generally speaking, the struggle is between the treaty revisionists and those who consider the treaties sacred.

On one side are Germany, Hungary, Austria, and Bulgaria championed by Italy, and on the other are France, the Little Entente, and Poland. England favors the latter group. Russia will favor the former. These two groups will tend to grow more openly and vehemently antagonistic, and the first serious skirmish, the testing out of relative strength, will take place in the Balkans."

Outside of Europe the outlook is anything but promising for world peace. The black, brown, and yellow races, numbering two thirds of the world's population, and for generations imperialized over by the Western Powers, are today in revolt. India's 360,000,000 are bent upon breaking away from Britain. China is determined to throw off Occidental yokes and influence. Africa, which is 97 per cent partitioned among the European powers is getting restive and looking for ways and means to break the foreign chains that bind her. White men are having a harder time of it with the passing of every month to keep their hold on the subject races that teem by hundreds of millions between Tangier, Rangoon, and Shanghai.

Back of Asia's revolt looms ominous and threatening the Russian Bear. Russia has definitely turned her back on the West and looks to the East for her future. She hopes to be able to lead the peoples of the earth, "downtrodden by the capitalistic nations," as she says, in a world-wide revolt against Occidentalism. She hopes to make the rivers of the world run red with the blood of Americans, Englishmen, Frenchmen, Germans, Italians, and all other "capitalists and imperialists," and the hordes of the East will be those who shall let the blood.

The prophecy of John in Revelation 16:12 and onward has led many earnest Bible students to believe that the great final battle of the earth will be precipitated by a clash between Orient and Occident. Certainly, the horizon of the

East today is lowering with the black clouds of revolution, rebellion, and future conflict on a gigantic scale. Heretofore the West has rested secure in the knowledge that the East knew little or nothing of modern industrialization, so vital to the mechanical and scientific warfare of the twentieth century. With Russia's great program of industrialization, however, and with the awakening of the East to the fact that they must have cannon, aircraft, poison gases, and all the other fearsome paraphernalia that science has given us, the future will not lend the West the comfort the past has. For when the countless millions of the East perfect themselves in modern warfare, the West will not be a match for them on the fields of war. Major K. A. Bratt in his book, "That Next War," says on this very point:

"Nobody knows what will occur if Asia is driven to militarism. But it is more than probable that in such case what has happened hitherto may be regarded as merely a foretaste of what is to come. If China became militarized, English and French rule in India would not last long. Pressed by East-Asiatic military forces, and with India in revolt, England and France would no longer be able to control the situation. But things will certainly not stop there. A bridge over to Egypt exists, and thence to the oppressed black races. The Asiatic revolt against European imperialism, against everything that European policy stands for, may be the impulse which will set the colored races in motion.

"The choice which confronts the West involves consequences far beyond its own boundaries. It is not only developments in Europe which are at stake. The revolt in Asia against the Europeans, and the effects which this revolt may produce on the colored races, is perhaps the most potent feature of the present situation."

Looking abroad on a world torn with hate and fear, and filled with wars and rumors of wars, hastening toward Armageddon itself, the editor of the Los Angeles *Times* has written:

"Unrest, overturnings, changes, uncertainties, stalk darkly through many nations. Azrael broods over a world in travail. On four continents the dragon's teeth are sprouting sabers and bayonets. The hemispheres are bathed in the red of a setting sun. Civilization halts and shudders in its onward march."

Another newspaper editor, William Philip Simms, exclaims:

"Wars and rumors of wars today hold the stage from one end of the earth to the other. Two thirds of the total population of the globe are at this moment engaged in killing one another, or are on the verge of it. The other third are on the side lines, fearful of what may happen.

"The whole world is tossing in a fever of unrest the outcome of which no man can tell, but whose possibilities are unthinkably dreadful."

It will not be long now, however, before "rumors of wars" will be turned to war itself, — war, grim and terrible — and none can be safe except those who have made God their trust, whose hope is in another world than this, even the new earth, wherein shall dwell the righteous. (Matthew 5: 5; 2 Peter 3: 13.)

Not till then will wars cease, and peace reign on earth from the rising even to the setting of the sun.

Talking Peace but Preparing *for* War

BIBLE prophets long ago foretold that in the epoch of the world's history in which Jesus Christ was to appear the second time, a strange and unparalleled thing would be seen in the earth; namely, that the world would be deluged with peace talk, and at the same time would be frantically preparing for a monster and bloody conflict. "But concerning the times and the seasons, brethren, ye have no need that aught be written to you. For yourselves know perfectly that the day of the Lord so cometh as a thief in the night. When they are saying, Peace and safety, then sudden destruction cometh upon them, as travail upon a woman with child; and they shall in no wise escape." 1 Thessalonians 5: 1-3.

Not only did Paul foresee such a state of affairs as reflected in the Scripture quoted above, but Old Testament prophets foresaw the same situation.

What the World Is Saying	What the World Is Doing
"And *many people* shall go and say, Come ye, and let us go up to the mountain of the Lord, to the house of the God of Jacob; and He will teach us of His ways, and we will walk in His paths: for out of Zion shall go forth the law, and the word of the Lord from Jerusalem. And	"Proclaim ye this among the Gentiles: *Prepare war,* wake up the mighty men, let all the men of war draw near; let them come up: beat your plowshares into swords, and your pruninghooks into spears: let the weak say, I am strong. Assemble yourselves, and

He shall judge among the nations, and shall rebuke many people: and they shall beat their swords into plowshares, and their spears into pruninghooks: nation shall not lift up sword against nation, neither shall they learn war any more." Isaiah 2: 3, 4.

come, all ye heathen, and gather yourselves together round about: thither cause Thy mighty ones to come down, O Lord. Let the heathen be wakened, and come up to the valley of Jehoshaphat: for there will I sit to judge all the heathen round about." Joel 3: 9-13.

Now let us look abroad upon our world to see if these daring Scriptural predictions are being fulfilled in our time. If so, then we may be assured that Armageddon, that final conflict of the earth, is hastening on, and that just beyond lies the blessed coming of our Lord and Saviour Jesus Christ.

Never has the world heard so much peace talk as since the World War ended on November 11, 1918. Several scores of international peace organizations have been formed to do away with war. Many peace and disarmament conferences have been called, at which the statesmen of the world have discussed for weary months the problem of bringing permanent peace to a world whose history has been but a series of wars. Books by the hundreds have poured from the presses of the world, extolling the virtues of peace and excoriating war. Newspapers and magazines have literally devoted millions of column inches of space to the great theme of world peace. The radio, — civilization's newest and most spectacular vehicle for the dissemination of knowledge and propaganda, — has been drafted into the campaign for world peace. Ministers have preached about peace, and the people have prayed for it. In short, to use the psychologist's pet phrase, the world has been made "peace conscious."

Talking Peace but Preparing for War

But what has it availed us?

Even in that stormy era of saber rattling just before 1914, never have the nations so strained every nerve in such a frenzy to prepare for that "next war." We have more men under arms today than before 1914. The nations of the world are today actually spending more money on their military establishments than in the pre-World-War era. Declares Henry Kittredge Norton in the New York *Times:*

"We know that the burden of national armaments is staggering. President Hoover is authority for the statement that there are today 30,000,000 men under arms, including active reserves — 10,000,000 more than before the Great War — this despite the fact that two of the greatest military powers of that time are now permitted only a few regiments."

James T. Shotwell, in the same paper, says:

"The civilized world is in this year of economic depression and hardship spending about $4,000,000,000 or $5,000,000,000 — probably much more — in preparation for the next war. This does not include that part of military and naval budgets which goes to meet the expenses of past wars. If pensions or allowances or war debts were added in, the amount would, of course, be many times greater. It refers merely to the actual cost of the armaments and men in military and naval establishments. It does not cover those potential armaments which are available in chemical and industrial mobilization. If refers only to those expenses which are a dead loss in the economic balance sheet of the nations incurring them, except for the single purpose of waging war.

"How heavy a burden this is upon a world struggling to avert economic bankruptcy can best be seen by a few comparisons. It means that every average family of Europe and the Americas is paying directly for the upkeep of the current war establishments, an amount that is somewhere between $30 and $40 a year."

Albion E. Johnson in the *Sunday Star*, Washington, D. C., has written:

"The big nations of the world are spending more money preparing for war today than ever before in peacetime history. Increasing by margins of more than a billion gold francs yearly, the armament expenditures of the six ex-allied powers — France, Great Britain, Italy, Russia, Japan, and the United States — promise even more startling gains during the next few years. While talking peace, nearly every government in the world is preparing [for war] with far greater seriousness than they did before 1914. . . ."

As a sample of the rampant war spirit, Benito Mussolini has boastingly declared: "The spirit of Locarno has vanished. All the nations are armed. Italy must arm. It must be in a position to mobilize five million men and arm them, and our air forces must be so numerous that they will darken the sun." And in another breath he declared that Italy's navy must be able to chase France's off the Mediterranean.

On the other hand, France is building a great line of steel and cement forts three fourths of a mile apart reaching all the way from the Moselle to the Rhine. Like China's Wall and Hadrian's ramparts in the north of England, these fortifications are planned by France to stop the invading hosts ere they despoil her fair land in the "next war" as they did in the last. She is building up her air force so that she can strike an instant and deadly blow at London, Rome, or Berlin, the moment the tocsin of war sounds again.

And so Europe has gone militarism mad again as she did in the days of the great race between Germany and France for a superior army, and between Germany and England for a superior navy, in those fierce competitive days before the the fateful summer of 1914.

But fearful as the World War was, it was child's play compared to what the war masters are preparing for the next catastrophe. They are mechanizing their forces to a degree hitherto unimagined. Faster and harder hitting rifles have been perfected, until in the next war every infantryman will be a veritable machine gun operator. Shells with greater explosive force have been perfected. Cannons with more distance and accuracy have been made. Great flocks of huge tanks with multiple turrets spewing shells and shrapnel at a prodigious rate, and with thick armor and wireless communication, are being made ready for action. Here is the way a newspaper dispatch described an experiment recently conducted by the United States army:

> "A war tank with a 338-horsepower Liberty airplane motor, the weight of the tank 20,000 pounds, raced through icy ponds, over big logs, through barbed wire entanglements and battered down brick walls two feet thick, at 45 miles an hour. Then, shedding its caterpillar track, it traveled over paved highways at 75 miles an hour."

But the most revolutionary and effective means of killing will be in the hands of the airmen and the chemical warfare service. Airplanes were first used in the Balkan War of 1912. They proved their right as a military arm of major importance in the World War. Then, however, they were but in their preliminary stages of development. Since then the strategists, military engineers, and air technicians have every day added something to their air reportoire that will mean faster and more widespread death to the enemy in that future conflict. Great bombing squadrons, each carrying five tons of high explosives, and flying two miles a minute, are ready for duty. Combat planes and scouting craft with speeds up to 250 miles an hour are ready for the fray. Tennyson's visionary poem of the last century will see ample fulfillment in another war, for the combination of air forces and lethal chemicals will spread death far and wide:

"Heard the heavens fill with shouting, and there rained a
 ghastly dew
From the nations' airy navies grappling in the central blue."

Albert Bushnell Hart, of Harvard University, writing in *Current History* magazine, says:

"The World War exceeded all other modern wars in the horrors of its destruction of the bodies and souls of troops in the trenches, in its reaction on the character of men, women, and children behind the lines, and in the systematic warfare on noncombatants, particularly by aerial warfare. Experts believe that if war should break out tomorrow between Great Britain and France, within a fortnight the principal cities in both countries would be in ruins. Ships of war would be at the bottom of the sea, and the armies would be driven into dugouts. Noncombatants are no longer free from the destructiveness of war. The next World War waged on the same basis as the last war, with the addition of more effective explosives and air warfare, would go far to exterminate millions of civil population. Such countries as Russia, under the direction of modern military science, might direct an endless swarm of airplanes to the destruction of Western civilization."

Colonel J. F. C. Fuller, in his book, "The Reformation of War," says:

"I believe that, in future warfare, great cities, such as London, will be attacked from the air, and that a fleet of 500 airplanes each carrying 500 ten-pound bombs of, let us suppose, mustard gas, might cause 200,000 minor casualties and throw the whole city into panic within half an hour of their arrival. Picture, if you can, what the results will be: London for several days will be one vast raving bedlam, the hospitals will be stormed, traffic will cease, the homeless will shriek for help, the city will be in pandemonium. What of the government at Westminister? It will be swept away by an avalanche of terror. Then will the enemy dictate his terms, which will be grasped at like a straw by a drowning man. Thus

International Newsreel
Swarms of bombing planes anticipate the advent of war.

may a war be won in forty-eight hours and the losses of the winning side may be actually nil!"

In similar vein writes the New York *Evening Post* about the role to be played by gas in the next war:

"Applied science has brought aviation to a day when a lone aviator, riding a mother plane, may drive before him through the sky lanes a convoy of death in the shape of pilotless planes. Under gas waves spread by them a great city or an army might be anesthetized for a day or sent into that sleep that knows no waking. In this winged brood of destruction, radio-guided, every plane will be able to drop bombs twenty times as destructive as the largest shell ever hurled from a gun muzzle. . . .

"Science has left no noncombatants in modern warfare, which has become a clash of nations rather than of armies. It has lifted war from the land and water, and from under the water, into a 'fourth dimension,' the air. Ancient conquerors ravaged the land with the sword and the torch and sowed with salt the ruined towns of their enemies. A modern conqueror hurls tons of nitrogen explosives at a nation and sows an invisible death out of the sky."

It is the opinion of Gen. E. D. Swinton, inventor of the tank, that a future war would not be between army and army, but between "people and people." He "conjectured that the fighting forces would be safer than the civilian population. He foresaw the sowing of disease germs in cities, the employment of airplanes without aviators to spread pestilence, the use of chemicals to destroy lives and staple crops. The outlawing of poison gas by the Washington Treaty was of no avail, he thought; poison gas will be used, and used more efficiently, than ever before. All treaties, for that matter, would be only so many scraps of paper; nations would march against one another without so much as a formal declaration of hostilities. The 'war to end war' had been a failure, and the disposition of the world today was not for peace, but for carnage."

An editorial in a well-known weekly adds additional light on the new turn modern warfare will take in the future clash between nations: "The next war will sweep down like a tropical storm, unannounced by any trumpet of thunder or herald of lightning. That is being planned by those who are studying the future.

"It is certain that if war is permitted again to deluge the earth — and to *permit* it, all we have to do is *fail to prevent* it — the tactics of the Great War will be as out of date as if they had been fought in ancient times. War will be less an affair of men and more an affair of machines. The individual soldier with his rifle is almost a thing of the past. Even battlefields, vast armies confronting each other in the same territory, belong to outworn methods. Invisible gases, the suffocation of whole cities without noise, silent horrors of every kind, stealthy assaults by a very few men armed with most potent powers, will be the new order. The forces of nature will be used more and more to supplant the muscular force of soldiers. Ray warfare is already the thesis of military study and experiment on a large scale. Light rays and heat rays are being trained to become allies of Mars. The old heroic manner of man fighting man will be largely done away; warfare will become world murder, with nature as accomplice — if nothing happens to prevent."

A German military authority, commander of an army corps during the World War, whose opinion is shared by a leading military expert of England as well as by a prominent member of the French general staff, stated, in an international discussion conducted by the New York *Herald* on "the next war," that "victory in the next war will depend largely on the destruction of helpless noncombatants, far in the rear of the fighting lines," and that "this destruction will be chiefly brought about by airplanes. Poisons, including both gases and death-dealing diseases germs, will be scattered over the cities. Thermite bombs will start fires, and explosive bombs will destroy factories and lines of communication, along with the civil population. . . . In case of another war, so much of civilization will be destroyed that a return to something resembling the 'Dark Ages' will not be improbable. European civilization might easily be blotted out."

Nicholas Murray Butler, the president of Columbia University, likewise declares:

"The happenings of 1914-18 and the subsequent scientific discoveries and mechanical inventions, which, were those happenings ever repeated, would multiply their destructiveness manyfold, have made it entirely clear that another such world-wide outbreak would demolish the existing political and economic system."

Major K. A. Bratt, the author of "That Next War," makes this truthful but startling asseveration:

"The white races, the civilized races, cannot survive the next great war, perhaps principally on account of the consequent revolutionary chaos in which the West will be submerged."

In his volume Major Bratt has this significant title to one of his chapters, — "On the Road to Annihilation."

Long ago John the Revelator, looking down to our very time, wrote of the war mania that would obsess us: "They are the spirits of devils, . . . which go forth unto the kings of the earth and of the whole world, to gather them to the battle of that great day of God Almighty. . . . And he gathered them together into a place called in the Hebrew tongue Armageddon." See Revelation 16: 14, 16.

As a striking parallel to this prophetic utterance let us consider a statement made by Ramsay MacDonald of Great Britain in the House of Commons some time ago:

"For the present general competition in arms among the nations it is difficult to say who is responsible. It would seem as if they were all bewildered, or laboring under some doom imposed upon them by devils or something else, going on and on until once again they are launched into war. . . . People are beginning to feel that there is something devilish in the operations now going on to increase armies, navies, and air forces."

How more graphically could the words of prophetic Scripture be fulfilled than we have seen in this chapter? God's word is carried out to the very letter in the war preparation and peace propaganda now absorbing the world.

Note this additional prophecy from John: "The nations were angry, and Thy wrath is come, and the time of the dead, that they should be judged, and that Thou shouldest give reward unto Thy servants the prophets, and to the saints, and them that fear Thy name, small and great; *and shouldest destroy them which destroy the earth.*" Revelation 11: 18.

Yes, the time is almost here when God will "destroy them which destroy the earth." And mark it well, that at the time when the nations are angry, and God must intervene to save the race from absolute annihilation — at that same time, all those who fear God, the small and the great, will receive their reward.

What is their reward? No small part of it is that after the glad day of His coming and His creation of new heavens and a new earth, they shall live forever in a world from which the war spirit, warriors, and war-making have been forever banished. In view of our undone condition today, is that not a sufficient reward to lead every man, woman, and child to seek God while He may be found, that at His second coming we may be without blame and faultless in His sight?

So the preparation for war that we see all about us today teaches us three lessons; namely, that Christ is coming soon, that His coming will put an eternal end to war, and that every soul should this day prepare to meet Him in peace.

Gospel *to* All Nations

NO great judgment has ever been brought upon the earth without a warning being given to those concerned. Before the flood the world was warned by Noah. Jonah was sent to Nineveh. Angels from heaven carried the message of impending doom to Sodom and Gomorrah. Isaiah and Jeremiah foretold the Babylonish captivity of the Jews, and the Saviour warned the Jews of the final overthrow of their city and nation.

Matthew 24:14 contains the statement that before the coming of Christ and the setting up of His everlasting kingdom, the gospel, or good news pertaining to it, shall go to all the nations of the world. It is a world-wide message. "And this gospel of the kingdom shall be preached in all the world for a witness unto all nations; and then shall the end come."

This text does not state that all the world will be converted. The Scriptures clearly show that but few will accept the message; but all will have the opportunity of hearing it and preparing to meet their Lord, if they desire to do so. In the great judgment day the unprepared will stand without excuse; for to earth's remotest bounds this gospel will be proclaimed, and this fact will be a witness against those who refuse to hear the message, and against those who reject it.

Already this gospel of the soon coming of our Lord has gone to nearly all nations of the earth. Believers in it are to be found among all denominations and in many pulpits. Missionaries are going to all lands. The Bible is printed and circulated in almost every known language, and God has forces already at command with which to close this message of Matthew 24:14 in a very short time. All this is but

A medical missionary proclaiming the gospel of the kingdom on the border of Tibet.

another evidence that the coming King is at the door.

"But of that day and hour knoweth no man." Matthew 24:36. We may not know the "day and hour," but Matthew 24 gives certain signs that precede that event, and, "when ye shall see all these things, know that it is near, even at the doors." Verse 33.

Hence we may know when our Lord's appearing is "near, even at the doors"; but we cannot know the exact time, for this the Lord has kept in His own hands.

But, says one, the coming of the Lord will be unexpected, for the apostle Paul writes: "Of the times and the seasons, brethren, ye have no need that I write unto you. For yourselves know perfectly that the day of the Lord so cometh as a thief in the night." 1 Thessalonians 5: 1, 2.

This is taken to prove that the matter has been fully settled, and so there is no need of giving it any further attention. But notice carefully what Paul says further on this subject: "But ye, brethren, are not in darkness, that that day should overtake you as a thief." Verse 4.

There is a class, however, to whom it will come as a thief. "When they shall say, Peace and safety; then sudden destruction cometh upon them; . . . and they shall not escape." V. 3.

Those who are studying God's word, will not be left in darkness. Hence in Mark 13:35 the Lord commands us to "watch." For what?—For evidences in His word that His coming is near, so that His people may know, and be prepared to receive Him "with joy" when He appears.

But to those who are not watching, who cry "peace and safety," and say that we can know nothing about it, the King will come as a thief, and their end will be destruction.

Of this class are those spoken of by the Saviour: "And if that evil servant shall say in his heart, My lord delayeth his coming; and shall begin to smite his fellow servants, and to eat and drink with the drunken; the lord of that servant shall come in a day when he looketh not for him, and in an hour that he is not aware of, and shall cut him asunder, and appoint him his portion with the hypocrites: there shall be weeping and gnashing of teeth." Matthew 24:48-51.

It is important to know when the coming of the Lord is near. Preparation is necessary for that event; and if we neglect the warning, that great day will overtake us as a thief, and we shall have the recompence of the ungodly.

But by those who have been watching and waiting for their Lord, that day will be hailed with joy, and the glad cry will go up, "Lo, this is our God; we have waited for Him, and He will save us: this is the Lord; we have waited for Him, we will be glad and rejoice in His salvation." Isaiah 25:9.

One Taken, Another Left

WHEN our Lord returns to this earth, He will find two classes of people. One class will have complied with the overtures of the gospel, and so will be accepted. The other class will have refused the offers of mercy, and will be rejected.

Some will doubtless be deceived as to their true condition up to the very coming of Christ to earth. He says: "Many will say to Me in that day, Lord, Lord, have we not prophesied in Thy name? And in Thy name have cast out devils? And in Thy name done many wonderful works? And then will I profess unto them, I never knew you: depart from Me, ye that work iniquity." Matthew 7: 22, 23.

There will therefore be a class of professed Christians who will be rejected of the Lord. The testimony on this point is plain: "Not every one that saith unto Me, Lord, Lord, shall enter into the kingdom of heaven; but he that doeth the will of My Father which is in heaven." Matthew 7: 21.

We may belong to the church; our profession may be as high as heaven; but these things will not be considered in the great judgment day. The question that will decide destinies for eternity is, Have you done "the will of My Father"?

The Bible is God's written will to us. It is His explanation to us of the only way by which we can be saved. In the judgment day our actions will be compared with the Book of Instruction, and our cases will be decided accordingly. If we have accepted the overtures of mercy as offered through Christ, and have done the will of the Father, an "abundant entrance" to the final reward will be granted us.

If we have chosen our own way, or have followed the teachings of men instead of the word of God, the sentence will be, "I never knew you: depart from Me."

Those who do the will of God belong to the kingdom of God. All who do not obey God belong to the kingdom of Satan, no matter how moral and upright they may be outwardly. Of such Christ says, "He that is not with Me is against Me; and He that gathereth not with Me scattereth abroad." Matthew 12: 30. There is no neutral ground.

A profession of religion and membership in the church will not save us, nor make our influence right here upon the earth. The Jews had a profession the highest the world has ever known, and their church requirements were very rigid; but their principles of service were wrong, and they crucified the Lord of life.

The Jews claimed that they were the children of Abraham; that they were heirs to the promises made to him, and so, of course, that they were perfectly safe. But John the Baptist told them not to make that claim, as it would not hold; for their hearts were not right before God, who, the Saviour declared, was "able of these stones to raise up children unto Abraham." (Matthew 3: 9.) The securing of eternal life is an individual work, regardless of birth, church relationship, or any profession we may make.

Neither does God judge from outward appearance. It is not our acts alone that will be taken into account. "For the Lord seeth not as man seeth; for man looketh on the outward appearance, but the Lord looketh on the heart." 1 Samuel 16: 7. Our character must be right before God can give us the final reward. Our thoughts and desires often influence our character more than do our words and actions.

The force and application of the words of Matthew 24: 40, 41, are very clear: "Then shall two be in the field; the one shall be taken, and the other left. Two women shall be

One Taken, Another Left 221

International Newsreel
"Two women shall be grinding at the mill; the one shall be taken, and the other left."

grinding at the mill; the one shall be taken, and the other left."

No matter how close the association may be, God knows those who are truly His. Two men may work side by side in the field, in the shop, or in the office. Both may have their names on the same church record. The one may have made his peace with heaven, while the other, by disbelief of the truth sent from the Lord, will stand among the rejected.

The old custom of grinding the family supply of flour is also taken to show the closeness of the final test. Two women help each other do their grinding of the day's supply of meal. The one may be a member of God's kingdom on earth, and so be fitted for the wonderful home Christ is preparing, while the other may still belong to the enemy.

The Revelation

"SURELY the Lord God will do nothing, but He revealeth His secret unto His servants the prophets." Amos 3: 7.

The fulfillment of this text may be verified from the Bible, from the days of Moses to the prophecies of John on the Isle of Patmos.

The world was warned of a flood through one hundred and twenty years of the preaching of Noah. For many years Israel was warned of their impending captivity to the Babylonians. Years before the birth of Cyrus he was called by name as the one who would overthrow Babylon and bring liberty to the Jews. The length of the Jewish captivity was foretold, and also the time of the return of this nation to Jerusalem. Daniel gave the date when Christ would begin His ministry, the time of His death, and the time when the apostles should begin their mission to the Gentiles. The Bible abounds in other instances fully as remarkable as these.

It is not reasonable to suppose that the most important event in all the history of the world,— the second coming of Christ,— would be overlooked, and the world be left in darkness regarding it. The reading of our text forbids such a supposition. As we search, we find that both Old and New Testaments abound in prophecies concerning this momentous event. Dr. Blickersteth, of England, affirms that one eighteenth of the New Testament is devoted to this subject.

Especially to the Christian era belongs the Book of the Revelation. Its prophecies reach from the days of John's exile to the coming of Christ, the resurrection, the New Jerusalem, and the earth made new.

By some this book is considered as one of the hidden mysteries of God. But such a view cannot be harmonized

The Revelation

with the opening verses of the first chapter. Let us read them:

"The Revelation of Jesus Christ, which God gave unto Him, to show unto His servants things which must shortly come to pass; and He sent and signified it by His angel unto His servant John: who bare record of the word of God, and of the testimony of Jesus Christ, and of all things that he saw." Revelation 1: 1, 2.

Such is the purpose of this book. It is given to reveal to God's people the most important events which were to occur during the time known as the Christian era. The very name of the book expresses its mission. Certainly that which is revealed in God's word should not be considered as hidden and obscured. Moses declares that "those things which are revealed belong unto us and to our children forever." (Deuteronomy 29: 29.)

And that the mission of the Revelation should not be belittled or misunderstood, the promise is given, "Blessed is he that readeth, and they that hear the words of this prophecy, and keep those things which are written therein: for the time is at hand." Revelation 1: 3. We cannot avoid the conclusion that the teachings of this book are of the utmost importance, and especially to us who live so near the coming of our Lord.

But to impress our minds more fully, the last chapter states, "These sayings are faithful and true: and the Lord God of the holy prophets sent His angel to show unto His servants the things which must shortly be done. Behold, I come quickly: blessed is he that keepeth the sayings of the prophecy of this book." Revelation 22: 6, 7.

It is true that much of the book of Revelation is symbolic. So also are many of the important prophecies of the Old Testament. Our Saviour taught in parables, and so pronounced was this method of teaching that on one occasion it is said that "without a parable spake He not unto them." (Matthew 13: 34.)

Yet to those who desire to understand them these parables were made plain. They were obscure only to those who rejected the messages which were thus brought to them. To the followers of Jesus in all ages these parables have been an unfailing source of edification and comfort.

God's word was given for the instruction of His people, and as a guide until our Lord shall take them home to their final great reward. But the truths contained in the parables and symbols of the prophecies are not, and can not be, plain to the mere casual reader. The wealth of the wisdom of the Bible is compared to a mine, in which we are to "search" and "dig" as for "hid treasures."

To the earnest student an unfailing interpreter is promised. "When He, the Spirit of truth, is come, He will guide you into all truth: . . . and He will show you things to come." John 16: 13.

In all time angels have been actively employed in carrying forward God's work in the earth. As such they are many times introduced in the prophecies. But in the Revelation they are especially presented in various ways and with different missions.

In chapters one to three, seven angels are represented as bringing special words of comfort, warning, and reproof to the church of Christ. These angels represent the faithful ministers who fail not to proclaim all the gospel to the church of God.

In chapter 7: 1, four angels are shown "holding the four winds of the earth." In symbolic language the blowing of the winds signifies war and strife among nations. The "four corners of the earth" embrace all the kingdoms of the world. In this verse the "four angels" symbolize the various agencies by which God restrains the war spirit of the nations until the number of His people are made up and "sealed" for His kingdom.

In chapter 8:2, 6, seven angels are presented to the prophet as proclaiming seven awful calamities which were to come upon the world.

In the fourteenth chapter three angels are introduced which have special messages to proclaim to the world just prior to the coming of the Lord. These messages apply to the times in which we live, and will be considered in succeeding chapters.

The First Angel's Message

"AND I saw another angel fly in the midst of heaven, having the everlasting gospel to preach unto them that dwell on the earth, and to every nation, and kindred, and tongue, and people, saying with a loud voice, Fear God, and give glory to Him: for the hour of His judgment is come: and worship Him that made heaven, and earth, and the sea, and the fountains of waters." Revelation 14: 6, 7.

In the visions of earlier chapters, many angels were presented to the prophet. Hence, when his attention is directed to the first of a new series, he naturally speaks of it as "another angel."

The messages of this chapter may be considered as "the three angels' messages of Revelation 14." We are justified in so numbering them, for of the last it is said, "the third angel followed them." The one preceding was therefore the the *second* angel, and the one preceding that would of course be the first.

The world through all ages has had but the one gospel of salvation through our Lord and Saviour Jesus Christ. It is the "everlasting gospel," for it is as old as the plan of redemption, and will continue in force until the mission of the gospel is accomplished and the number of the saved is made up.

The three messages of this chapter are to prepare a people to stand "faultless before the presence of His glory" in the kingdom of God. (See Jude 24.) Hence the preparation for so great an event demands a revival of vital godliness, and a perfection of character which can be brought about only by a powerful proclamation of the "everlasting gospel." This is to fit a people for translation.

The First Angel's Message

Angels do not come in person as teachers and preachers This work has been intrusted to men. Hence the angels in this chapter must be symbolic, each representing a body of religious teachers who proclaim the message they represent.

The feature that gives definiteness to the message is the proclamation of "the hour of His judgment." It is this which arouses the world. One author on the prophecies writes: "The burden of this angel was to be the same gospel which had been before proclaimed, but connected with it was the additional motive of the proximity of the kingdom."

This message could not have been given in the early days of the church, for it embraces the "judgment," and that takes place during the closing days of earth's history. In the days of Paul the judgment was not in progress, for he reasoned before Felix of "righteousness, temperance, and *judgment to come*." (Acts 24: 25.)

Neither can "the hour of His judgment" be deferred until Christ shall appear. The judgment begins during the sounding of the first angel's message. Two others are to follow, and the mission of the three is to prepare a people for the coming of their Lord. He will not come until the work of these messages is completed. Each message requires time in its proclamation, for they are all world-wide. The judgment is in progress during the proclamation of all three of these messages, for it is ushered in by the first. Hence, it begins years before our Lord appears in the clouds of heaven.

Upon whom, then, will this judgment begin? Surely not upon the living, for they are still in the valley of decision. Their future still depends upon their acceptance or rejection of these three testing messages.

It must, therefore, begin with the "great majority," the vast army of the dead. These are the only ones whose race is run, whose life-work is finished, whose record is complete, whose probation is ended. It is the investigative judgment now in progress in the courts of heaven. (For full explanation of the investigative judgment see following chapter on "The Sanctuary.")

And when the work of the three messages is finished, and all have decided for or against the truths proclaimed therein, the probation of the living will cease, and their cases will come up before the great tribunal of heaven for judgment. From this time the characters of all will be forever fixed. Then the fiat will go forth: "He that is unjust, let him be unjust still: and he which is filthy, let him be filthy still: and he that is righteous, let him be righteous still: and he that is holy, let him be holy still." Revelation 22: 11.

All this takes place prior to the second coming of Christ. That is the next event, as brought out in the verse which immediately follows: "And, behold, I come quickly; and My reward is with Me, to give every man according as his work shall be." He comes to bring the reward previously decided in the judgment.

This message was to go to "every nation, and tongue, and people." This feature was accurately fulfilled in the great advent movement of 1840-1844. It was a world-wide, two-fold message, embracing a revival of the "everlasting gospel," and the proclamation of "the hour of His judgment."

In many places godly men arose, preaching a revival of a pure gospel, connecting with it the soon coming of the Messiah, which coming they associated with the work of the "judgment," as contained in the message in the text at the head of the chapter. It is a noticeable fact that this wonderful movement sprang up almost simultaneously in many countries, often without connection or understanding between those who carried the message.

Of the great advent movement in America, Uriah Smith writes in his commentary, "Thoughts on Daniel and the Revelation":

The First Angel's Message

"But the strongest and most conclusive evidence that the message belongs to the present time will consist in finding some movement in this generation through which its fulfillment has been accomplished, or is going forward. On this point we refer to a movement of which it would now be hard to find any one who is wholly ignorant. It is the great advent movement of the present century. As early as 1831, Wm. Miller, of Low Hampton, N. Y., by an earnest and consistent study of the prophecies, was led to the conclusion that the gospel dispensation was near its close. He placed the termination, which he thought would occur at the end of the prophetic periods, about the year 1843. This date was afterward extended to the autumn of 1844.

"We call his investigations a consistent study of the prophecies, because he adopted that rule of interpretation which will be found lying at the base of every religious reformation, and of every advance movement in prophetic knowledge; namely, to take all the language of the Scriptures, just as we would that of any other book, to be literal, unless the context or the laws of language require it to be understood figuratively; and to let scripture interpret scripture. True, on a vital point he made a mistake, as will be explained hereafter; but in principle, and in a great number of particulars, he was correct. He was on the right road, and made an immense advance over every theological system of his day.

"When he began to promulgate his views, they met with general favor, and were followed by great religious awakenings in different parts of the land. Soon a multitude of colaborers gathered around his standard, among whom may be mentioned such men as F. G. Brown, Chas. Fitch, Josiah Litch, J. V. Himes, and others, who were then eminent for piety, and men of influence in the religious world.

"The period marked by the years 1840-1844 was one of intense activity and great progress in this work. A message was proclaimed to the world which bore every characteristic of a fulfillment of the proclamation of Revelation 14: 6, 7. The preaching was emphatically such as might be called the everlasting (age-lasting) gospel. It pertained to the closing up of this age, and the incoming of the everlasting age of the King of righteousness.

"It was that gospel of the kingdom which Christ declared should be preached in all the world for a witness unto all nations, and then the end should come. (Matthew 24: 14.) The fulfillment of either of these scriptures involves the preaching of the nearness of the end. The gospel could not be preached to all nations as a *sign* of the end unless it was understood to be such, and the proximity of the end was at least one of its leading themes.
. . .
"Perhaps no movement ever exhibited greater activity than this respecting the soon coming of Christ, and in no cause was ever more accomplished in so short a space of time. A religious wave swept over this country, and the nation was stirred as no people have been stirred since the opening of the great Reformation of the sixteenth century."—"*Daniel and the Revelation,*" *pp. 591, 592, 594.*

Of the extent of this work in England, Mourad Brook, an English writer, is quoted as saying:

"It is not merely in Great Britain that the expectation of the near return of the Redeemer is entertained, and the voice of warning raised, but also in America, India, and on the continent of Europe. In America, about three hundred ministers of the word are thus preaching 'this gospel of the kingdom'; while in this country [Great Britain], about seven hundred of the Church of England are raising the same cry."

D. T. Taylor speaks as follows in regard to the diffusion of the advent sentiments in other parts of the world:

"In Wurtemburg, there is a Christian colony numbering hundreds, who look for the speedy advent of Christ; also another of like belief on the shores of the Caspian; the Molokaners, a large body of dissenters from the Russian Greek Church, residing on the shores of the Baltic— a very pious people, of whom it is said, 'Taking the Bible alone for their creed, the *norm* of their faith is simply the

Holy Scriptures'— are characterized by 'the expectation of Christ's immediate and visible reign upon earth.' In Russia, the doctrine of Christ's coming and reign is preached to some extent, and received by many of the lower class.

"It has been extensively agitated in Germany, particularly in the south part among the Moravians. In Norway, charts and books on the advent have been circulated extensively, and the doctrine has been received by many. Among the Tartars in Tartary, there prevails an expectation of Christ's advent about this time. English and American publications on this doctrine have been sent to Holland, Germany, India, Ireland, Constantinople, Rome, and to nearly every missionary station on the globe. At the Turk's Islands, it has been received to some extent among the Wesleyans.

"Mr. Fox, a Scottish missionary to the Telugu people, was a believer in Christ's soon coming. James McGregor Bertram, a Scottish missionary of the Baptist order at St. Helena, has sounded the cry extensively on that island, making many converts and premillennialists; he has also preached it at South Africa at the missionary stations there. David N. Lord informs us that a large proportion of the missionaries who have gone from Great Britain to make known the gospel to the heathen, and who are now laboring in Asia and Africa, are millenarians.

"Joseph Wolff, D. D., according to his journals, between the years 1821 and 1845, proclaimed the Lord's speedy advent in Palestine, Egypt, on the shores of the Red Sea, Mesopotamia, the Crimea, Persia, Georgia, throughout the Ottoman empire, in Greece, Arabia, Turkestan, Bokhara, Afghanistan, Cashmere, Hindustan, Tibet, Holland, Scotland, and Ireland, at Constantinople, Jerusalem, St. Helena, also on shipboard in the Mediterranean, and at New York City to all denominations. He declares he has preached among Jews, Turks, Mohammedans, Parsees, Hinds, Chaldeans, Yeseedes, Syrians, Sabeans, to pashas, sheiks, shahs, the kings of Organtsh and Bokhara, the queen of Greece, etc.; and of his extraordinary labors, the *Investigator* says, 'No individual has, perhaps, given greater publicity to the doctrine of the second coming of the Lord Jesus Christ than has this well-known missionary to the world. Wherever he goes, he proclaims the approaching advent of the Messiah in glory.'"—*"Voice of the Church," pp. 342-344.*

"In Scandinavia also the advent message was proclaimed, and a widespread interest was kindled. Many were roused from their careless security, to confess and forsake their sins, and seek pardon in the name of Christ. But the clergy of the State church opposed the movement, and through their influence some who preached the message were thrown into prison. In many places where the preachers of the Lord's soon coming were thus silenced, God was pleased to send the message, in a miraculous manner, through little children. As they were under age, the law of the State could not restrain them, and they were permitted to speak unmolested.

"The movement was chiefly among the lower class, and it was in the humble dwellings of the laborers that the people assembled to hear the warning. The child-preachers themselves were mostly poor cottagers. Some of them were not more than six or eight years of age, and while their lives testified that they loved the Saviour, and were trying to live in obedience to God's holy requirements, they ordinarily manifested only the intelligence and ability usually seen in children of that age. When standing before the people, however, it was evident that they were moved by an influence beyond their own natural gifts. Tone and manner changed, and with solemn power they gave the warning of the judgment, employing the very words of Scripture, 'Fear God, and give glory to Him; for the hour of His judgment is come.' They reproved the sins of the people, not only condemning immorality and vice, but rebuking worldliness and backsliding, and warning their hearers to make haste to flee from the wrath to come.

"The people heard with trembling. The convicting Spirit of God spoke to their hearts. Many were led to search the Scriptures with new and deeper interest, the intemperate and immoral were reformed, others abandoned their dishonest practices, and a work was done so marked that even ministers of the State church were forced to acknowledge that the hand of God was in the movement. It was God's will that the tidings of the Saviour's coming should be given in the Scandinavian countries; and when the voices of His servants were silenced, He put His Spirit upon the children, that the work might be accomplished."—"*Great Controversy,*" *pp. 366, 367.*

It is to Wm. Miller that America looks as the father of the advent movement of 1840-1844. He was born at Pittsford, Mass., Feb. 15, 1782. Hence at the "disappointment" of 1844 he was 62 years of age.

His early years were spent in work on his father's farm at Low Hampton, N. Y., to which place the Miller family removed in 1786. His opportunities for an education were limited, yet by the light of a pitch-pine torch at the primitive fireplace he stored his mind with historical and other knowledge which became the foundation of his future active and important life-work.

As Mr. Miller grew to manhood, he was highly respected for his intelligence and sturdy integrity. He filled numerous positions of trust and responsibility among his fellow townsmen. He enlisted in the war of 1812, and received a captain's commission. His regiment was engaged in active service, and during the war there was much to admire in Mr. Miller as a soldier.

In his early manhood Mr. Miller became associated with a class of men who, though good citizens as the world goes, were deeply affected with skeptical principles and deistical theories. Ever a student, he read the popular infidel works of his day, and at length avowed himself a deist. But in 1816, at the age of 34 years, he began a careful reading of the Bible. He soon became convinced of the authenticity of the Scriptures, and of the divinity of Jesus Christ. At last he accepted Him as his Saviour.

Of this experience he wrote with much satisfaction and joy:

"I was constrained to admit that the Scriptures must be a revelation from God. They became my delight; and in Jesus I found a friend. . . . The Bible now became my chief study, and I can truly say I searched it with great delight."

Child preachers proclaimed the judgment message in Scandinavia.

His method of study carries a lesson to every Bible student. Of this, one who was actively engaged in his wonderful religious awakening of 1844, and conversant with Mr. Miller's experience, writes:

"Endeavoring to lay aside all preconceived opinions, and dispensing with commentaries, he compared scripture with scripture by the aid of the marginal references and the concordance. He pursued his study in a regular and methodical manner; beginning with Genesis, and reading verse by verse, he proceeded no faster than the meaning of the several passages so unfolded as to leave him free from all embarrassment.

"When he found anything obscure, it was his custom to compare it with every other text which seemed to have any reference to the matter under consideration. Every word was permitted to have its proper bearing upon the subject of the text, and if his view of it harmonized with every collateral passage, it ceased to be a difficulty. Thus whenever he met with a passage hard to be understood, he found an explanation in some other portion of the Scriptures. As he studied, with earnest prayer for divine enlightenment, that which had before appeared dark to his understanding was made clear. He experienced the truth of the psalmist's words, 'The entrance of Thy words giveth light; it giveth understanding unto the simple.'

"With intense interest he studied the books of Daniel and the Revelation, employing the same principles of interpretation as in the other Scriptures, and found, to his great joy, that the prophetic symbols could be understood. He saw that the prophecies, so far as they had been fulfilled, had been fulfilled literally; that all the various figures, metaphors, parables, similitudes, etc., were either explained in their immediate connection, or the terms in which they were expressed were defined in other scriptures; and when thus explained were to be literally understood. 'Thus I was satisfied,' he says, 'that the Bible was a system of revealed truth so clearly and simply given that the wayfaring man, though a fool, need not err therein.' Link after link of the chain of truth rewarded his efforts, as step by step he traced down the great lines of prophecy. Angels of Heaven were guiding his mind and opening the Scriptures to his understanding. . . .

"His attention was especially directed to those Scriptures which refer to the second coming of Christ. As a result he became convinced that the events which were generally expected to take place before the coming of Christ, such as the universal reign of peace, and the setting up of the kingdom of God upon the earth, were to be subsequent to the second advent. Furthermore, all the signs of the times and the condition of the world correspond to the prophetic description of the last days. He was forced to the conclusion, from the study of Scripture alone, that the period allotted for the continuance of the earth in its present state was about to close."—"*Great Controversy,*" *pp. 320, 323.*

As Wm. Miller pursued the study of the Book of Daniel, he came to the text, "Unto two thousand and three hundred days; then shall the sanctuary be cleansed." Daniel 8:14. Believing this "sanctuary" to be the earth, he sought earnestly for a starting point for the 2300 days, but for a long time without success.

The prophet Daniel had also been left in perplexity regarding this same period. The angel, even Gabriel, had been bidden of God to "make this man [Daniel] to understand the vision." (Verse 16.)

The vision of the eighth chapter embraced many symbols, and Gabriel began his work of explanation. He made everything plain and clear so far as he went. He proceeded through all the symbols referring to the kingdoms of this world as given in the first twelve verses. This explanation is found in verses 13-26. At this point Daniel could endure no more. The strain upon him was too great, and "he fainted, and was sick certain days."

The prophet further states, "I was astonished at the vision, but none understood it." Verse 27. This failure to understand can refer only to the unexplained portion of the vision, regarding the 2300 days, as the rest of the vision had been fully and clearly explained, as can be verified by a reading of the chapter.

Daniel's heart was burdened for his people Israel. He knew that the seventy years allotted to their captivity, as foretold in Jeremiah 29:10, were about finished, but feared lest their sins had utterly separated them from God. He was also perplexed regarding the unexplained portion of the vision of the eighth chapter. So in a very earnest manner he sought his God in his trouble and perplexity. He said, "And I set my face unto the Lord God, to seek by prayer and supplications, with fasting, and sackcloth, and ashes." Daniel 9:3.

At the conclusion of this prayer the angel Gabriel stood by his side, and said, "O Daniel, I am now come forth to give thee skill and understanding. At the beginning of thy supplications the commandment came forth, and I am come to show thee; for thou art greatly beloved: therefore understand the matter, and consider the vision." Daniel 9: 22, 23.

In chapter 8:16, Gabriel was commissioned to make Daniel "understand the vision." But one part of the vision remained unexplained. God's purposes will be carried out. So in the ninth chapter Gabriel again appears to Daniel, and says, "I am now come forth to give thee skill and understanding. . . . Therefore understand the matter, and consider the vision." This must be to call the attention of the prophet to the unexplained portion of the previous vision, which referred to time. So we may expect the explanation from Gabriel to begin with time. What are, therefore, his first words?

"Seventy weeks are determined upon thy people and upon thy holy city. . . . Know therefore and understand, that from the going forth of the commandment to restore and to build Jerusalem unto the Messiah the Prince shall be seven weeks, and threescore and two weeks: the street shall be built again, and the wall, even in troublous times. And after threescore and two weeks shall Messiah be cut off, but not for Himself. . . . And He shall confirm the covenant with many for one week: and in the midst of the week He shall cause the sacrifice and the oblation to cease." Daniel 9: 24-27.

Says the learned Dr. Hales, in commenting upon the seventy weeks, "This chronological prophecy was evidently designed to explain the foregoing vision, especially the chronological part of the 2300 days."—*"Chronology," Vol. II, p. 517.*

Gesenius, in his Hebrew Lexicon, says that the original here translated "determined" means properly *to cut off*.

"Seventy weeks have been cut off upon thy people, and upon thy holy city."—*Whiting's Translation.*

Dr. Gill, on Daniel 9: 24, says: "That is, such a space of time is fixed upon; *cut out*, as the word signifies." In plain words, seventy weeks, or 490 days are cut off from the 2300 days of chapter 8: 14.

The 2300 days, the 70 weeks, and similar periods brought into the eighth and ninth chapters of Daniel, must be considered as prophetic, each day standing for a year. Great events in the history of God's people, as well as with the nations of earth, are embraced within this period of the 2300 days. To compress all this within the scope of 2300 literal days would be impossible. If we follow the rule of symbolic prophecy, allowing a day to represent a year, the difficulty vanishes, and the time thus computed fits with history.

"The explanation of these prophetic periods is based on what is called the 'year-day principle'; that is, making each day stand for a year, according to the Scriptural rule for the application of symbolic time. (Ezekiel 4: 6; Numbers 14: 34.) That the time in these visions of Daniel 8 and 9 is symbolic is evident from the nature and scope of the prophecy. The question calling out the answers on this point was, 'How long the vision?'" The vision, reckoning from 538 B.C. to our own time, sweeps over a period more than 2400 years in length. But if the 2300 days of the vision are literal days, we have a period of only a little over six years and a half for the duration of the kingdoms and the transaction of the great events brought to view, which is absurd. The year-day principle numbers among its supporters such names as Augustine, Tichonius, Primasius, Andreas, the Venerable Bede, Ambrosius, Ansbertus, Berengaud, and Bruno Astensis, besides the leading modern expositiors. (See Elliott's "Horæ Apocalypticæ," Vol. III, p. 241; and "The Sanctuary and its Cleansing," pp. 45-52.) But what is more conclusive than all else is the fact that the prophecies have actually been fulfilled on this principle,— a demonstration of its

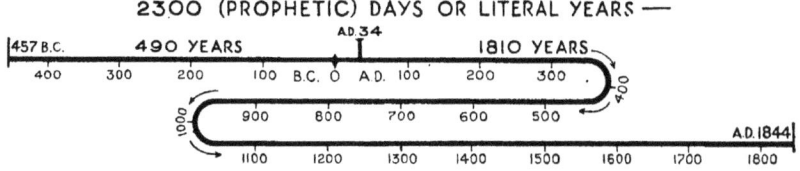

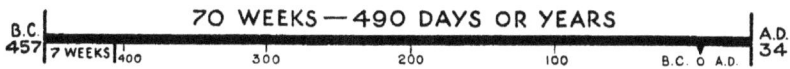

A chart illustrating the 2300-day prophecy

correctness from which there is no appeal. This will be found in the prophecy of the seventy weeks throughout, and all the prophetic periods of Daniel 7 and 12, and Revelation 9, 12, and 13."—"*Daniel and the Revelation,*" *pp. 197, 198.*

From the 2300 days, we find in chapter 9: 24 that seventy weeks, or 490 days, were cut off and set apart for the people of the Jews. This seventy weeks is again cut up in verses 25, 27, into three periods of seven weeks, sixty-two weeks, and one week, the sum aggregating seventy weeks as before. Hence, the 2300 days, the seventy weeks, and the seven weeks of verse 25, all begin at the same time. When was this?—The answer is plain: "From the going forth of the commandment to restore and to build Jerusalem." Verse 25.

In Ezra 6: 14 we read that "they builded, and finished it [the house of the Lord], according to the commandment . . . of Cyrus, and Darius, and Artaxerxes king of Persia."

The first decree, by Cyrus, embraced only the rebuilding of the temple. (See Ezra 1: 2-4.)

The second decree, by Darius, confirmed the decree of Cyrus, which had been hindered, and provided liberally for the construction of the temple, but no more. (See Ezra 6: 1-12.)

But the prophetic period must date from a "commandment to restore and to build Jerusalem." This complete decree was issued by Artaxerxes Longimanus, B.C. 457, and included the full rebuilding of the temple, the city of Jerusalem, and the restoration of the government of the Jews. (See Ezra 7: 12-26.)

Will the dates with which we have been dealing correspond with history? Let us see:

In Daniel 9: 25, we are told that there were to be "seven weeks," or forty-nine literal years in which "the street shall be built again, and the wall, even in troublous times." In regard to this period Prideaux says:

"In the fifteenth year of Darius Nothus ended the first seven weeks of Daniel's prophecy. For then the restoration of the church and state of the Jews in Jerusalem and Judea was fully finished, in that last act of reformation which is recorded in the thirteenth chapter of Nehemiah, from the twenty-third verse to the end of the chapter, *just forty-nine* years after it had been commenced by Ezra in the seventh year of Artaxerxes Longimanus."—"*Connections,*" *Vol. I. p. 322.*

This brings us to B.C. 409.

We also find in verse 25, that "seven weeks, and threescore and two weeks" were to extend to "the Messiah the

Prince." These sixty-nine weeks stand for 483 literal years. Beginning as before at B.C. 457, they end in A.D. 27. There seems to be a discrepancy of one year in this date. But if we should begin with the first day of B.C. 457, and end with the last day of A.D. 26, we would have just 483 years. But as the Jews on their return did not reach Jerusalem until the autumn of B.C. 457, the time from which this date was taken, the 483 years would carry us to A.D. 27, the year in which Jesus was baptized.

In Luke 3: 23 we read that Jesus "began to be about thirty years of age" at the time of His baptism. How can this be harmonized with the date of A.D. 27, as given above? By a mistake, the date of the Christian era did not begin until Jesus was three years of age. Hence He was thirty years of age in the year A.D. 27, when He was baptized. See "Hale's Chronology," Vol. I. pp. 83, 84.

What occurred at the baptism of Christ is thus described by the gospel writer: "Now when all the people were baptized, it came to pass, that Jesus also being baptized, and praying, the heaven was opened, and the Holy Ghost descended in a bodily shape like a dove upon Him, and a voice came from heaven, which said, Thou art My beloved Son; in Thee I am well pleased." Luke 3: 21, 22; margin, A.D. 27. After this, Jesus came "preaching the gospel of the kingdom of God, and saying, *The time* is fulfilled." (Mark 1: 14, 15.)

"*The time* here mentioned must have been some specific, definite, and predicted period; but no prophetic period can be found then terminating, except the sixty-nine weeks of the prophecy of Daniel, which were to extend to the Messiah the Prince. The Messiah had now come; and with His own lips He announced the termination of that period which was to be marked by His manifestation."—"*Daniel and the Revelation,*" *p. 202.*

"And He shall confirm the covenant with many for one week: and in the midst of the week He shall cause the sacrifice and the oblation to cease." Daniel 9:27. This was the last week of the seventy, or the last seven years of the 490.

In the midst of the week He was to "cause the sacrifice and the oblation to cease." All the offerings in the temple service were typical of Christ, "the Lamb of God, slain from the foundation of the world." At His death, type met antitype, the real offering for sin was made, and the sacrificial services of the temple were of no more avail. At the death of Christ an unseen hand rent the veil of the temple from top to bottom.

The "midst of the week" would be three and one-half years. In the autumn of A.D. 27, Jesus was anointed to His ministry by the descent of the Holy Ghost at His baptism. In the spring of A.D. 31, at the time of the Passover, just three and one-half years after His baptism, He was crucified.

"And He shall confirm the covenant with many for one week." This is the last week of the seventy, and the last seven years of the period allotted especially to the Jews. It terminated A.D. 34.

During the first three and one-half years of this week, the covenant with Israel had been confirmed by the ministry of Jesus himself. During the last half of the week, it was confirmed by the disciples. Their instruction had been, "Go not into the way of the Gentiles, and into any city of the Samaritans enter ye not; but go rather to the lost sheep of the house of Israel." Matthew 10: 5, 6. This instruction was heeded by the disciples until A.D. 34. Then the public action of the Jews closed the door of the gospel to them as a nation, and opened it to the Gentiles.

> "At that time, through the action of the Jewish Sanhedrim, the nation sealed its rejection of the gospel, by the martyrdom of Stephen and the persecution of the followers of Christ. Then the message of salvation, no longer restricted to the chosen people, was given to the

The First Angel's Message

world. The disciples, forced by persecution to flee from Jerusalem, 'went everywhere preaching the word.'"—*"Great Controversy," p. 328.*

"Unto two thousand and three hundred days; then shall the sanctuary be cleansed." Having fixed beyond all controversy the dates connected with the seventy weeks, it becomes an easy matter to settle the ending of the 2300 days. Subtract the seventy weeks, or 490 years, from 2300, and the remainder will be 1810. As the seventy weeks ended in the autumn of A.D. 34, we have only to add 1810 to 34, which brings us to the autumn of 1844, the time emphasized by Mr. Miller and others who joined him in giving the first message as "the hour of God's judgment."

The following dialogue is characteristic of Mr. Miller's method of meeting objectors:

"Having heard that a physician in his neighborhood had said 'Esquire Miller,' as he was familiarly called, 'was a fine man and a good neighbor, but was a monomaniac on the subject of the advent,' Mr. Miller was humorously inclined to let him prescribe for his case.

"One of his children being sick one day, he sent for the doctor, who, after prescribing for the child, noticed that Mr. Miller was very mute in one corner, and asked what ailed him.

"'Well, I hardly know, doctor. I want you to see what does, and prescribe for me.'

"The doctor felt of his pulse, and could not decide respecting his malady; and inquired what he supposed was his complaint.

"'Well,' said Mr. Miller, 'I don't know but I am a monomaniac; and I want you to examine me, and see if I am; and if so, cure me. Can you tell when a man is a monomaniac?'

"The doctor blushed, and said he thought he could.

"Mr. Miller wished to know how.

"'Why,' said the doctor, 'a monomaniac is rational on all subjects but one; and when you touch that particular subject, he will become raving.'

"'Well,' said Mr. Miller, 'I insist upon it that you see whether I am in reality a monomaniac; and if I am, you shall prescribe for and cure me. You shall, therefore, sit down with me two hours, while I present the subject of the advent to you, and, if I am a monomaniac, by that time you will discover it.'

"The doctor was somewhat disconcerted; but Mr. Miller insisted, and told him, as it was to present the state of mind, he might charge for his time as in regular practice.

"The doctor finally consented; and at Mr. Miller's request, opened the Bible and read from the eighth of Daniel. As he read along, Mr. Miller inquired what the ram denoted, with the other symbols presented. The doctor had read Newton, and applied them to Persia, Greece, and Rome, as Mr. Miller did.

"Mr. Miller then inquired how long the vision of those empires was to be.

"'2300 days.'

"'What!' said Mr. Miller, 'could those great empires cover only 2300 literal days?'

"'Why,' said the doctor, 'those days are years, according to all commentators; and those kingdoms are to continue 2300 years.'

"Mr. Miller then asked him to turn to the second of Daniel, and to the seventh; all of which he explained the same as Mr. Miller. He was then asked if he knew when the 2300 days would end. He did not know, as he could not tell when they began.

"Mr. Miller told him to read the ninth of Daniel. He read down till he came to the twenty-first verse, when Daniel saw 'the man Gabriel,' whom he had 'seen in the vision.'

"'In what vision?' Mr. Miller inquired.

"'Why,' said the doctor, 'in the vision of the eighth of Daniel.'

"'Wherefore, understand the matter and consider the vision.' He had now come, then, to make him understand that vision, had he?"

"'Yes,' said the doctor.

"'Well, seventy weeks are determined; what are these seventy weeks a part of?'

"'Of the 2300 days.'
"'Then do they begin with the 2300 days?'
"'Yes,' said the doctor.
"'When did they end?'
"'In A.D. 33.'
"'Then how far would the 2300 extend after 33?'
"The doctor subtracted 490 from 2300, and replied, 1810. Why,' said he, 'that is past.'
"'But,' said Mr. Miller, 'there were 1810 from 33; in what year would that come?'
"The doctor saw at once that the 33 should be added, and set down 33 and 1810, and, adding them replied, '1843.'
"At this unexpected result the doctor settled back in his chair and colored; but immediately took his hat and left the house in a rage.
"The next day he again called on Mr. Miller, and looked as though he had been in the greatest mental agony.
"'Why, Mr. Miller,' said he, 'I am going to hell. I have not slept a wink since I was here yesterday. I have looked at the question in every light, and the vision must terminate about A.D. 1843; and I am unprepared, and must go to hell.'
"Mr. Miller calmed him, and pointed him to the ark of safety; and in about a week, calling each day on Mr. Miller, he found peace to his soul, and went on his way rejoicing, as great a monomaniac as Mr. Miller. He afterward acknowledged that, till he made the figures 1843, he had no idea of the result to which he was coming."

This dialogue occurred when Mr. Miller still thought the closing year was 1843. He afterward changed it to 1844. (See page 239). Also he held that the earth was the sanctuary, and that its cleansing was to be its purification by fire at Christ's coming. Hence he concluded that the close of the 2300 days was the time of the second advent.

The Sanctuary

WHAT is the sanctuary, and what is its cleansing? When Israel was encamped before Sinai, the Lord said to Moses, "Let them make Me a sanctuary; that I may dwell among them." Exodus 25: 8.

The apostle Paul, referring to the same time and the same religious system, writes, "Then verily the first covenant had also ordinances of divine service, and a worldly sanctuary." Hebrews 9: 1.

This earthly sanctuary is often spoken of as the tabernacle, or tent. It was a portable structure, erected according to divine instruction. In the days of Solomon this tabernacle gave place to the beautiful and permanent temple at Jerusalem.

This sanctuary, whether inclosed in the tent built in the wilderness of Sinai, or in the temple at Jerusalem, was divided into two apartments, called the holy and most holy places. Each apartment had its furniture prepared for the special service to be carried on therein. Regarding this furniture the apostle says:

"For there was a tabernacle made; the first [or first apartment], wherein was the candlestick, and the table, and the shewbread; which is called the sanctuary [margin, the holy]. And after the second veil the tabernacle which is called the Holiest of all; which had the golden censer, and the ark of the covenant overlaid round about with gold, wherein was the golden pot that had manna, and Aaron's rod that budded, and the tables of the covenant; and over it the cherubim of glory shadowing the mercy seat." Hebrews 9: 2-5.

All these things were real to the prophet Daniel, for he was a Jew of the royal line, and before the captivity was familiar with the temple at Jerusalem, its furniture, and the service of the sanctuary; and with these he would naturally connect the words of the angel, "Unto two thousand and three hundred days; then shall the sanctuary be cleansed."

"It will be safe for us," as one writer has aptly said, "to put ourselves in imagination in the place of Daniel, and view the subject from his standpoint. What would he understand by the term 'sanctuary' as addressed to him?" "His mind would inevitably turn, on the mention of that word, to the sanctuary of that dispensation; and certainly he well knew what that was. His mind did turn to Jerusalem, the city of his fathers, which was then in ruins, and to their 'beautiful house,' which, as Jeremiah laments, was burned with fire. And so, as was his wont, with his face turned toward the place of their once venerated temple, he prayed God to cause His face to shine upon His sanctuary, which was desolate. By the word 'sanctuary' Daniel evidently understood their temple at Jerusalem."

It is written of both Jew and Gentile that "all have sinned and come short of the glory of God." (Romans 3: 23.) It is also true of all that "the wages of sin is death." (Romans 6: 23.) But a Saviour had been promised, and the service in this earthly sanctuary had to do with the forgiveness of sins.

"The blood is the life" (Deuteronomy 12: 23), and the shedding of the blood of the sacrifice signified that the sinner was worthy of death. Hence the Lord said to Israel: "The life of the flesh is in the blood: and I have given it to you upon the altar to make an atonement for your souls: for it is the blood that maketh an atonement for the soul. Therefore I said unto the children of Israel, No soul of you shall eat blood." Leviticus 17: 11, 12.

How forceful, then, are the words of Paul to the Hebrews: "Almost all things are by the law purged with blood; and without shedding of blood is no remission." Hebrews 9: 22.

But since "it is not possible that the blood of bulls and of goats should take away sins," the offerings in the earthly sanctuary were only typical of the offering to be made by Christ, and of His work in the heavenly sanctuary.

During the old dispensation the sinner confessed his sins upon the head of the offering, and the sacrifice was slain, and some of the blood carried into the sanctuary. By this blood, and in some offerings by the eating of the flesh by the priests, the sins were in a figure transferred from the individual to the sanctuary. This was an everyday work. Paul says that "the priests went always into the first tabernacle [the holy place], accomplishing the service of God." (Hebrews 9:6.) By this daily ministry the sanctuary became the resting place of the sins of the people, and was "defiled" thereby.

The ministration in the most holy place was performed only once a year. Aaron was warned not to come "at all times into the holy place within the veil before the mercy seat, which is upon the ark; that he die not." (Leviticus 16:2.)

Paul writes that "into the second [the most holy place] went the high priest alone once every year, not without blood, which he offered for himself, and for the errors of the people." (Hebrews 9:7.)

Upon "the seventh month, on the tenth day of the month" the high priest entered into the most holy place "to make an atonement for the children of Israel for all their sins once a year." (Leviticus 16:29, 34.)

Paul says that the earthly sanctuary was "purified" by this yearly service. It was "cleansed" from the defilment of sin which had been confessed by the people throughout the year. By a sin offering, by his confession, and by the ministry of the priest, the guilt, or sin, of the penitent was transferred from the transgressor to the sanctuary. Thus, day by day, until the last day of the ecclesiastical year, the sins of the people were carried into the sanctuary, which thus became the receptacle of guilt.

"But this," remarks one writer, "was not the final disposition of these sins. The accumulated guilt was removed by a special service, which was called the cleansing of the sanctuary. This service, in the type, occupied one day in the year; and the tenth day of the seventh month, on which it

The high priest laid the sins of the people on the head of the scapegoat, and it was turned out to die.

was performed, was called the day of atonement. On this day, while all Israel refrained from work and afflicted their souls, the priest brought two goats, and presented them before the Lord at the door of the tabernacle of the congregation. On these goats he cast lots; one lot for the Lord, and the other lot for the scapegoat. The one upon which the Lord's lot fell, was then slain, and his blood was carried by the priest into the most holy place of the sanctuary, and sprinkled upon the mercy seat. And this was the only day on which he was permitted to enter into that apartment. "Coming forth, he was then to lay both his hands upon the head of the scapegoat, confess over him all the iniquities of the children of Israel, and all their transgressions in all their sins, and, thus putting them upon his head (Leviticus 16: 21), he was to send him away by the hand of a fit man into a land not inhabited, a land of separation, or forgetfulness, the goat never again to appear in the camp of Israel, and the sins of the people to be remembered against them no more. The service was for the purpose of cleansing the people from their sins, and cleansing the sanctuary and its sacred vessels. (See Leviticus 16: 30, 33.) By this process, sin was removed, —but only in figure; for all that work was typical."

At Sinai the Lord gave Moses the most definite and minute instruction as to the construction of the earthly sanctuary or tabernacle. "According to all that I show thee, after the pattern of the tabernacle, and the pattern of all the instruments thereof, even so shall ye make it." Exodus 25: 9. It was to be as nearly a reproduction of the heavenly sanctuary as the circumstances of earth and the conditions under which it was to be used would allow. Paul says that the earthly sanctuary and its ministration were "the patterns of things in the heavens." (Hebrews 9: 23.)

In prophetic vision John saw this heavenly sanctuary: "I looked, and, behold, the temple of the tabernacle of the testimony in heaven was opened." And again: "The temple of God was opened in heaven, and there was seen in His temple the ark of His testament." Revelation 15: 5; 11: 19. And Paul speaks of it as "the true tabernacle, which the Lord pitched, and not man," and as "a greater and more perfect tabernacle." (Hebrews 8: 2; 9: 11.)

The priests of the earthly tabernacle served only "unto the example and shadow of heavenly things." Of Christ as Priest of the new dispensation, Paul writes: "We have such an High Priest, who is set on the right hand of the throne of the Majesty in the heavens; a minister of the sanctuary, and of the true tabernacle, which the Lord pitched, and not man." Hebrews 8: 5, 1, 2.

In the old dispensation of types and shadows the blood of animals was shed in atonement for sin. Of the new dispensation we read that "every high priest is ordained to offer gifts and sacrifices: wherefore it is of necessity that this Man have somewhat also to offer." (Hebrews 8:3.) This offering was His own blood, for we read:

"But Christ being come an High Priest of good things to come, by a greater and more perfect tabernacle [the temple in heaven], not made with hands, that is to say, not of this building; neither by the blood of goats and calves, but by His own blood He entered in once into the holy place, having obtained eternal redemption for us." Hebrews 9: 11, 12.

The ministry in the heavenly sanctuary did not begin until Christ came and in Himself provided an offering. Paul explains that "the way into the holiest of all was not made manifest, while as the first tabernacle was yet standing: which was a figure for the time then present, in which were offered both gifts and sacrifices, that could not make him that did the service perfect." (Hebrews 9: 8, 9.)

While the service in the earthly sanctuary cleansed the sinner typically, relying upon the ratification by the coming sacrifice, "the Lamb of God," Paul asserts that "much more shall the blood of Christ, who through the eternal Spirit offered Himself without spot to God, purge your conscience from dead works to serve the living God." (Hebrews 9: 14.)

At the death of Christ the service of the earthly sanctuary ceased to avail for sin, in testimony of which the veil of the temple was rent in twain. When He ascended to His Father the service in the temple in heaven began, with Christ as both Priest and Sacrifice. Upon this subject Paul writes:

On the day of atonement all Israel gathered around the sanctuary while the high priest made atonement for the people at the altar.

The Sanctuary

"And they truly were many priests, because they were not suffered to continue by reason of death: but this Man, because He continueth ever, hath an unchangeable priesthood. Wherefore He is able also to save them to the uttermost that come unto God by Him, seeing He ever liveth to make intercession for them. For such an High Priest became us, who is holy, harmless, undefiled, separate from sinners, and made higher than the heavens; who needeth not daily, as those high priests, to offer up sacrifice, first for His own sins, and then for the people's: for this He did once, when He offered up Himself." Hebrews 7: 23-27.

By confession, through all the years of Christ's ministration, the sins of God's people have been transferred to the sanctuary above. Of every sin and every repentance a faithful record has been kept "in the books" of heaven. In this sense the heavenly sanctuary is "defiled" and must at some time be cleansed as was done once a year in type in the earthly sanctuary. This final "cleansing" is a thorough investigation of the life-work of all who have ever started in the service of God. It is a work of judgment. It is to decide who have been faithful to their profession, and are worthy of the final great reward.

"In the typical system," says Uriah Smith, "which was a shadow of the sacrifice and priesthood of Christ, the cleansing of the sanctuary was the last service performed by the high priest in the yearly round of ministration. It was the closing work of the atonement — a removal or putting away of sin from Israel. It prefigured the closing work of the ministration of our High Priest in heaven, in the removal or blotting out of the sins of His people, which are registered in the heavenly records. This service involves a work of investigation, a work of judgment; and it immediately precedes the coming of Christ in the clouds of heaven with power and great glory; for when He comes, every case has been decided. Says Jesus, 'My reward is with Me, to give every man according as his work shall be.' Revelation 22:12. It is this work of judgment, immediately preceding the second advent, that is announced in the first angel's message of Revelation 14:7: 'Fear God, and give glory to Him; for the hour of His judgment is come.'"

In the earthly, typical ministration, the work of cleansing the sanctuary was performed once a year. In the antitypical service Christ our High Priest enters "once for all." This is the important work introduced in our text, "Unto two thousand and three hundred days; then shall the sanctuary be cleansed."

The date at which this period begins is considered in the previous chapter, which places its close in the autumn of 1844. From the evidences presented it is plain that the cleansing of the sanctuary in heaven, which is the investigative judgment, began at that time. It was then our Saviour entered upon His ministration in the most holy place of the sanctuary above. It is the beginning of the end. Its investigations will continue until the case of every individual is settled for time and for eternity.

To adopt the admirable statement of "Thoughts on Daniel and the Revelation," our position is that "one year's round of service in the earthly sanctuary represented the entire work of the sanctuary above. In the type, the cleansing of the sanctuary was the brief closing work of the year's service. In the antitype, the cleansing of the sanctuary must be the closing work of Christ, our great High Priest, in the tabernacle on high. In the type, to cleanse the sanctuary, the high priest entered into the most holy place to minister in the presence of God before the ark of His testament. In the antitype, when the time comes for the cleansing of the sanctuary, our High Priest, in like manner, enters into the most holy place to make a final end of His intercessory work

The Sanctuary 255

in behalf of mankind. We confidently affirm that no other conclusion can be arrived at on this subject without doing despite to the unequivocal testimony of God's word."

To those who are looking for the soon coming of our Lord, the disappointment of Wm. Miller and those who, with him, expected Christ to come in 1844, is a subject of considerable interest.

It is evident that God's hand covered some feature of the sanctuary question, and behind that hand they could not penetrate. Some link in their chain of reasoning was defective. But of this they were certain — the time had passed, and their Lord had not come as expected.

Again and again the leaders in this movement went over the prophecies in their endeavor to discover some error in the computation of the time. But no inaccuracy could be found, and the date could not be changed. Nor were they alone in their interpretation of the time feature of the prophecies. Others agreed with them in this respect, but had various theories as to the nature of the event.

Dr. Geo. Bush, Professor of Hebrew and Oriental Literature in the New York City University, in a letter addressed to Mr. Miller, and published in the *Advent Herald* for March, 1844, says:

"Neither is it to be objected, as I conceive, to yourself or your friends, that you have devoted much time and attention to the study of the chronology of prophecy, and have labored much to determine the commencing and closing dates of its great periods. If these periods are actually given by the Holy Ghost in the prophetic books, it was doubtless with the design that they should be studied, and probably in the end, fully understood; and no man is to be charged with presumptuous folly who reverently makes the attempt to do this. . . . In taking a day as the prophetic term for a year, I believe you are sustained by the soundest exegesis, as well as fortified by the high names of Mede, Sir Isaac Newton, Bishop Newton,

Kirby, Scott, Keith, and a host of others, who have long since come to substantially your conclusions on this head. They all agree that the leading periods mentioned by Daniel and John do actually expire about this age of the world, and it would be a strange logic that would convict you of heresy for holding in effect the same views which stand forth so prominently in the notices of these eminent divines.

"Your results in this field of inquiry do not strike me as so far out of the way as to effect any of the great interests of truth and duty. . . . Your error, as I apprehend, lies in another direction than your *chronology*. . . . You have entirely mistaken *the nature of the events* which are to occur when those periods have expired. This is the head and front of your expository offending. . . . The great event before the world is not its physical conflagration, but its moral regeneration. Although there is doubtless a sense in which Christ may be said to come in connection with the passing away of the fourth empire of the Ottoman power, and His kingdom to be illustriously established, yet that will be found to be a spiritual coming in the power of the gospel, in the ample outpouring of His Spirit, and the glorious administration of His providence."

The doctrine of a temporal millennium as advocated by Dr. Bush was considered a harmful delusion by Mr. Miller, and as such was strenuously opposed by him. Both men were correct in their dates, and both were mistaken in the event. Christ did not appear in the clouds of heaven in 1844, neither was the "moral regeneration" of the earth, as anticipated by Dr. Bush, ushered in at that time, for constantly since then have "evil men and seducers waxed worse and worse, deceiving, and being deceived."

The grievous disappointment of the Adventists in 1844 does not militate against the genuineness of the message they had borne. There is sometimes victory in defeat. No people ever suffered a more crushing disappointment than did the disciples at the crucifixion of Christ. They expected Him to take the throne of David, when in fact He stood in the very shadow of the cross. Yet after His resurrection they discovered that His death was the crowning victory and glory of His mission. It was essential to the whole plan of salvation.

Earnest, God-fearing men, directed by the Holy Spirit, proclaimed the message of 1844. After their disappointment, earnest believers sought carefully for their error in the interpretation of the prophecies. They were led to see that the sanctuary to be cleansed was not the earth as they had supposed, but was "the true tabernacle" in heaven, "which the Lord pitched, and not man," with Jesus Christ as High Priest.

It then became plain that the cleansing of the sanctuary was not the purifying of the earth, but the investigative judgment of which the yearly day of atonement in the earthly sanctuary was a type.

They also found that the ark of the Most Holy place was the receptacle of the "tables of the testimony," the law of God. They found that the Bible taught clearly that the law is immutable, changeless, and perpetual in its obligations. Thus their very disappointment resulted in throwing a flood of light on Scriptures not previously understood.

But let none harbor the thought that the Advent movement of 1844 was the work of a few irresponsible fanatics. On the contrary it was a movement which stirred the world. It was symbolized by an angel flying in the midst of heaven "having the everlasting gospel to preach," and proclaiming, "Fear God, and give glory to Him; for the hour of His judgment is come." It embraced in its promulgation some of the brightest minds of the age. In England and America, often in the most conservative churches, there were more than one thousand ministers enlisted in the proclamation of "this gospel of the kingdom," and the Spirit of God gave witness to the word spoken by them.

17

The Second Angel's Message

"AND there followed another angel, saying, Babylon is fallen, is fallen, that great city, because she made all nations drink of the wine of the wrath of her fornications." Revelation 14: 8.

This message closely follows that of the first angel of this series of three, but does not displace it. The work of the first angel continues during the sounding of the second angel. In like manner the first and second continue their work through the sounding of the third, thus forming a great threefold message.

When Christ came to earth, He, by His teaching, swept away the darkness and blindness of the religious system of His day, and brought to light "the mystery of the kingdom of God." (Mark 4: 11. See also, Romans 16: 25; Ephesians 3: 3-5; 1 Timothy 3: 16; Colossians 1: 27.)

But only twenty-three years after the crucifixion, Paul saw an evil coming into the church which he denominates "the mystery of iniquity." He warns most earnestly against it in these words:

"Let no man deceive you by any means: for that day [the second coming of Christ] shall not come, except there come a falling away first, and that man of sin be revealed, the son of perdition; who opposeth and exalteth himself above all that is called God, or that is worshipped: so that he as God sitteth in the temple of God, showing himself that he is God. . . . And now ye know what withholdeth that he might be revealed in his time. *For the mystery of iniquity doth already work:* only he who now letteth [Greek, restrains] will let, until he be taken out of the way." 2 Thessalonians 2: 3-7.

[258]

These words can refer only to the great apostasy which, beginning in the days of the apostles, came into full swing in the fourth century. By this apostasy the religion of Christ was perverted, and the "mystery of godliness" was, during the centuries of the Dark Ages, hidden under the pall of the "mystery of iniquity."

As a result of this "falling away" from the pure gospel,

The second angel denounces the church for its fallen condition.

pagan forms, observances, and doctrines were brought into the church, thus combining Christianity and paganism, the result being a confused, mongrel system of religion, Christian in name, but pagan in its nature. As a further result, pride and ostentation took the place of the simplicity of early Christianity, and little true godliness was found in the church. The word of God was, so far as possible, withheld from the people, being taken away from such as possessed even portions of it, and dignitaries of the church impiously assumed the authority and prerogatives of God.

This apostate church is symbolized in the Revelation by a fallen, impure woman. Of her we read, "And upon her forehead was a name written, Mystery, Babylon the great, the mother of harlots and abominations of the earth." Revelation 17:5.

The word Babylon signifies "confusion" and is derived from "Babel; because the Lord did there confound the languages of all the earth: and from thence did the Lord scatter them abroad upon the face of all the earth." (Genesis 11:9.)

If this church which had departed from God was "Babylon, . . . the mother," who are the harlot daughters? But one answer can be given: They must be professed churches of Christ which hold to the errors of their Babylonish "mother." They in turn become "Babylon" when they reject the advancing light of God's word.

During and after the Reformation the bodies which came out of the "mother" church brought into their creeds many errors from the black pool of darkness from which they had sprung.

As time passed, godly men saw some of these errors, and stepped out into new light as it was revealed to them. Then a new denomination would be formed, and, unfortunately, a new creed would be made. Few are the instances where a denomination has advanced beyond its creed. Hence, new light meant a new denomination, and then, again, a new creed. And so the work of reformation resulted in the formation of the many denominations which constitute the churches of today. How aptly does the term "Babylon" apply to such a mixed multitude.

But the time came when God would call out a people that should be especially His, and to which He could reveal, point by point, all His precious truths, unfettered by creeds, and which would lead back, step by step, to the old paths, and reinstate in its completeness the "mystery of godliness," which had been so long obscured.

This was the mission of the first angel's message of Revelation 14: 6, which proclaimed the "everlasting gospel." This is the gospel of the ages, stripped of all the combined errors of heathensim and a false Christianity. It is to fit a people for the second coming of Christ. It is to prepare a people for translation when He shall come.

Those who sounded the first message did not seek to found a new church, or promulgate a new creed. They labored for all churches alike, and sought to awaken the people by preaching a pure gospel. Upon this point William Miller himself wrote:

"In my labors I never had the desire or thought to establish any separate interest from that of existing denominations, or to benefit one at the expense of another. I thought to benefit all. Supposing that all Christians would rejoice in the prospect of Christ's coming, and that those who could not see as I did would not love any the less those who should embrace this doctrine, I did not conceive there would ever be any necessity for separate meetings. My whole object was a desire to convert souls to God, to notify the world of a coming judgment, and to induce my fellow men to make that preparation of heart which will enable them to meet their God in peace. The great majority of those who were converted under my labors united with the various existing churches."

"As his work tended to build up the churches," writes one who participated in this movement, "it was for a time regarded with favor. But as ministers and religious leaders decided against the Advent doctrine, and desired to suppress all agitation of the subject, they not only opposed it from the pulpit, but denied their members the privilege of attending preaching upon the second advent, or even of speaking of their hope in the social meetings of the church. Thus the believers found themselves in a position of great trial and perplexity. They loved their churches, and were loath to separate from them; but as they saw the testimony of God's word suppressed, and their right to investigate the prophecies denied, they felt that loyalty to God forbade them to submit. Those who sought to shut out the testimony of God's word they could not regard as constituting the church of Christ, 'the pillar and ground of the truth.' Hence they felt themselves justified in separating from their former connection."

During the proclamation of the first message great light had gone to the world. The "everlasting gospel" had been preached with power. Those who were earnest and sincere were reached by this message. "Pride and conformity to the world were swept away; wrongs were made right; hearts were united in the sweetest fellowship; and love and joy reigned supreme. If the doctrine did this for the few who did receive it, it would have done the same for all if all had received it."

Of our Saviour's mission He said, "If I had not come and spoken unto them, they had not had sin: but now they have no cloak for their sin." John 15: 22.

To those not spiritually blind the beneficial results of the message of 1840-1844 could be seen in the churches wherever it was proclaimed. But the leaders soon rejected the light and turned from it. When a person deliberately turns from the light, a loss of spirituality — a moral fall — must follow. And, as in the days of our Saviour, those who did this "had no cloak for their sin."

"About this time," writes one who was acquainted with the religious conditions of that period, "a marked change was apparent in most of the churches throughout the United States. There had been for many years a gradual but steadily increasing conformity to worldly practices and customs, and a corresponding decline in real spiritual life; but in that year [1844] there were evidences of a sudden and marked declension in nearly all the churches of the land."

There were godly men who at that time held their membership in the churches of all denominations who felt keenly the rapidly lowering spiritual vitality among professed Christians, and sounded vigorously the alarm. Mr. Barnes, author of the widely used commentary which bears his name, in a meeting of the presbytery of Philadelphia, was reported as saying:

"There are no awakenings, no conversions, not much apparent growth in grace in professors, and none come to my study to converse about the salvation of their souls. With the increase of business, and the brightening prospects of commerce and manufactures, there is an increase of worldly-mindedness. Thus it is with all denominations."

In the month of February of the same year, Professor Finney, of Oberlin College, said:

"We have had the fact before our minds, that, in general, the Protestant churches of our country, as such, were apathetic or hostile to nearly all the moral reforms of the age. There are partial exceptions, yet not enough to render the fact otherwise than general. We have also another corroborative fact,— the almost universal absence of revival influence in the churches. The spiritual apathy is almost all-pervading, and is fearfully deep; so the religious press of the whole land testifies. Very extensively, church members are becoming devotees of fashion, joining hands with the ungodly in parties of pleasure, in dancing, in festivities, etc. But we need not expand this painful subject. Suffice it that the evidence thickens and rolls heavily upon us, to show that the churches generally are becoming sadly degenerate. They have gone very far from the Lord, and He has withdrawn Himself from them."

"We have never witnessed," said a writer in the *Religious Telescope*, "such a general declension as at present. Truly, the church should awake, and search into the cause of this affliction; for affliction everyone that loves Zion must view it. When we call to mind how few and far between cases of true conversion are, and the almost unparalleled impenitence and hardness of sinners, we almost involuntarily exclaim, 'Has God forgotten to be gracious? or is the door of mercy closed?' "

While many who deplored the lack of godliness in the churches did not understand the cause, it was apparent to those who had taken their stand for the truth. Hence, in all parts of the land they raised the cry of the second angel's message, "Babylon is fallen." Those who rejected the light sustained a spiritual fall. Those who accepted the demands of the message, soon connected with it the movement brought to view in Revelation 18: 1-4, and sounded the call, "Come out of her, My people." As a result "about fifty thousand severed their connection with the denominations where they were not allowed to hold and proclaim their views in peace." Babylon had fallen.

Like causes produce like results, and today though a new generation is upon the stage of action, Babylon, both mother and daughters, still clings to her errors, and the frown of God still rests upon her. It is true there are found in the various churches many who are truly pious and who deplore the low spiritual condition; but as a whole Babylon is unchanged; and shorn of a large part of the spiritual power that once was hers notwithstanding her errors, we see her tending more and more toward the world, and exemplifying less and less the spirit and fruits of true religion.

The Lord "would have healed Babylon, but she is not healed." (Jeremiah 51: 9.) And erelong, under the closing work of the three angels, when they shall be joined by "another angel" "having great power," the message will again go forth in still greater power than in 1844, "Babylon the great is fallen, is fallen." "Come out of her, my people, that ye be not partakers of her sins, and that ye receive not of her plagues." (See Revelation 18: 1-4.)

The Third Angel's Message

"AND the third angel followed them, saying with a loud voice, If any man worship the beast and his image, and receive his mark in his forehead, or in his hand, the same shall drink of the wine of the wrath of God, which is poured out without mixture into the cup of His indignation; and he shall be tormented with fire and brimstone in the presence of the holy angels, and in the presence of the Lamb: and the smoke of their torment ascendeth up for ever and ever: and they have no rest day nor night, who worship the beast and his image, and whosoever receiveth the mark of his name. Here is the patience of the saints: here are they that keep the commandments of God, and the faith of Jesus." Revelation 14: 9-12.

"The third angel followed them." That is, he follows the angels of verses six and eight. This is the last of the series of three messages given in this chapter. From this time forward to the close of probation these three messages blend in a last warning to the world of the great final crisis which is so near at hand. When these three angels shall cease their work, probation ends, and the angels brought to view in chapter sixteen begin to pour out the seven last plagues upon an impenitent and doomed world.

The message of the third angel embraces three distinct features:

First, a warning against turning from the true God to the worship of a specious counterfeit, called the beast, and of an image, or likeness of the beast.

Second, is recorded the terrible punishment that will be meted out to those who, notwithstanding the warning, do worship the beast and his image.

Third, a company is pointed out who reject this false worship and remain loyal to God.

The rise of this beast and its evil work are thus described in Revelation 13: 1-8: "And I stood upon the sand of the sea, and saw a beast rise up out of the sea, having seven heads and ten horns, and upon his horns ten crowns, and upon his

The prophet John saw a beast with seven heads rise up out of the sea.

heads the name of blasphemy. . . . And there was given unto him a mouth speaking great things and blasphemies. . . . And he opened his mouth in blasphemy against God, to blaspheme His name, and His tabernacle, and them that dwell in heaven. . . . And it was given unto him to make war with the saints, and to overcome them: and power was given him over all kindreds, and tongues, and nations. And all that dwell upon the earth shall worship him, whose names are not written in the book of life of the Lamb slain from the foundation of the world."

In prophecy the seas, or waters, are used as symbols of peoples and nations of the earth. (See Revelation 17:15.) A beast represents a worldly power or kingdom. (See Daniel 7.) Usually a political, or civil power is thus symbolized, but sometimes a beast represents a power both civil and religious, or a government in which church and state are united.

The beast of our text must symbolize a power in which the religious element predominates. It binds upon its followers a system of worship contrary to God's commands, for the wrath of God and awful punishments are pronounced against those who participate in that worship.

In all the Bible there is but one power brought to view which can meet the foregoing specifications. It is the power which had its rise in the apostasy of the early centuries. (See chapter, "Great Tribulation," pp. 105-111 of this book.) It is papal Rome,—the embodiment of the "mystery of iniquity" referred to by Paul in 2 Thessalonians 2:7. It is "MYSTERY, BABYLON THE GREAT, THE MOTHER OF HARLOTS AND ABOMINATIONS OF THE EARTH" described by John in Revelation 17:5.

This power assumes the authority to forgive sins, and claims for its head the names and attributes of deity. These prerogatives God has reserved to Himself, and their assumption by any man or people is the acme of blasphemy.

Rome, under its papal phase, became also the most relentless persecutor of the faithful followers of Jesus that the world has ever known. The blood of tens of millions of martyrs witnesses to this fact.

And John tells us that all the world, except the few who remain true to God, shall yet bow in worship before this power. (See "The Second Angel's Message," pp. 258-264.)

An image is a similitude or likeness of some original after which it is modeled. An image of the papal beast must be a body composed of, or derived from, other professedly religious organizations which hold to distinguishing errors promulgated by the system designated as the beast. In fact, the image does practically the same evil things done by the beast of which it is a likeness.

The beast of the third angel's message is the same as Babylon of Revelation 17:5, the fallen daughters of whom, bearing the same family name, and doing a similar work, are brought to view in the second angel's message of Revelation 14:8. Both these scriptures refer to the same great apostasy.

When the second angel proclaimed his message, the various churches of Christendom were closely identified with Babylon, all holding errors derived from the "mother church." When the light of that message was rejected, those churches became the fallen, harlot daughters of their Babylonian mother. Having thus fallen, they become more and more like their mother, until by an unholy alliance with the civil power they develop an image, or likeness of the beast against the worship of which the third angel utters his solemn and awful warning:

"If any man worship the beast and his image, and receive his mark in his forehead, or in his hand, the same shall drink of the wine of the wrath of God, which is poured out without mixture into the cup of His indignation." Revelation 14:9, 10. Fearful the fate of him who allows himself to be led into error by this deceitful power.

The attention of John is then called to another company whose members have not joined in the great apostasy of Babylon. Of them he says, "Here is the patience of the saints: here are they that keep the commandments of God, and the faith of Jesus." Revelation 14:12.

This company did not share in the moral fall of Babylon as announced in the second angel's message, and as repeated in Revelation 18:2. The announcement made in this text is followed by a "voice from heaven, saying, Come out of her, My people, that ye be not partakers of her sins, and that ye receive not of her plagues." (V. 4.) For an explanation of the moral and spiritual fall which did take place at, and subsequent to, the message of the second angel, see references in chapters of this book, "The Second Angel's Message," pp. 258-264, and, "Iniquity Shall Abound," pp. 140-156.)

The feature which distinguishes and separates this people from Babylon is evidently "the commandments of God." These they hold in reverence and obey, while others regard them lightly and openly trample upon them. The inference of the text is plain; Babylon has rejected the law of God, by rejecting some of its precepts. "For whosoever shall keep the whole law, and yet offend in one point, he is guilty of all." James 2: 10.

It is a lamentable fact that the binding claims of God's law, as recorded in the twentieth chapter of Exodus, are being held more and more lightly as the years go by. This is true not only of the rank and file of professed Christians, but of ministers, and even more forcibly of instructors in the schools of theology. Thus open and defiant rebellion against God is the answer by the professed Christianity of today to the message of the second angel of Revelation 14: 8,—"Babylon is fallen." And Babylon sinks lower and still lower continually until in the language of Revelation 18: 2, she becomes "the habitation of devils, and the hold of every foul spirit, and a cage of every unclean and hateful bird." And with mighty power and with telling effect the message is repeated, "Come out of her, My people."

When Adam fell, two ways were open for the salvation of the race. Either God's law must be amended to meet the changed condition of man, or One who is equal with the Author of law must bear the guilt of man's transgression and thus open a way of escape to the penitent sinner.

The first proposition was not possible, for God cannot deny Himself. The principles of His law are as broad as the universe and as unchangeable as the Creator himself. God was right, and His law was right. God could not change; He says, "I am the Lord, I change not." Malachi 3:6. Neither could He change His law without stultifying Himself and destroying the principles of His own government. Such a change would be to bring evil into the whole universe which He had created. To cut off every possibility of such a thought He states plainly, "My covenant will I not break, nor alter the thing that has gone out of My lips." Psalm 89:34. While the covenant here introduced may refer in its restricted sense to the covenant made with David, yet the statement is true in a broader sense of the covenant of God's law which He makes the foundation of every other covenant or promise. For God to alter His law would be to destroy Himself and His government—a thing unthinkable.

God's "covenant" is His law. This application is made plain in the account of the giving of the law on Sinai: "And He wrote upon the tables the words of the *covenant*, the *ten commandments*." Exodus 34:28. And again, "He declared unto you His *covenant*, which He commanded you to perform, even *ten commandments*; and He wrote them upon two tables of stone." Deuteronomy 4:13.

The Ruler of the universe is very jealous for His law. It represents His government. David recognized this when He wrote, "Thou hast magnified Thy word above all Thy name." Psalm 138:2.

To change God's law would mean that God's government was defective. As God's word, or law, could not be changed, Christ, taking the place of sinful man, must suffer in order to save him from the penalty of sin. Thus the alternative was met squarely. God could not change His law; man must be saved; hence the death of Christ. If any other way could have been provided, Infinite Wisdom would have searched it out. In the death of Christ, God's law was vindicated, and a way of escape was opened for mankind.

But notwithstanding the death of Christ in vindication of the divine law, from the pulpit, from the rostrums of theological schools, and in the columns of religious papers it is taught that the Old Testament is obsolete, and God's law abolished!

And yet, thirty-five years this side the crucifixion, Paul wrote to Timothy, "From a child thou hast known the holy Scriptures, which are able to make thee wise unto salvation through faith which is in Christ Jesus. All Scripture is given by inspiration of God, and is profitable for doctrine, for reproof, for correction, for instruction in righteousness: that the man of God may be perfect, throughly furnished unto all good works." 2 Timothy 3: 15-17.

It will be remembered that the New Testament was not written in the days when Timothy was a student. All the Scripture which he had to study was the Old Testament. Yet Paul tells this young minister that what he had studied embraced all the elements necessary to furnish him "unto all good works." The Old Testament contains all the truths of the gospel. The New Testament elaborates and makes clearer these truths, and presents an actual dead, risen, and living Saviour as foretold by the prophets of the Old Testament. We thank God for the Old Testament; we thank Him for the New Testament; we thank Him for a whole, complete, harmonious Bible.

Of those who would discredit and destroy the divine law, David wrote, "It is time for Thee, Lord, to work; for they have made void Thy law." Psalm 119: 126.

And our Saviour, in His sermon on the mount, speaking of the unchanging nature of that law, says, "Think not that I am come to destroy the law, or the prophets: I am not come to destroy, but to fulfill. For verily I say unto you, Till heaven and earth pass, one jot or one tittle shall in no wise pass from the law, till all be fulfilled." Matthew 5: 17, 18.

Again Paul, in his argument to the Romans upon the binding claims of the law, sums up with the statement: "Wherefore the law is holy, and the commandment holy, and just, and good." Romans 7: 12.

The following from "Great Controversy," pp. 583, 584, vividly shows the result of rejecting the law of God:

"In rejecting the truth, men reject its Author. In trampling upon the law of God, they deny the authority of the Lawgiver. It is as easy to make an idol of false doctrines and theories as to fashion an idol of wood or stone. By misrepresenting the attributes of God, Satan leads men to conceive of Him in a false character. With many, a philosophical idol is enthroned in the place of Jehovah; while the living God, as He is revealed in His word, in Christ, and in the works of creation, is worshiped by but few.

"Thousands deify nature, while they deny the God of nature. Though in a different form, idolatry exists in the Christian world today as verily as it existed among ancient Israel in the days of Elijah. The god of many professedly wise men, of philosophers, poets, politicians, journalists,— the god of polished fashionable circles, of many colleges and universities, even of some theological institutions,— is little better than Baal, the sun-god of Phœnicia.

"No error accepted by the Christian world strikes more boldly against the authority of heaven, none is more directly opposed to the dictates of reason, none is more pernicious in its results, than the modern doctrine, so rapidly gaining ground, that God's law is no longer binding upon men. Every nation has its laws, which command respect and obedience; no government could exist without them; and can it be conceived that the Creator of the heavens and the earth has no law to govern the beings He has made?

The Third Angel's Message

"Suppose that prominent ministers were publicly to teach that the statutes which govern their land and protect the rights of its citizens were not obligatory,— that they restricted the liberties of the people, and therefore ought not to be obeyed; how long would such men be tolerated in the pulpit? But is it a graver offense to disregard the laws of states and nations than to trample upon those divine precepts which are the foundation of all government?

"It would be far more consistent for nations to abolish their statutes, and permit the people to do as they please, than for the Ruler of the universe to annul His law, and leave the world without a standard to condemn the guilty or justify the obedient. Would we know the result of making void the law of God? The experiment has been tried. Terrible were the scenes enacted in France when atheism became the controlling power. It was then demonstrated to the world that to throw off the restraints which God has imposed is to accept the rule of the cruelest of tyrants. When the standard of righteousness is set aside, the way is open for the prince of evil to establish his power in the earth."

When Christ comes He will vindicate the law, and terribly punish its enemies and those who have thought to change it. The third angel declares that they "shall be tormented with fire and brimstone."

Of their punishment the prophet Isaiah writes, "For the indignation of the Lord is upon all nations, and His fury upon all their armies: He hath utterly destroyed them, He hath delivered them to the slaughter. Their slain also shall be cast out, and their stink shall come up out of their carcases, and the mountains shall be melted with their blood. . . .

"For it is the day of the Lord's vengeance, and the year of recompenses for the controversy of Zion. And the streams thereof shall be turned into pitch, and the dust thereof into brimstone, and the land thereof shall become burning pitch." Isaiah 34: 2-9.

In Revelation 18, John recounts the sins of modern Babylon, and shows her final doom: "Therefore shall her plagues come in one day, death, and mourning, and famine; and she shall be utterly burned with fire: for strong is the Lord God who judgeth her." V. 8.

Why this awful destruction? "They have transgressed the laws, changed the ordinance, broken the everlasting covenant. Therefore hath the curse devoured the earth, and they that dwell therein are desolate: therefore the inhabitants of the earth are burned." Isaiah 24: 5, 6.

Sabbath Rest

EARNEST warnings are given in Isaiah 58. To the watchmen God says, "Cry aloud, spare not, lift up thy voice like a trumpet, and show My people their transgressions, and the house of Jacob their sins. Yet they seek Me daily, and delight to know My ways, as a nation that did righteousness, and forsook not the ordinances of their God." They fast for "strife and debate," and "smite with the fist of wickedness." (See vs. 2-4.) But God calls them to repentance.

"And they that shall be of thee shall build the old waste places: thou shalt raise up the foundations of many generations; thou shalt be called, The repairer of the breach, The restorer of paths to dwell in." V. 12.

What "paths" will they "restore"? What "breach" will they "repair"? What "foundations" that have lain unimproved for "many generations" will they "raise up"? The answers to these questions will be found in the following verses:

"If thou turn away thy foot from the Sabbath, from doing thy pleasure on My holy day; and call the Sabbath a delight, the holy of the Lord, honorable; and shalt honor Him, not doing thine own ways, nor finding thine own pleasure, nor speaking thine own words: then shalt thou delight thyself in the Lord; and I will cause thee to ride upon the high places of the earth, and feed thee with the heritage of Jacob thy father: for the mouth of the Lord hath spoken it." Vs. 13, 14.

The lessons of this chapter are plain. In verses 1-7 a class of professed followers of God is introduced, but they have forsaken the ordinance of their God, and their religion is largely a man-made form. Of them, this same prophet writes, "They have transgressed the laws, changed the ordinance, broken the everlasting covenant." Isaiah 24: 5.

What ordinance of God's law has been so treated? Chapter 58: 13 shows plainly that it is the Sabbath commandment. This Sabbath was instituted at creation to commemorate that great work:

"Thus the heavens and the earth were finished, and all

Sabbath rest and worship

the host of them. And on the seventh day God ended His work which He had made; and He rested on the seventh day from all His work which He had made. And God blessed the seventh day, and sanctified it: because that in it He had rested from all His work which God created and made." Genesis 2: 1-3. To sanctify is to set apart to a holy or religious use.

And when the great moral law of ten commandments was given at Sinai, the Sabbath of the Lord was made the heart of that law.

Sabbath Rest

"Remember the Sabbath day, to keep it holy. Six days shalt thou labor, and do all thy work: but the seventh day is the Sabbath of the Lord thy God: in it thou shalt not do any work, thou, nor thy son, nor thy daughter, thy manservant, nor thy maidservant, nor thy cattle, nor thy stranger that is within thy gates: for in six days the Lord made heaven and earth, the sea, and all that in them is, and rested the seventh day: wherefore the Lord blessed the Sabbath day, and hallowed it." Exodus 20: 8-11.

But we now see almost the whole Christian world observing the first day of the week instead of the seventh — the Sabbath of Jehovah. They certainly have forsaken the Sabbath "ordinance," or, as expressed in Isaiah 24: 5, "changed the ordinance, broken the everlasting covenant."

But a people will arise who shall "build the old waste places," and "raise up the foundations of many generations." There will be a company that will respect the law of God, and honor His Sabbath.

For nearly fourteen centuries ("many generations") has papal Rome pressed its counterfeit Sabbath upon the world, presenting it as the badge of its authority. So successful has been its work that nearly the whole Christian world has accepted this symbol of the Papacy, and rejoices in it. Neither the Reformation nor the advancing light upon God's word has broken its hold.

To evade the claims of the divine law, while enforcing the observance of the false Sabbath, this power reconstructed the ten commandments to suit its purpose. On the following page, in parallel columns, is given the law of God as spoken on Sinai, and the same as amended by the Papacy.

In the amended version of the law it will be seen that the second commandment is omitted in order to allow the worship of images; the fourth is so changed as to remove from it every vestige of the true Sabbath; and the tenth is divided

THE LAW OF GOD

As Given by Jehovah

'I will not alter the thing that is gone out of My lips.'

I.
Thou shalt have no other gods before Me.

II.
Thou shalt not make unto thee any graven image, or any likeness of anything that is in heaven above, or that is in the earth beneath, or that is in the water under the earth; thou shalt not bow down thyself to them, nor serve them; for I the Lord thy God am a jealous God, visiting the iniquity of the fathers upon the children unto the third and fourth generation of them that hate Me, and showing mercy unto thousands of them that love Me, and keep My commandments.

III.
Thou shalt not take the name of the Lord thy God in vain; for the Lord will not hold him guiltless that taketh His name in vain.

IV.
Remember the Sabbath day to keep it holy. Six days shalt thou labor, and do all thy work; but the seventh day is the Sabbath of the Lord thy God: in it thou shalt not do any work, thou, nor thy son, nor thy daughter, thy manservant, nor thy maidservant, nor thy cattle, nor thy stranger that is within thy gates; for in six days the Lord made heaven and earth, the sea, and all that in them is, and rested the seventh day; wherefore the Lord blessed the Sabbath day, and hallowed it.

V.
Honor thy father and thy mother, that thy days may be long upon the land which the Lord thy God giveth thee.

VI.
Thou shalt not kill.

VII.
Thou shalt not commit adultery.

VIII.
Thou shalt not steal.

IX.
Thou shalt not bear false witness against thy neighbor.

X.
Thou shalt not covet thy neighbor's house, thou shalt not covet thy neighbor's wife, nor his manservant, nor his maidservant, nor his ox, nor his ass, nor any thing that is thy neighbor's.

(*See Exodus 20: 3-17.*)

As Changed by Man

"He shall think himself able to change times and laws."__ Daniel 7: 25.
Douay Bible.

I.
I am the Lord thy God: thou shalt not have strange gods before Me.

II.
Thou shalt not take the name of the Lord thy God in vain.

III.
Remember thou keep holy the Sabbath day.

IV.
Honor thy father and thy mother.

V.
Thou shalt not kill.

VI.
Thou shalt not commit adultery.

VII.
Thou shalt not steal.

VIII.
Thou shalt not bear false witness.

IX.
Thou shalt not covet another's wife.

X.
Thou shalt not covet another's goods.

(*See "Larger Catechism," Translated from the Italian by Bishop Byrne, of Nashville, Tenn., copyright, 1906, or any Catholic Catechism.*)

to make up the number ten, because of the omission of the second.

The vision of Daniel was literally fulfilled, that this power shall "think to change times and laws." Daniel 7:25. And truly it can be said, "They have transgressed the laws, changed the ordinance, broken the everlasting covenant." Isaiah 24:5.

And as the Protestant churches were formed as the result of the great Reformation of the sixteenth century, they brought with them many of the errors of the Dark Ages, prominent among which is the Sunday Sabbath. And while denouncing the Papacy they have clung, and are clinging, to the first-day Sabbath which the Papacy puts forth as the evidence of its authority, as shown from the following quotations from their own publications:

"*Ques.*—How prove you that the church hath power to command feasts and holy days?

"*Ans.*—By the very act of changing the Sabbath into Sunday, which Protestants allow of; and therefore they fondly contradict themselves, by keeping Sunday strictly, and breaking most other feasts commanded by the same church."—"*Abridgment of Christian Doctrine,*" *p. 58.*

"*Ques.*—Have you any other way of proving that the church has power to institute festivals of precept?

"*Ans.*—Had she not such power, she could not have done that in which all modern religionists agree with her,—she could not have substituted the observance of Sunday, the first day of the week, for the observance of Saturday, the seventh day, a change for which there is no Scriptural authority."—"*Doctrinal Catechism,*" *p. 351.*

Are the foregoing claims true or false? How do the Sunday-keeping Protestant churches relate themselves to this question?

The following by Rev. Isaac Williams, B. D., represents the sentiments of the Protestant Episcopal Church of Europe and America:

"There are some points of great difficulty respecting the fourth commandment; and wherever there is any difficulty in Scripture, we may be sure that it is intended to draw our attentive consideration to it, as a matter of great importance and profit.

"In the first place we are commanded to keep holy the seventh day; but yet we do not think it necessary to keep the seventh day holy; for the seventh day is Saturday. It may be said that we keep the first day instead; but then surely this is not the same thing; the first day cannot be the seventh day; and where are we told in Scripture that we are to keep the first day at all? We are commanded to keep the seventh; but we are nowhere commanded to keep the first.

"There is another difficulty on this subject; we Christians, in considering each of the commandments, turn to what our Lord says in explanation of them; for in the Sermon on the Mount, He says, that 'not one jot or tittle of the law shall fail,' that He has come 'not to destroy, but to fulfill the law'; and then He shows in the instances of the sixth, seventh, and third commandments, how He will require them to be fulfilled by Christians, not in the letter only, but in the spirit, in the heart and thoughts, far more strictly than the Jews thought it necessary. . . .

"How is it that the observance of the seventh day is done away with, although there is no warrant in Holy Scriptures for doing so? . . . The reason why we keep the first day of the week holy instead of the seventh is for the same reason that we observe many other things, not because the Bible, but because the church, has enjoined it."—*"The Church Catechism," pp. 333-336.*

There is no point of difficulty, as suggested above, respecting the fourth commandment when we surrender our will to God and obey His law. The only difficulty to be met is where men cling to the first-day Sabbath of the Papacy, and then attempt to justify such a course. In the foregoing quotations the same stand is taken that is taken by the Catholics, and, acknowledging that they have no Bible proof for the Sunday Sabbath, the whole responsibility

Sabbath Rest

for the observance of the day is placed upon the church. But there *is* a serious difficulty to be met by those who assume such an attitude. In the days of Christ the Jews had accepted tradition to the extent of making void the precepts of Jehovah.

At one time the Pharisees asked Jesus, "Why do Thy disciples transgress the tradition of the elders?" He answered, "Why do ye also transgress the commandment of God by your tradition?" He then states the condition of those who do this: "In vain they do worship Me, teaching for doctrines the commandments of men." Matthew 15: 9.

This principle holds good in this generation as well as in the days of Christ. By their own statement Sunday worshipers stand condemned as holding to a man-made institution contrary to God's command, simply and only "because the church has enjoined it." Christ says that "in vain" do such "worship Me."

In a book by Rev. Amos Binney and Rev. Daniel Steele, D. D., issued by the Methodist Episcopal Publishing House, under the heading, "The Sabbath," occur the following statements:

"By this [the Sabbath] is meant,

"1. The day appointed of God, at the close of creation, to be observed by man as a day of rest from all secular employment, because that in it God himself had rested from His work. (Genesis 2: 1-3.) Not that God's rest was necessitated by fatigue (Isaiah 40: 28); but He rested, that is, ceased to work, on the seventh day as an example to man; hence assigned it as a reason why man should rest on that day (Exodus 20: 11; 31: 17). God's blessing and sanctifying the day, meant that He separated it from a common to a religious use, to be a perpetual memorial or sign that all who thus observed it would show themselves to be the worshipers of that God who made the world in six days and rested on the seventh. (Exodus 20: 8, 11; 31: 16, 17; Isaiah 56: 6, 7.)

"2. The Sabbath is indispensable to man, being promotive of his highest good, physically, intellectually, socially, spiritually, and eternally. Hence its observance is connected with the best of promises, and its violation with the severest penalties. (Exodus 23:12; 31:12-18; Nehemiah 13:15-22; Isaiah 56:2-7; 58:13, 14; Jeremiah 17:21-27; Ezekiel 20:12, 13; 22:26-31.) Its sanctity was very distinctly marked in the gathering of the manna. (Exodus 16:22-30.)

"3. The original law of the Sabbath was renewed and made a prominent part of the moral law, or ten commandments, given through Moses at Sinai. (Exodus 20:8-11.)

"4. This seventh-day Sabbath was strictly observed by Christ and His apostles previous to His crucifixion. (Mark 6:2; Luke 4:16, 31; 13:10; Acts 1:12-14; 13:14, 42, 44; 17:2; 18:4.)

"5. Jesus, after His resurrection, changed the Sabbath from the seventh to the first day of the week; thus showing His authority as Lord even of the Sabbath, (Matthew 12:8); not to abrogate or break it, but to preside over and modify, or give new form to it, so as to have it commemorate His resurrection, when He ceased from His redeeming work as God did from His creation work (Hebrews 4:10).

"When Jesus gave instructions for this change we are not told, but very likely during the time when He spake to His apostles of the things pertaining to His kingdom. (Acts 1:3.) This is probably one of the many unrecorded things which Jesus did. (John 20:30; 21:25.)

"6. That the Sabbath was actually changed from the seventh to the first day of the week appears from the example of the apostles, who, after the resurrection of Christ, celebrated the first day as the Sabbath. (John 20:19, 26; Acts 20:7; 1 Corinthians 16:2.) Hence this is called the *Lord's* day. (Revelation 1:10.)"—*"Binney's Theological Compend,"* pp. 169-171.

No just criticism can be offered to the first four of the propositions here quoted. They are logical, and unequivocally sustained by the word of God. No observer of the seventh-day Sabbath could state them more clearly. But from that point the arguments are illogical, the positions untenable, and the statements untrue as to fact.

Jesus did not, as affirmed in proposition five, change the Sabbath, either before or after His resurrection. No shred of evidence can be found, either in the words of Christ or the history or teaching of the apostles, to substantiate such a proposition.

God's law *could not be changed.* All efforts to do so are but man-made, and do not affect its validity. But more; if it had been or could have been changed, the record of such change would of necessity have been as clear and positive as the record of making it and the commandment enforcing it.

The author of this proposition undoubtedly gave the best argument he had, namely, "This [the announcement of the change of the Sabbath] is *probably one of the many unrecorded things which Jesus did.*" But, are we willing to meet our God and Judge over His broken law with as flimsy an excuse as this for disregarding the Sabbath of the fourth commandment?

At the close of the fifth proposition a contrast is drawn between Christ the Redeemer and God the Creator, which in fact does not exist, since Christ is Creator as well as Redeemer. One text makes this truth plain: "He was in the world, and the world was made by Him, and the world knew Him not." John 1: 10.

As to the example of the apostles brought out in proposition six, the texts quoted contain no proof whatever that the disciples observed the first day of the week as the Sabbath. Let us examine them.

The first text referred to is John 20: 19: "Then the same day at evening, being the first day of the week, when the doors were shut where the disciples were assembled *for fear of the Jews*, came Jesus and stood in the midst, and saith unto them, Peace be unto you."

This was at the close of the day of the resurrection. The disciples did not believe that Jesus had been raised, so this could not have been a meeting to commemorate that event. They were not holding a religious meeting, as some have supposed, but were simply together in their own hired room where they lodged and took their meals, as we learn from Acts 1: 13. (See Mark 16: 11; Luke 24: 37.) The statement is often made that Jesus came to this "meeting" with a benediction because of their assembling on this first new Sabbath. But this is not the case. He "upbraided them with their unbelief" in His resurrection. (Mark 16: 14.) In the plain words of the text they had retired into that upper room because it was for the time being their home, and under the circumstances they spent more time there than they had formerly done "for fear of the Jews," and not to commemorate the resurrection of their Saviour, in which they did not believe.

The second text is John 20: 26: "And after eight days again His disciples were within, and Thomas with them: then came Jesus, the doors being shut, and stood in the midst, and said, Peace be unto you."

It is claimed that this was the Sunday after the first meeting. But the veriest school boy will tell you that eight days from Sunday is Monday. "After eight days" may have been Tuesday or any other day so far as the wording of the text goes. It certainly could not have been seven days,—the next Sunday.

The third text is Acts 20: 7: "And upon the first day of the week, when the disciples came together to break bread, Paul preached unto them, ready to depart on the morrow; and continued his speech until midnight." This is the only New Testament instance of a religious meeting on the first day.

This text is presented as a link in the chain of evidence showing that it was the custom of the apostles to meet on the first day of the week for religious worship. Hence, in some "unrecorded" way, this day *must* have become the Christian Sabbath in the place of the seventh day of the fourth commandment.

Not stopping to question the soundness of the argument,

Paul preached till daybreak and the next day walked nineteen miles.

we ask, When did this meeting occur? It was a night meeting, for "there were many lights in the upper chamber, where they were gathered together." (V. 8.) And it was "upon the first day of the week." (V. 7.)

When did the "first day" begin? "And the evening and the morning were the first day." Genesis 1: 5. This is the way God started the weekly cycle for this earth. The Jews knew of no other way. When the sun sets one day, that day is ended and the next one begins. "From even unto even, shall ye celebrate your Sabbath." Leviticus 23: 32. Hence there could not have been a night meeting on the first day of the week except on the night following the seventh.

This was Paul's farewell meeting with the church at Troas. He preached all night, and on Sunday morning started on his long walk of nineteen miles to meet the ship which had gone before to Assos. This shows conclusively that Paul did not attach any sacredness to the day.

The following diagram will explain Paul's movements:

FIRST DAY OF THE WEEK, OR SUNDAY

In the evening, or dark part, Paul preached all night.	In the morning, or light part, Paul went on foot to Assos.

"AND THE EVENING - - - - - - AND THE MORNING WERE THE FIRST DAY." GENESIS 1: 5.

It is easy to see that the time of Paul's meeting at Troas was simply a matter of convenience, and not because the day was the Sabbath.

We are not alone in our understanding of the circumstances of this text, as the following quotations will show:

"The sole doubt will be what evening this was. . . . For my own part I conceive clearly that it was upon Saturday night, as we falsely call it, and not on the coming Sunday night. . . . Because St. Luke records that it was upon the first day of the week when this meeting was. . . . Therefore it must needs be on the Saturday, not on our Sunday evening, since the Sunday evening in St. Luke's and the Scripture account was no part of the first, but of the second day, the day ever beginning and ending at evening."—*William Prynne, in "Dissertation of the Lord's Day Sabbath," pp. 36-41, A. D. 1633.*

"It was in the evening which succeeded the Jewish Sabbath."—*Conybeare and Howson's "Life of Paul," p. 626, people's edition, 1878.*

"I conclude, therefore, that the brethren met on the night after the Jewish Sabbath. . . . On Sunday morning, Paul and his companions resumed their journey." —*Prof. McGarvey, "Commentary on Acts."*

The fourth text is 1 Corinthians 16: 2: "Upon the first day of the week let every one of you lay by him in store, as God hath prospered him."

It is claimed that this text refers to a collection to be taken at the public meetings held upon the newly-made first-day Sabbath. But unfortunately for this argument, such an interpretation does violence to the text. "Lay by him in store" cannot possibly mean to put away from you into the contribution box.

Upon the proper rendering of the text Mr. J. W. Morton, former Presbyterian missionary to Haiti, bears the following testimony:

"The whole testimony turns upon the meaning of the expression, 'by him'; and I marvel greatly how you can imagine that it means 'in the collection box of the congregation.' Greenfield, in his lexicon, translates the Greek term, *'With one's self, i. e., at home.'* Two Latin versions, the Vulgate and that of Castellio, render it *'apud se,'* with one's self; at home. Three French translations, those of Martin, Osterwald, and De Sacy, *'chez soi,'* at his own house; at home. The German of Luther, *'bei sich selbst,'* by himself; at home. The Dutch, *'by hemselven,'* same as the German. The Italian of Diodati, *'appresso di se,'* in his own presence; at home. The Spanish of Fileppe Scio, *'en su casa,'* in his own house. The Portuguese of Ferreira, *'para isso,'* with himself. The Swedish, *'near sig self,'* near himself."

The fifth text is Revelation 1: 10: "I was in the Spirit on the Lord's day."

It is assumed that the "Lord's day" in the text is Sunday, and so Sunday must be the Sabbath. But this is assuming a point that should be proved. What day is the Lord's day?—"The seventh day is the Sabbath of the Lord thy God." Exodus 20: 10. "If thou turn away thy foot from the Sabbath, from doing thy pleasure on *My* holy day." Isaiah 58: 13. "Therefore the Son of man is Lord also of the

Sabbath." Mark 2: 28. Why is Christ Lord of the Sabbath?—Because He made it. "All things were made by Him; and without Him was not anything made that was made." "He was in the world, and the world was made by Him." John 1: 3, 10. (See also Col. 1: 16.)

It was the word spoken by Christ which created the world. Then it is Christ of whom it is said, "For in six days the Lord made heaven and earth, the sea, and all that in them is, and rested the seventh day; wherefore the Lord blessed the Sabbath day, and hallowed it." Exodus 20: 11.

It was Christ who made the earth "in six days." It was Christ who "rested the seventh day." It was Christ who "blessed the Sabbath day and hallowed it." And for these reasons He is "Lord also of the Sabbath." Nowhere in the Bible is any other day than the Sabbath of the commandment called the "Lord's day." This text proves that, far away on the Isle of Patmos, the beloved disciple observed and reverenced the day which the Lord made at creation, and has always called His own; and which He requires all men now to regard and observe as "a delight, the holy of the Lord, honorable," because it is His holy, blessed, sanctified day.

In a book by Rev. J. Q. Bittinger, published by the Congregational Sunday-school and Publishing Society, the following statements occur:

> "Christ's endorsement of the Decalogue must be accepted as revealing His view of the permanency of the Sabbath. This endorsement is several times repeated. In the opening part of the Sermon on the Mount He uses this language: 'Think not that I am come to destroy the law, or the prophets: I am not come to destroy, but to fulfill.' The 'law and the prophets' is understood as denoting the Old Testament. . . .
>
> "But any lingering doubt of Christ's position on the Sabbath is put to rest by His own express words—'The

Sabbath was made for man,' not for man in any limited period or in any stage of his history, but for man universally and always. The Sabbath can never cease to be a memorial of divine rest. . . .

"Many works of beneficence were done on the Sabbath, which brought the day into prominent discussion. The Gospels, accordingly, abound in frequent reference to the subject. A different state of things existed when the Epistles were written.

"There did not seem to be any special occasion for calling attention to the Sabbath. The day was kept. Its validity was not questioned. . . . Paul, in his Epistle to the Romans is expounding the doctrine of justification by faith. Why should he canvass the Sabbath question? And yet in this discussion the law necessarily forms a prominent feature. Is there any reason for believing that he did not hold the law intact? Or that he emasculated it by taking from it a single precept? 'Do we then make void the law through faith? God forbid: yea, we establish the law.' Romans 3: 31. Subsequently he cites some of the provisions of this law, and sums up the whole in the exact language of the Great Master,—'And if there be any other commandment, it is briefly comprehended in this saying, namely, Thou shalt love thy neighbor as thyself.' . . . (Romans 13: 9.)

"In ancient writers frequent mention is made of religious assemblies on Saturday. Athanasius says, 'They met on the Sabbath, not that they were infected with Judaism, but to worship Jesus, the Lord of the Sabbath.' . . .

"The obligation of the Sabbath law comes to us from the Old Testament, and in the New this obligation is not annulled. Neither the Old nor the New leave any standing ground for those who maintain that the Sabbath was a temporary arrangement, to serve a special purpose, or to meet a special emergency. But we find it ordained from the first, imbedded in the Decalogue on an equal footing with the other commands, accepted and obeyed by Christ and His disciples, and maintained by the entire Christian church, as perpetually obligatory upon man. Not a word is said, or even hinted, that the day was annulled or set aside."—"*A Plea for the Sabbath and for Man,*" *pp. 87, 88, 90-92, 96, 97*.

Be it remembered, that the preceding quotation is taken from the pages of a book advocating the observance of Sunday as the Sabbath. Yet after the clear statements of such grand truths, by some legerdemain, no one seems to know how, the Sabbath of the law, so strenuously maintained throughout, is transferred from the seventh to she first.

With a law which cannot be done away, with a Sabbath instituted for the express and only purpose of celebrating the great work of creation, and with this Sabbath imbedded in the very heart of an immutable law, and with no evidence that any change was made by Christ or the apostles, how can arguments for another day be maintained in the same book? How can modern Sunday keepers be satisfied with the excuse of the Papacy, "because the church has enjoined it"? The first-day Sabbath is frankly acknowledged to be a man-made institution, therefore those who observe it come under the Saviour's stern rebuke, "In vain they do worship Me, teaching for doctrines the commandments of men." Matthew 15:9.

The following statements are from the pen of W. W. Everts, D. D., Presbyterian, regarding the Sabbath:

"To guard the inviolability of His laws, God had signally punished Saul, Nabab, and Abihu. How then could He have been pleased with the substitution of the first for the seventh day, if not provided for in His new revelation? How can the apostles have encouraged by precept and example the observance of the Lord's Day, if set apart without divine authority, while warning the churches against the bondage of merely human appointment? . . .

"But clear apostolic example abundantly justifies the universal substitution of the first for the seventh as the Christian Sabbath. This change may have been one of the things pertaining to the kingdom of God, concerning which Luke tells us Jesus spoke to His disciples after the resurrection."—*"The Sabbath: Its Permanence, Promise, and Defence," pp. 50-52.*

Such argument is vain and even self-condemnatory, revealing as it does some sense of the sacredness and unchanging character of the divine law. How dare men, with the open Bible in their hands, reason thus? In vain do we ask to be cited to this "apostolic example" which so "abundantly justifies the universal substitution of the first for the seventh as the Christian Sabbath." The authors of books published by different denominations of Sunday keepers, as previously quoted, unite in the acknowledgement that there is no Bible authority for the change of the Sabbath.

Yet notwithstanding the admitted fact that there is no Bible evidence of any change, and notwithstanding evidence is all against the supposition that any such change was ever made by divine authority, men are so wedded to the false Sabbath that in sheer desperation they tell us that it "*may be* one of those unrecorded things which Luke says Jesus told His disciples."

As evidence that the apostles regarded Sunday as sacred, we are cited to the fact that they held religious meetings upon that day. But how many meetings did they ever hold upon Sunday so far as the record goes? Only one; namely, Paul's farewell meeting at Troas, upon the dark part of the first day, corresponding to our Saturday night. No sacredness was asserted as belonging to the day. It was only a casual meeting, as we might meet Wednesday night for prayer and social meeting, or on any other day which the conditions would make convenient or necessary.

In addition to this lone meeting at Troas it is sometimes urged that Christ "uniformly met with His disciples upon the first day of the week after His resurrection." But how often did He so "meet with them"?—Not once as that term

Autotype Fine Art Co., Ltd.
Paul preached to the Gentiles on the Sabbath at Antioch.

is generally understood; a meeting presupposes appointment or previous arrangement. But these so-called meetings were rather appearances. Upon the day of His resurrection, Jesus "appeared first to Mary Magdalene." Mark 16: 9. "After that He appeared in another form unto two of them, as they walked, and went into the country." Verse 12. "Afterward He appeared unto the eleven as they sat at meat, and upbraided them with their unbelief and hardness of heart, because they believed not them which had seen Him after He was risen." Verse 14. These appearances all occurred upon the same first day, namely, the day of the resurrection, and not one of them was upon the occasion of a religious meeting, but incidentally as the disciples were following their usual bent, not even believing that the Saviour was risen.

The weekly Sabbath, whenever referred to in the New Testament, always means the seventh day, or Saturday. Sunday is invariably spoken of as "the first day of the week." But the fact that Christ rose from the grave on Sunday, is offered by many as a reason for observing that day as the Sabbath.

But the Gospels were written at various dates after the resurrection, and show that at those times no change had been made in the Sabbath. Matthew about six years after, in writing of the resurrection, says: "In the end of the Sabbath, as it began to dawn toward the first day of the week, came Mary Magdalene and the other Mary to see the sepulcher." Matthew 28: 1. Here a sharp distinction is drawn between the Sabbath and "the first day."

Mark, about ten years after the event, writes: "And when the Sabbath was past, Mary Magdalene, and Mary the mother of James, and Salome, had bought sweet spices, that they might come and anoint Him. And very early in the morning the first day of the week, they came unto the sepulcher at the rising of the sun." Mark 16: 1, 2. Mark had not yet heard of any change in the Sabbath.

Luke, writing twenty-eight years after the resurrection, evidently knew of no change, for he says: "And they returned [from the burial of Christ], and prepared spices and ointments; and rested the Sabbath day *according to the commandment* [See Exodus 20: 8-11]. Now upon the first day of the week, very early in the morning, they came unto the sepulcher, bringing the spices which they had prepared, and certain others with them." Luke 23: 56; 24: 1.

The gospel of John is supposed to have been written sixty-three years after the resurrection. In chapter 19: 42 he speaks of laying the body of Jesus in the sepulcher on "the Jews' preparation day," which was Friday. Chapter 20: 1 passes over the intervening Sabbath and speaks of Sunday, the resurrection day, as "the first day of the week." He mentions it as we would any ordinary working day, on which they would be at perfect liberty to bring the spices and ointments prepared on Friday, and do the work necessary in caring for the body of their Lord as was the custom for their dead.

When Constantine made his famous decree, more than three hundred years after Christ, that all people in cities and villages should rest from work on the first day of the week, even he did not call it the Sabbath, but called it the "Venerable Day of the Sun"; from which heathen festival the name "Sunday" originated.

It was not till at least one thousand five hundred years after Christ that Sunday began to be called the Sabbath in common usage.

And in nearly all the old family Bibles occurs the accompanying table in which Saturday is

DAYS OF THE WEEK
1st day of the week Sunday
2nd day of the week Monday
3rd day of the week Tuesday

called the "seventh day, or the Sabbath."

So, clear down to the time when our old family Bibles were printed, it was accepted that the word Sabbath signified the seventh day, or Saturday.

4th day of the week Wednesday
5th day of the week Thursday
6th day of the week Friday
7th day of the week or Sabbath, Saturday

If the examples of the apostles be appealed to as evidence as to their understanding of this Sabbath question, we may be permitted to introduce the apostle Paul. In one of his famous tours through the Gentile churches, he came to Thessalonica, in Macedonia, "where was a synagogue of the Jews." Here he, "as his manner was, went in unto them, and three Sabbaths days reasoned with them out of the Scriptures." (Acts 17: 1, 2.)

At Antioch Paul preached to both the Jews and Gentiles on the Sabbath. (Acts 13: 14.) At the close of the discourse the Gentiles asked him to preach the same things to them the next Sabbath. (Verse 42.) And the next Sabbath nearly the whole city came out to hear him. (Verse 44.)

At Philippi Paul met the people on the Sabbath, and there preached to them. (Acts 16: 13.)

When Paul came to Corinth he made his home with Aquilla and Priscilla. "And because he was of the same craft, he abode with them, and wrought: for by their occupation they were tent-makers. And he reasoned in the synagogue *every Sabbath* and persuaded the Jews and the Greeks." Acts 18: 3, 4.

How long he continued his work at Corinth we do not know. It must have been many weeks, considering the work accomplished and the movement of other apostles as directed by Paul from that place.

Rev. J. Q. Bittinger, Congregationalist, in his book, "A Plea for the Sabbath," as previously quoted, speaking of the Sabbath in the days of the apostles as recorded in the Epistles, says: "There did not seem to be any special occasion for calling attention to the Sabbath. The day was kept. Its validity was not questioned."

Certainly apostolic example is with the Sabbath of Jehovah, given to commemorate the finished work of creation. So long as it remains a fact that God created the earth in six days and rested the seventh, just so long will it be that God's Sabbath memorial cannot be changed.

One more quotation will be added from first-day authors. It is from the pen of A. W. Weston, of the Disciple Church:

"The Lordian supper was instituted by the Saviour, whereas the Lordian Sabbath [Sunday] was not. . . .

"There was vastly greater propriety that the institutions designed for man to honor Christ, should originate with man himself. . . .

"We are not of those who think that either the value or the authority of the day depends upon divine command. . . .

"It [the Sunday Sabbath] is the day of all days, immensely, immeasurably, infinitely superior to the Sabbath in every lesson which it teaches."—*"Evolution of a Shadow,"* pp. 188, 190, 191, 200.

These statements have the appearance of the climax of defiance to the law of Jehovah, reaching closely to the borders of blasphemy. But the writer has only stated in plain terms the real position of others who reach the same conclusion in milder words.

Some day Jehovah will wonderfully surprise those who by specious words and defiant acts trample upon His holy day while offering in its stead a man-made institution. In thunder tones as at Sinai, He will demand of them, "Who hath required this at your hand?" "For whosoever shall keep the whole law, and yet offend in one point, he is guilty of all." James 2: 10.

A Sealing Message

"AND I saw another angel ascending from the east, having the seal of the living God: and he cried with a loud voice to the four angels, to whom it was given to hurt the earth and the sea, saying, Hurt not the earth, neither the sea, nor the trees, till we have sealed the servants of our God in their foreheads." Revelation 7: 2, 3.

The sealing work here introduced has its consummation at the close of probation. Then the last message of salvation has gone "to every nation, and kindred, and tongue, and people"; but it has been rejected by the many. Those who accept this message and are sanctified by it, are sealed for the kingdom. Then the door of mercy is closed, probation is ended, and the decree goes forth:

"He that is unjust, let him be unjust still: and he which is filthy, let him be filthy still: and he that is righteous, let him be righteous still: and he that is holy, let him be holy still." Revelation 22: 11.

The seal brought by the "angel ascending from the east," is to be placed upon the "foreheads" of the "servants of our God." It must, therefore, represent some message sent to them, the acceptance of which separates them from the world and marks them as God's peculiar people. The climax is reached when their obedience to this sealing message has fitted them for translation when Jesus comes. This work of sealing is the culmination of the threefold message of Revelation 14. It brings out a company staunch, tried, and true, of whom it is said, "Here is the patience of the saints: here are they that keep the commandments of God, and the faith of Jesus." V. 12. Their unquestioning obedience presents them to God as "more than conquerors through

Him that loved us." These characteristics become the badge, or seal, of their service to God.

The word *seal* in the original is defined as "a signet ring; a mark, stamp, badge; a token, a pledge." Webster defines the word as "an engraved or inscribed stamp, used for making impressions in wax or other soft substances, to be attached to a document, or otherwise used by way of authentication or security."

One author states that a seal is used "always in connection with some law or enactment that demands obedience, or upon documents that are to be made legal, or subject to the provisions of law. The idea of law is inseparable from a seal."

Most legal documents are not binding unless they bear the seal of the notary. The decrees of kings and governments require the seal of state to make them valid and obligatory. The seal attests the authenticity and authority of the document to which it is attached.

A record of God's law is found in the statute book of His word,— the Bible. On Sinai it was graven on tables of stone by the finger of God. Where in that code do we find the seal of the Lawgiver, giving His name, disclosing His identity, and stating His authority?

The first three commandments contain the name of *God*, but they do not designate who He is. Paul says, "There be gods many, and lords many." 1 Corinthians 8: 5. Idolaters can claim these precepts as the law of their gods of wood and stone. The heathen of Africa can claim them for the gods of their fetish worship. There is nothing to designate the true God in these three precepts.

Passing over the fourth commandment, the fifth contains the words, "Lord God," but does not in any way define them. The last five precepts do not contain the name of God at all.

A Sealing Message

Turning back to the fourth, we find the desired information: "For in six days the Lord made heaven and earth, the sea, and all that in them is."

One writer states that in the fourth commandment "the Author of this law has designated who He is, the extent of His dominion, and His right to rule; for every created intelligence must at once assent that He who is the Creator of all, has the right to demand obedience from all His creatures. Thus with the fourth commandment in its place, this wonderful document, the Decalogue, the only document among men which God ever wrote with His own finger, has a signature; it has that which renders it intelligible and authentic; it has a seal. But without the fourth commandment, it lacks all these things."

The Scriptures speak plainly as to this claim regarding the fourth commandment. The Lord said to Israel, "Verily My Sabbaths ye shall keep: for *it is a sign between Me and you* throughout your generations; *that ye may know that I am the Lord* that doth sanctify you." Exodus 31:13. In Bible parlance the terms *sign, token, mark,* and *seal* are synonymous.

But let us not think of this instruction entirely as pertaining to the literal Israel that was overthrown at the destruction of Jerusalem. Paul says to the Romans, "For he is not a Jew, which is one outwardly; neither is that circumcision, which is outward in the flesh: but he is a Jew, which is one inwardly; and circumcision is that of the heart, in the spirit, and not in the letter; whose praise is not of men, but of God." Romans 2:28, 29.

To the Gentiles of Galatia the apostle writes, "If ye be Christ's, then are ye Abraham's seed, and heirs according to the promise." Galatians 3:29.

And in his epistle to the church at Ephesus he says that "the Gentiles should be fellow heirs, and *of the same body*, and partakers of His promise in Christ by the gospel." (Ephesians 3:6.)

Only by taking the place which the Jews would have occupied if they had remained faithful, can the Gentiles share in this "promise made to Abraham," and by this promise alone are we saved. The position that God has made one mode of salvation for the Jew, and has given a new gospel for the Gentile, is absolutely untenable. The believing Gentiles are "graffed in" to the stock of Israel and thus partake "of the root and fatness of the olive tree." (Read Romans 11:16-24.)

The effects of this sealing message are summed up by Uriah Smith in the following words:

"Having now ascertained that the seal of God is His holy Sabbath, having His name, we are prepared to proceed with the application. By the scenes introduced in the verses before us; namely, the four winds apparently about to blow, bringing war and trouble upon the land, and this work restrained till the servants of God should be sealed, as though a preparatory work must be done for them to save them from this trouble, we are reminded of the houses of the Israelites marked with the blood of the paschal lamb, and spared as the destroying angel passed over to slay the first-born of the Egyptians (Exodus 12) also of the mark made by the man with a writer's inkhorn (Ezekiel 9) upon all those who were to be spared by the men with the slaughtering weapons who followed after; and we conclude that the seal of God, here placed upon His servants, is some distinguishing mark, or religious characteristic, through which they will be exempted from the judgments of God that fall on the wicked around them.

"As we have found the seal of God in the fourth commandment, the inquiry follows, Does the observance of that commandment involve any peculiarity in religious practice?—Yes, a very marked and striking one. It is one of the most singular facts to be met with in religious history that in an age of such boasted gospel light as the present, when the influence of Christianity is so powerful and widespread, one of the most striking peculiarities in practice which a person can adopt, and one of the greatest crosses he can take up, even in the most enlightened and Christian lands, is the simple observance of the law of God. For the fourth commandment requires the observance of the seventh day of each week as the Sabbath of the Lord; but almost all Christendom, through the combined influences of paganism and the papacy, have been beguiled into the keeping of the first day. A person has but to commence the observance of the day enjoined in the commandment, and a mark of peculiarity is upon him at once. He is distinct alike from the professedly religious world and the unconverted world.

"We conclude, then, that the angel ascending from the east, having the seal of the living God, is a divine messenger in charge of a work of reform to be carried on among men in reference to the Sabbath of the fourth commandment. The agents of this work on the earth are of course ministers of Christ; for to men is given the commission of instructing their fellow men in Bible truth; but as there is order in the execution of all the divine counsels, it seems not improbable that a literal angel may have the charge and oversight of this work.

"We have already noticed the chronology of this work as locating it in our own time. This is further evident from the fact that, as the next event after the sealing of the servants of God, we behold them before the throne, with palms of victory in their hands. The sealing is therefore the last work to be accomplished for them prior to their redemption."—"*Daniel and the Revelation,*" *pp. 442, 443.*

As the seal of God is the badge of entry into God's everlasting kingdom, so the mark of the beast subjects those who bear it to the awful punishments of the last day. Of such it is written:

"If any man worship the beast and his image, and receive his mark in his forehead, or in his hand, the same shall drink of the wine of the wrath of God, which is poured out without mixture into the cup of His indignation." Revelation 14:9, 10.

The worship of the beast and his image must be a heinous sin in the eyes of Jehovah, for the penalties against it are the most severe of any recorded between the lids of the Bible. The receiving of the mark must take place at the same time that the servants of God are sealed; namely, in the last days.

This symbol of a mark is taken from an ancient custom as described by Bishop Newton:

"It was customary among the ancients for servants to receive the mark of their master, and soldiers of their general, and those who were devoted to any particular deity, of the particular deity to whom they were devoted. These marks were usually impressed on their right hand or on their forehead, and consisted of some hieroglyphic character, or of the name expressed in vulgar letters, or of the name disguised in numerical letters, according to the fancy of the imposer."—"*Dissertations on the Prophecies,*" *Vol. 3, p. 241*.

According to Prideaux, Ptolemy Philopater commanded that all Jews of Alexandria who applied for citizenship, should have the mark of an ivy leaf (the badge of his god, Bacchus) impressed upon them with a hot iron.—"*Connections,*" *Vol. II, p. 78*.

The original word for mark is defined as "a graving, sculpture; a mark cut in or stamped."

This ancient custom of placing a significant mark upon individuals is used as a type of a moral mark which will be so indelibly impressed upon the characters of the rebels against the law and government of God that it will be plain in the sight of all earthly and heavenly intelligences, and separate them from the righteous as plainly as the distinguishing brand of the ancients separated those who received it from their fellows. It will be something that cannot be concealed.

A Sealing Message

Commentators generally agree that the beast here mentioned is the papacy. The mark of the beast must be some form or observance by which the authority of that power is acknowledged. To what characteristic of that power does this mark respond?

Daniel, in describing the papal power under the symbol of the little horn, says: "And he shall speak great words against the Most High, and shall wear out the saints of the Most High, and *think to change times and laws.*" Daniel 7: 25.

The papacy has in past ages been the ruling factor in many earthly governments, and has not only thought to change their statutes but has actually done so at will. So this attempted change of law cannot refer to human statutes. But when this power reaches forth its sacrilegious arm to change the precepts of Jehovah, it encounters a power it cannot subvert. It can think it has accomplished the change, but in point of fact God's law stands intact. This power can lead nearly the whole world to follow in its errors, but the words of the Saviour, "One jot or one tittle shall in no wise pass from the law," set bounds beyond which no earthly power can actually pass. Whatever claims may be set up to the contrary are only futile imaginings. God will search them out by and by.

Paul refers to this power as "that man of sin, . . . the son of perdition; who opposeth and exalteth himself above all that is called God, or that is worshiped." (2 Thessalonians 2: 3, 4.)

An earthly power might assume equality with Jehovah by claiming for its precepts equal authority with the precepts of the Creator. But here we have a power presented which exalts itself above God. It asserts its power to change the law of God, and demands and enforces, so far as possible, its changed law in opposition to God's original law.

The "mark of the beast" is given to those who "worship the beast." The "seal of God" is placed upon those who worship God. How shall it be determined which power the people are worshiping?— This is distinctly shown by the law they are keeping.

By an examination of the law of God side by side with the law as changed by the papacy (see page 278) this feature is made very clear. Hence when the question is asked, "What constitutes the mark of the beast?" the answer is plain,"The mark of the beast is the change that the beast has attempted to make in the fourth commandment."

Daniel did not say that this power would make a new law, but that it would "think to change" some law already in existence. God has but one unchanging law, — the ten commandments. This law the papacy has endeavored to change, by substituting in the fourth commandment the first-day Sabbath for the seventh-day Sabbath of Jehovah.

By this attempted change the seal of God has been stripped from His law, and the mark of the beast has been substituted. The evidence of God's authority as Creator has been removed, and the badge of the power of the papacy to change has been put in its place. This power does not claim that God instituted or commanded this change in the Sabbath, but that it was made by the "church," and history substantiates their claim. A few statements from reliable Catholic writers will make plain this claim to authority:

"The word of God commandeth the seventh day to be the Sabbath of our Lord, and to be kept holy; you Protestants, without any precept of Scripture, change it to the first day of the week, only authorized by our traditions. Divers English Puritans oppose, against this point, that the observation of the first day is proved out of Scripture, where it is said, the first day of the week. (Acts 20: 7; 1 Corinthians 16: 2; Revelation 1: 10.) Have they not spun a fair thread in quoting these places? If we should produce no better for purgatory and prayers for the dead, invocation of saints, and the like, they might have good cause, indeed, to laugh us to scorn; for where was it written that these were Sabbath days in which those meetings were kept? Or where is it ordained that they should be always observed? Or, which is the sum of all, where is it decreed that the observance of the first day should abrogate, or abolish, the sanctifying of the seventh day, which God commanded everlastingly to be kept holy? Not one of these is expressed in the written word of God."—"*Treatise of Thirty Controversies.*"

In the face of the foregoing claims the Sunday-keeping Protestant churches are silent. Many acknowledge that there is no Bible authority for the change, but accept it solely "upon the authority of the church." Many years ago the Catholics published an offer of one thousand dollars to any one who would, from the Bible, produce evidence that the Sabbath has been changed from the seventh to the first day of the week, but no one has taken it. The Sunday Sabbath is a man-made institution, and the papacy boasts of the change as the badge, or "mark" of its authority, as shown by the following:

"*Ques.* — What does God ordain by the commandment?

"*Ans.* — He ordained that we sanctify, in a special manner, this day on which He rested from the labor of creation.

"*Ques.* — What is this day of rest?

"*Ans.* — The seventh day of the week, or Saturday; for He employed six days in creation, and rested on the seventh. Genesis 2: 2; Hebrews 4: 1; etc.

"*Ques.* — It is, then, Saturday we should sanctify, in order to obey the ordinance of God?

"*Ans.*—During the old law, Saturday was the day sanctified; but the church, instructed by Jesus Christ and directed by the Spirit of God, has substituted Sunday for Saturday; so now we sanctify the first, not the seventh day. Sunday means, and now is, the day of the Lord."

—"*Catechism of the Christian Religion*," by *Stephen Keenan* (*Boston, Patrick Donahue, 1857*), *p. 206.*

Jehovah has given His Sabbath as the badge of His authority as Creator. The little horn power of Daniel 7: 25, which we have identified as the papacy, not only ruthlessly tramples upon this divine institution, making God's chosen Sabbath the busiest day of the week, but it has erected in its place a counterfeit institution to which it points as evidence of authority to command men under sin. As in the fourth commandment as given by the Creator we find the seal of God, so in that precept as applied to the false Sabbath by an apostate power, we find the badge of the papacy, the mark of the beast.

The Coming King

THERE is no one truth of Scripture to which so much prominence is given as that of the second coming of Christ. The New Testament is especially eloquent upon this subject, over three hundred references to it being found upon its pages.

There is a reason for this prominence. The coming of Christ is the consummation of the Christian's hope; the event which changes the Christian's experience from mortality to immortality, from the sorrows, labors, privations, and agonies of the present life, to the joys and everlasting felicities of the life to come.

Other hopes are set before us in the Scriptures; but the hope of the coming of Christ is the crowning hope of all, in that it brings the realization of all other hopes. Thus Paul, writing to Titus, represents Christians as ever "looking for that blessed hope, and the glorious appearing of the great God and our Saviour Jesus Christ." (Titus 2: 13.)

Christians should not only look for the appearing of Christ, but they should love to contemplate it. What man was a more true and devoted follower of Christ than the apostle Paul? To him, in life and in death, the coming of Christ was a joyful theme, a "blessed hope." As he drew near to the end of his laborious life, and was soon to stand by the headsman's block, the thought of the coming of his divine Master filled all the chambers of his soul with gladness. Condemned to death by an unrighteous judge, he looked forward to the glad time when the righteous Judge would come to judge the world in righteousness. (See 2 Timothy 4: 6-8.) Like Abraham, he believed that the Judge of all the earth would do right. (See Genesis 18: 25.)

This righteous judgment, so full of hope and promise to the children of God, brings to those who have slighted the gracious offers of salvation and have followed their own evil ways, no ray of hope, no joy, no blessedness, nothing but destruction. The heart that will not be moved to repentance by the love of God, can be reached in no other way. God has no reserve power by which to save such.

Jesus declares that His coming will be to the wicked like the flood which destroyed the unbelieving and wicked antediluvians, who mocked Noah and rejected his message of warning. (Read Luke 17: 26, 27.)

Says Paul: "And to you who are troubled rest with us, when the Lord Jesus shall be revealed from heaven with His mighty angels, in flaming fire taking vengeance on them that know not God, and that obey not the gospel of our Lord Jesus Christ: who shall be punished with everlasting destruction from the presence of the Lord, and from the glory of His power; when He shall come to be glorified in His saints, and to be admired in all them that believe (because our testimony among you was believed) in that day." 2 Thessalonians 1: 7-10.

To the wicked, the day of the Lord's appearing will be one of terror and distress. It is said of them in that day: "And the kings of the earth, and the great men, and the rich men, and the chief captains, and the mighty men, and every bondman, and every free man, hid themselves in the dens and in the rocks of the mountains; and said to the mountains and rocks, Fall on us, and hide us from the face of Him that sitteth on the throne, and from the wrath of the Lamb: for the great day of His wrath is come; and who shall be able to stand?" Revelation 6: 15-17.

In the preceding chapters we have shown that the relation of our Saviour to this earth has been varied, to meet the needs of a fallen humanity and to bring back the world to allegiance to God.

As Creator, the word of God as spoken by Him called the world into existence.

As the great central figure of the plan of salvation, He is the "Lamb slain from the foundation of the world." The gospel of Christ was the hope of the patriarchs and prophets of the Old Testament, and He, in person, was the leader of ancient Israel.

He is the greatest teacher that the world ever knew.

He became the Man of sorrows on earth, taking the nature of man and living as a man, passing through all the experiences that a man must meet, that He might be able to reach men in whatever condition they might be.

He bore the sins of the world in Gethsemane, and died on Calvary, that pardon might be made possible to all who would accept the offering made at so great a cost.

Raised from the dead on the third day, He made the great coming resurrection day possible.

As our mediator and advocate, He pleads His blood in behalf of the repenting sinner, and by it brings to him forgiveness, justification, and righteousness.

As high priest, He now presents His own sacrifice, His own blood, as a perfect atonement for the sins of His people on earth, and thus the claims of His Father's law are fully met, sinners are saved, and the justice of God vindicated.

But the time is very near when our Saviour will lay off His priestly garments, assume His kingly crown, put on his royal robes, and take to Himself the kingdom which He has redeemed from the power of the enemy. He is soon coming to earth to raise the righteous dead of all generations, change the faithful living from mortality to immortality, and with those redeemed by His great sacrifice, reign forever.

To this great event the children of God have ever looked forward as the culmination of the hopes and desires of the ages.

When He comes, it will be the same One who once walked the earth a stranger; the same One who died on the cross for sinners; the same One who ascended to heaven in the sight of His astonished and sorrowful disciples. "This same Jesus!" Do you believe it? Jesus said, "I will come again." The angels said, "This *same* Jesus" will come again, "in like nanner as ye have seen Him go." He went away bodily; He will return in the same manner. "For the Lord himself shall descend from heaven." 1 Thessalonians 4: 16. He was borne away in a cloud; He will come in the same way. "Behold, He cometh with clouds; and every eye shall see Him." Revelation 1: 7. Angels escorted Him to heaven; they will also return with Him. "The Son of man shall come in His glory, and all the holy angels with Him." Matthew 25: 31.

But He will not come in His own glory alone. When He comes to receive to Himself His faithful ones, He will then appear in all the glory of heaven. He will "come in His own glory, and in His Father's, and of the holy angels." (Luke 9: 26.) His own glory is above the brightness of the sun. (Read Acts 26: 13.) The glory of the Father can be no less, and the glory of a single angel is described by the revelator as follows:

"And I saw another mighty angel come down from heaven, clothed with a cloud: and a rainbow was upon his head, and his face was as it were the sun, and his feet as pillars of fire." Revelation 10: 1.

When Jesus comes as King, accompanied by ten thousand times ten thousand, and thousands of thousands of these resplendent beings, shining in all the glory of Himself and His Father, He will indeed be "wrapped in a blaze of boundless glory."

How different such a coming from that witnessed at His first advent. He came then a stranger to His own professed people; He will come again to be "admired in all them that believe." Then He came in weakness; now He comes in power to scatter His enemies. He was then a babe in Bethlehem's manger, wrapped in swaddling clothes, and lived to wear a crown of thorns; now He comes a king, wearing a crown of glory, and attended by all the shining angels. Then he came to bear the burden of sin, to suffer and to die; now He comes without sin, nevermore to die, but bearing crowns of life for all His people. Thank God that this time—

> "He comes not an infant in Bethlehem born,
>   He comes not to lie in a manger;
> He comes not again to be treated with scorn,
>   He comes not a shelterless stranger;
> He comes not to Gethsemane,
>   To weep and sweat blood in the garden;
> He comes not to die on the tree,
>   To purchase for rebels a pardon;
> Oh, no! glory, bright glory, environs Him now."

And we shall see Him. What a thought! See Him as He is; He whose head and hairs are white like wool, as white as snow; whose eyes are as a flame of fire; whose feet are like unto fine brass, as if they burned in a furnace; whose voice is as the sound of many waters, and whose countenance is as the sun shineth in his strength. See Revelation 1: 14-16. But this is too much for our understanding. We must wait for the glad day of His actual coming, when our eyes may behold Him in all His splendor; for "it doeth not yet appear what we shall be: but we know that, when He shall appear, we shall be like Him; for we shall see Him as He is." 1 John 3: 2.

The King's Reward

"BEHOLD, I come quickly; and My reward is with Me, to give every man according as his work shall be." Revelation 22: 12.

The blessed Lord said to His disciples, "I will come again and receive you unto Myself." John 14: 3. To have Christ and be with Him eternally, is no small reward. But this promise was not for the disciples alone. When "Paul the aged" was in prison, waiting for his death sentence to be carried out, he wrote: "I am now ready to be offered, and the time of my departure is at hand. I have fought a good fight, I have finished my course, I have kept the faith: henceforth there is laid up for me a crown of righteousness, which the Lord, the righteous Judge, shall give me at that day: and not to me only, but unto *all them also that love His appearing.*" 2 Timothy 4: 6-8.

A crown of righteousness is a part of the great reward which the King will bestow. This is called by some writers a "crown of life." (James 1: 12; Revelation 2: 10.) Another says, "When the Chief Shepherd shall appear, ye shall receive a crown of glory that fadeth not away." 1 Peter 5: 4.

But in order for this crown to be received by all for whom it is intended, some must be called from the dead; for many who now sleep in the dust have been righteous. The Lord, however, has made provision for all these. "For this we say unto you by the word of the Lord, that we which are alive and remain unto the coming of the Lord shall not prevent [go before] them which are asleep. For the Lord himself shall descend from heaven with a shout, with the voice of the archangel, and with the trump of God: and *the dead in Christ shall rise first.*" 1 Thessalonians 4: 15, 16.

Thank God that though good men may die, the grave cannot hold them when the Lord comes and calls for them. No, indeed; for "all that are in the graves shall hear His voice, and shall come forth." (John 5: 28, 29.) Not only this, but at the very instant when they come out of their graves the gift of immortality is theirs. This is the Lord's promise: "Behold, I show you a mystery; We shall not all sleep, but we shall all be changed, in a moment, in the twinkling of an eye, at the last trump: for the trumpet shall sound, and the dead shall be raised incorruptible [immortal], and we shall be changed." 1 Corinthians 15: 51, 52.

Glorious change indeed; no more sickness, sorrow, pain, or death, "for the former things are passed away." (Revelation 21: 4.) "Death is swallowed up in victory" (1 Corinthians 15: 54), and all things are made new — a new life, a new home, a new occupation, a new song — and best of all, these may be enjoyed throughout the eternal ages.

Is all this worth looking after? Who does not desire such a reward? Oh, to be able to receive it! But in order to have this, each one must be "counted worthy" of it. When the Lord comes, only the "dead in Christ" arise at His call. (1 Thessalonians 4: 16.) The rest of the dead do not rise till a thousand years afterward. (See Revelation 20: 5.) This shows that the righteous are separated from the wicked when the Lord comes. But even this is done in a moment, in the "twinkling of an eye." There is no time for the judgment, then. No; before the Lord comes, He looks over the cases of those who profess to know Him, and decides who are faithful; all the rest are left out, and when the King comes, the faithful alone are raised to life. After these are taken to dwell with Him, the wicked have their resurrection, and are brought forth to be punished. (John 5: 29.)

After the decision has been made as to who are worthy to come up in the resurrection of the just, then the Lord comes to give them the reward of everlasting life. Let us remember, then, that we must be ready to meet the Lord before this decision is rendered; for if we wait until the Lord is seen coming, it will be too late. We shall then be obliged to cry, "The harvest is past, the summer is ended, and we are not saved." Jeremiah 8: 20.

The Lord gives us a solemn warning on this point. He says to all: "Take heed to yourselves, lest at any time your hearts be overcharged with surfeiting, and drunkenness, and cares of this life, and *so that day come upon you unawares.* For as a snare shall it come on all them that dwell on the face of the whole earth." Luke 21: 34, 35.

We have seen that our resurrection, our immortality, our being with Christ, our crown of inheritance, all depend upon, and are to be given at, His second coming. How important, then, that coming is! If the coming were to prove a failure, all would be lost. But that can never be. All through the dim ages of the past, as the saints have fallen one by one by the stroke of death, angels have marked their places of rest. And when the command of the returning Lord shall be heard, "Go, gather My saints together unto Me," with what joyful haste will the angels fly to meet those who have burst the tomb at the sound of the voice of the Son of of God!

Oh, glorious awakening! Perhaps the first sight to greet the vision of those opening eyes in the dawn of eternity will be the face of an angel, radiant with glory. It must surely be an awakening of song, when death is thus "swallowed up in victory," and the sweet voice of Him who is our Redeemer is heard to sing, "I will declare Thy name unto My brethren, in the midst of the church will I sing praise unto Thee." Hebrews 2: 12. Then will the very heavens ring with the jubilee of that assembled throng.

The New Jerusalem

CHRIST, when about to leave His disciples, comforted them with these words: "Let not your hearts be troubled. . . . In My Father's house are many mansions: if it were not so, I would have told you. I go to prepare a place for you. And if I go and prepare a place for you, I will come again, and receive you unto myself; that where I am, there ye may be also." John 14: 2, 3.

There is a glorious city being built in heaven for the faithful. Mansions are being prepared in it for the overcomers. This wondrous city was already under construction when Christ was on earth. On His return to heaven, He promised to continue this work; and as the years passed, new mansions were to be added to meet the demands of the saints, even down to the very time when the King shall come and claim His own. Then, at the resurrection of the just, these mansions shall be given them.

Then the resurrected saints and the living righteous will be caught up "in the clouds, to meet the Lord in the air." (See 1 Corinthians 15: 51, 52; 1 Thessalonians 4: 16, 17.) Borne from earth to the mansions prepared for them in the city of God, they will there live and reign "with Christ a thousand years." (Revelation 20: 4.)

During this thousand years the saints will "judge the world," as stated by Paul in 1 Corinthians 6: 2, and as recorded in Daniel 7: 22. At the end of the thousand years the wicked dead will be raised. (See Revelation 20: 5, 6.) The New Jerusalem will come down to earth from heaven. "And I John saw the holy city, New Jerusalem, coming down from God out of heaven, prepared as a bride adorned for her husband." Revelation 21: 2.

For a thousand years Satan will be confined to this earth. During this time his subjects will all be dead, and he can deceive them no longer, for there will be none alive to be deceived, so the earth will be a dreary prison for him. This is called the binding of Satan. (Read Revelation 20: 2.)

But with the resurrection of all the wicked who have ever lived, a field opens again in which Satan can work, and he is thus "loosed out of His prison." (Revelation 20: 7.) Thus having opportunity once again to deceive "the nations" (verse 8), the earth no longer confines him as in a prison.

The glorious new Jerusalem is before him. He once before waged war with heaven (Revelation 12: 7), and he now determines to marshall his forces and, if possible, capture the city. It is a desperate undertaking, but it is his last opportunity, and he hopes to win. This hope he presents to the vast throng of the resurrected wicked. In this multitude are the great warriors of every age. He deceives them with the vain hope of success in his enterprise.

The earth rings with the preparation for war. When all is ready, the mighty army is gathered "to battle, the number of whom is as the sand of the sea. And they went up on the breadth of the earth, and compassed the camp of the saints about, and the beloved city." (Revelation 20: 8, 9.)

But as they are about to wage impious war upon Christ and the redeemed host, fire comes "down from God out of heaven," and devours them. (Verse 9.) Thus will end the kingdom of Satan, and the reign of wickedness.

This purifying fire will cleanse the earth, and it will be made perfect and lovely as on the day when it came from the hand of the Creator, and He pronounced it "good."

Peter, speaking of this event, says that "the elements [the atmosphere surrounding the earth] shall melt with fervent heat, the earth also [shall melt] and the works that are therein shall be burned up. . . . Nevertheless we, ac-

cording to His promise, look for new heavens and a new earth, wherein dwelleth righteousness." (2 Peter 3: 10, 13.)
The earth will melt with the burning of that day. The "works" of man "that are therein shall be burned up"; but from it will come a new earth, glorious in all the beauty that an all-wise Creator can give it. The "heavens," or atmosphere which surrounds it, will be made "new," free from all the poisonous elements which now contaminate it.

The New Jerusalem has been preserved through these terrible scenes by the power of God. When the holy city comes "down from God out of heaven," our Saviour precedes it and prepares a place for it. "And His feet shall stand in that day upon the Mount of Olives, which is before Jerusalem on the east, and the Mount of Olives shall cleave in the midst thereof toward the east and toward the west, and there shall be a very great valley." Zechariah 14: 4.

It is reasonable to suppose that in this wonderful valley, so miraculously prepared, the New Jerusalem will descend. It is the largest city the world has ever known, and requires spacious grounds.

The mount of Olives is surrounded by memories the most sacred. It is close by Jerusalem, in which was the temple where God was wont to meet His faithful people. Here the Saviour loved to go with His disciples. Whole nights He spent upon its sides in prayer, and from it He ascended to heaven when His mission to earth was finished.

When He returns, accompanied by the New Jerusalem, how appropriate that His feet should first rest upon the spot from which He ascended. How appropriate that the New Jerusalem, the capital city of the new earth, should rest upon the spot where the earthly Jerusalem once stood.

Hallowed by the presence of Christ, and transformed by His power, this spot of earth is purified and made ready without the action of the fires of the great burning. So while

The joys and glories of the new earth

the surrounding earth is being melted and made new, the city of our God remains unmolested, the peaceful home of Christ and the redeemed throng.

God has seen fit to give us a minute description of this glorious city. It lies foursquare, and it is twelve thousand furlongs, or fifteen hundred miles, around it. This makes three hundred and seventy-five miles on every side. It has a wall about two hundred and fifty feet high, built of jasper. This wall has twelve foundations, made up of the rarest and most beautiful stones. In this wall are twelve gates, each one made of a single pearl. The mansions are made of transparent gold.

The river of life issues from "the throne of God and of the Lamb," and runs through the main street of the city. The river flows beneath the tree of life, which grows on either side. From the description given in Revelation 22: 2, we understand that this wonderful tree has two trunks — one on each side of the river. Its branches join at the top, forming a beautiful arch over the river.

"And the leaves of the tree were for the healing of the nations." Verse 2. Sin has dwarfed and enfeebled mankind; but the leaves of this tree will restore the race to its original condition before the curse of sin rested upon it. Thus all effects of the curse will be removed.

The fruit of the tree ripens every month, and it bears "twelve manner of fruits." (Revelation 22: 2.) And as the saints come up "from one new moon to another" (Isaiah 66: 23), it is reasonable to infer that this tree will be found loaded with a different variety of fruit each month. The fruit of this tree perpetuates the life of those who eat of it.

The New Jerusalem is the city residence of the saved. In it are mansions for all. Outside the city, to earth's remotest bounds, the nations of the saved dwell in peace, plenty, and happiness.

But they are not idle. They have their occupations and individual interests as we have now. (Read Isaiah 65: 21-25.) They will "build houses" to suit their own tastes, and they will live in them forever. "They shall not build, and another inhabit." They will attend to farming pursuits; for "they shall plant vineyards, and eat the fruit of them." "They shall not plant, and another eat." There will then be no mortgages to foreclose, nor rents to pay, nor taxes to be collected.

Their occupation will be varied by frequent visits to their city home in the New Jerusalem; for "from one new moon to another, and from one Sabbath to another, shall all flesh come to worship before Me, saith the Lord." Isaiah 66: 23. But there will be order in this new realm, and there will be those who will govern the various provinces of the empire of Christ; for it is stated that "the kings of the earth do bring their glory and honor into it." Revelation 21: 24.

"And God shall wipe away all tears from their eyes; and there shall be no more death, neither sorrow, nor crying, neither shall there be any more pain: for the former things are passed away." Revelation 21: 4. Forever made free from death, the saved will live an eternal life, in duration as the life of God, with whom "they shall reign forever and ever." (Revelation 22: 5.)

Lost in amazement as we contemplate these wonderful themes, we can only join with Paul in exclaiming, "Eye hath not seen, nor ear heard, neither have entered into the heart of man, the things which God hath prepared for them that love Him." 1 Corinthians 2: 9.

TEACH Services, Inc.
P U B L I S H I N G

We invite you to view the complete
selection of titles we publish at:
www.TEACHServices.com

We encourage you to write us
with your thoughts about this,
or any other book we publish at:
info@TEACHServices.com

TEACH Services' titles may be purchased in
bulk quantities for educational, fund-raising,
business, or promotional use.
bulksales@TEACHServices.com

Finally, if you are interested in seeing
your own book in print, please contact us at:
publishing@TEACHServices.com

We are happy to review your manuscript at no charge.

www.ingramcontent.com/pod-product-compliance
Lightning Source LLC
Chambersburg PA
CBHW071654160426
43195CB00012B/1462